Piaget's theory of
intellectual development
AN INTRODUCTION

HERBERT GINSBURG and SYLVIA OPPER
Cornell University

Prentice-Hall, Inc., Englewood Cliffs, New Jersey

Piaget's theory of intellectual development

AN INTRODUCTION

THE PRENTICE-HALL SERIES IN DEVELOPMENTAL PSYCHOLOGY
John C. Wright, editor

Piaget and Knowledge by Hans Furth
The Cognitive Process: Readings by R.J.C. Harper, C.C. Anderson,
    C.M. Christensen, and S. Hunka
Psychopathology of Childhood by Jane W. Kessler

Piaget's theory of intellectual development
AN INTRODUCTION
by Herbert Ginsburg and Sylvia Opper

P-13-493007-X
C-13-493017-X

Library of Congress Catalog Card Number 76–76312

Printed in the United States of America

Current printing (last digit):
19   18   17   16   15   14   13

Prentice-Hall International, Inc., *London*
Prentice-Hall of Australia, Pty. Ltd., *Sydney*
Prentice-Hall of Canada, Ltd., *Toronto*
Prentice-Hall of India Private Ltd., *New Delhi*
Prentice-Hall of Japan, Inc., *Tokyo*

acknowledgments

The authors wish to thank the following publishers for permission to reprint copyrighted materials in this book:

The Child's Conception of Number (with Alina Szeminska), translated by C. Gattegno and F.M. Hodgson (London: Routledge & Kegan Paul Ltd., 1952), pp. 45, 50, 75, 79, 82, 124–125, reprinted by permission of Routledge & Kegan Paul Ltd. and W.W. Norton & Company, Inc.

The Child's Conception of the World, translated by J. and A. Tomlinson (New York: Harcourt, Brace & World, Inc., 1929), pp. 258–259, 274, reprinted by permission of Routledge & Kegan Paul Ltd. and Humanities Press, Inc.

The Construction of Reality in the Child, translated by M. Cook (New York: Basic Books, Inc., Publishers, 1954), pp. 14, 25, 51, 76, 77, 79–80, reprinted by permission of Routledge & Kegan Paul Ltd. and Basic Books, Inc., Publishers.

The Early Growth of Logic in the Child, translated by E.A. Lunzer and D. Papert (London: Routledge & Kegan Paul Ltd., 1964), pp. 21, 102, 109, reprinted by permission of Routledge & Kegan Paul Ltd. and Harper & Row, Publishers.

"Equilibration and the Development of Logical Structures," in *Discussions on Child Development: The Fourth Meeting of the World Health Organization, Study Group on the Psychobiological Development of the Child,* edited by J.M. Tanner and B. Inhelder (London: Tavistock Publications, Ltd., 1956), p. 102, reprinted by permission of the World Health Organization.

The Growth of Logical Thinking from Childhood to Adolescence, translated by A. Parsons and S. Seagrin (New York: Basic Books, Inc., Publishers, 1958), pp. 56, 60, 70–71, 75, 103, 116–117, 129, 130, reprinted by permission of Routledge & Kegan Paul Ltd. and Basic Books, Inc., Publishers.

Judgment and Reasoning in the Child, translated by M. Warden (New York: Harcourt, Brace & World, Inc., 1926), pp. 17–18, 87, 88, 123, reprinted by permission of Routledge & Kegan Paul Ltd. and Humanities Press, Inc.

The Language and Thought of the Child, translated by M. Gabain (London: Routledge & Kegan Paul Ltd., 1926), pp. 35, 37, 41, 126, 130, 149, reprinted by permission of Routledge & Kegan Paul Ltd. and Humanities Press, Inc.

The Moral Judgment of the Child, translated by M. Gabain (New York: Harcourt, Brace & World, Inc., 1932), pp. 55, 60, 122, 126, 141, reprinted by permission of Routledge & Kegan Paul Ltd. and Crowell-Collier, Inc.

The Origins of Intelligence in Children, translated by M. Cook (New York: International University Press, 1952), reprinted by permission of Delachaux & Niestlé.

Play, Dreams, and Imitation in Childhood, translated by C. Gattegno and F.M. Hodgson (New York: W.W. Norton & Company, Inc., 1951, 1962), pp. 10, 30, 31, 46–47, 55–56, 63, 65, 96, 218, 222, 224, 225, 231, 232, by permission of Routledge & Kegan Paul Ltd. and W.W. Norton & Company, Inc.

The Psychology of Intelligence, translated by M. Percy and D.E. Berlyne (London: Routledge & Kegan Paul Ltd., 1950), pp. 6, 7, reprinted by permission of Routledge & Kegan Paul Ltd. and Humanities Press, Inc.

foreword

Today Piaget seems to be *the* child psychologist in the eyes of the American public. His name crops up in countless publications and his ideas are discussed in many different circles—psychological, educational, philosophical, psychiatric. In spite of his popularity, however, he remains a difficult author, especially for an English-speaking reader. *Piaget's Theory of Intellectual Development: An Introduction* is therefore very welcome. Thanks to the joint efforts of a Piagetian-trained psychologist and an American professor of developmental psychology, we now have a book which brings out and explains the difficulties so often encountered by students of Piaget. Not to feel disturbed at any misinterpretation of his thought is a rare pleasure when reading a book about Piaget, and I was delighted to find that the authors have not fallen into the two most common pitfalls: they have not oversimplified, nor have they been content to adopt the difficult Piagetian terminology without adequate explanation.

The undergraduate students of Piagetian theory, for whom this book is intended, are really fortunate to have this book to help them understand some of the more abstruse concepts; even our Genevan students do not find his theory easy to grasp. Each time Piaget comes across a behavior, however trivial it may seem, he seeks to explain it with reference to his theoretical framework, which is thus continuously being refined and enriched; with Piaget the empirical is never separated from the theoretical.

It is this continuing development which students find difficult, and which is so clearly brought to light in this book. The authors in fact adopt this technique, passing from theory to example and vice versa, in a way which is both clear and comprehensible. Their examples of children's behavior have been most carefully selected and I particularly like the use of various aspects of one example to illustrate different theoretical points. I also think it useful that the authors have included other interpretations of some Piagetian concepts, thus giving the reader an idea of Piaget's position in contemporary psychology.

In fact, although this well-written book is primarily destined for students, it is quite clear that it will enable many readers already well acquainted with Piaget's theory to explore his reasoning more deeply. It is not concerned with lengthy discussion or criticism, but provides, as it was intended to, a concise description and clear analysis of Piaget's thought and work.

Geneva, Switzerland   BÄRBEL INHELDER
March 1969   *Professor of*
                                                         Developmental Psychology

preface

Since the early 1950s, it has become increasingly clear to child psychologists, educators, and others in diverse areas that Jean Piaget is the foremost contributor to the field of intellectual development. From 1920 until the present, Piaget and his collaborators have produced more worthwhile research and theory than any other individual or group of investigators in child psychology. The sheer volume of Piaget's output is staggering. He has produced more than thirty full-length books and more than a hundred articles in the field of child psychology.

But numbers alone do not tell the full story. Piaget has captured the interest of modern psychologists and educators for several important reasons. First, he has introduced a score of new and interesting problems which previously went unnoticed. For example, it was Piaget who discovered the profoundly complex problem of *conservation*, which has caught the imagination of many investigators. This problem taps one aspect of the child's ability to construct a reality which transcends the mere appearance of things. Second, Piaget's theories have reoriented current conceptions of the child's development. His ideas are novel, imaginative, and comprehensive. Some persons now feel that his theories are the first to offer a successful challenge, or at least a viable alternative, to the trend dominant in American child psychology, namely the stimulus-response behaviorist tradition. And finally, of all theories of child development,

Piaget's is the one most securely founded upon the study of the child. None of the investigators whose theories have been used to explain the development of children—Freud, Lewin, Hull, Miller and Dollard, Skinner, Werner—has studied children as extensively as has Piaget. In fact, some of these figures—e.g., Freud, Hull, Skinner—hardly studied children at all. Gesell did study children, but did not produce a serious theory. By contrast, Piaget has for nearly fifty years observed, interviewed, and tested children of all ages, and this enormous set of empirical data is the foundation of his theory.

Clearly then, persons interested in child development should at the least be familiar with Piaget's work. Unfortunately, this is no simple task. For the most part, Piaget is an extremely difficult writer: his ideas are novel and hard to assimilate; his style of writing is not the ultimate in lucidity; many of his theoretical terms sound strange to the ears of the professional psychologist or educator, and certainly to the novice; and his later contributions are stated in terms of symbolic logic and mathematics. These difficulties have several unfortunate consequences. One is that the job of learning about Piaget is very onerous indeed. The interested reader seems to require a text introducing him to Piaget's ideas before he is able to profit from the primary sources themselves.

We have written this book in the hope of assisting the beginning student of Piaget. It is a brief introduction to his basic ideas and findings concerning the child's intellectual development. We hope that the book will be useful to students, particularly undergraduates, in psychology, education, and allied fields. The book may be used as supplementary reading, in whole or part, in courses dealing with child psychology, cognition, educational psychology, and so on. We hope, too, that the book may be read with profit by the general reader.

Despite the fact that the book is an introduction, and a brief one at that, we have tried to present the material in some depth. That is, we have assumed that the reader, although knowing little about psychology and Piaget, is intelligent and willing to work a bit to understand Piaget's ideas. Secondly, we have assumed that the reader should not be shielded from difficult aspects of Piaget's theory, like the use of symbolic logic.

Naturally, in a book of this type, we have had to be selective. No doubt readers familiar with Piaget will notice that we have omitted a number of important topics. For example, we do not describe the work on perception, or the research on concepts of geometry. We make no pretense at offering a comprehensive treatment of Piaget's work. Rather, we have tried to present, as lucidly as possible, Piaget's major theoretical notions concerning intellectual development, as well as some of the research on which they are based. Since the aim of this book is to present clearly the basics of Piaget's ideas, we have kept our own critique to a minimum. For the same reason, we have not referred extensively to independent investigators' research on Piaget's ideas.

Chapter One begins with a brief biography of Piaget and outlines some of his basic ideas. Chapter Two deals with his account of development in infancy. The focus is on an aspect of the theory which has not been sufficiently stressed; namely, the account of learning and motivation. Chapter Three describes Piaget's early research and theory concerning the child from about 2 to 11 years. Among the topics covered are the development of symbolism, the child's methods of communication, and moral judgment. Chapter Four also deals with the child of about the same age, but discusses Piaget's later work on rather different substantive problems. The emphasis is on the child's understanding of classes, relations, and number. Chapter Five discusses adolescent thought and describes Piaget's use of logic as a model for the adolescent's thinking. Chapter Six ends the book with a discussion of Piaget's work in "genetic epistemology," and of the implications of his work for education. We hope that by the end of the book students will have some insight into Piaget's views, and will appreciate the magnitude of his contribution.

A number of persons have contributed to the writing of this book, although they bear no responsibility for its defects. First, we wish to thank our teachers. Herbert Ginsburg studied Piaget under Lise Wallach, William Kessen, William Charlesworth, and Halbert Robinson. Sylvia Opper had the good fortune of studying Piaget with Piaget, and with Bärbel Inhelder. Several students and colleagues have read preliminary drafts of the manuscript and have offered useful comments: Ross Geoghegan, David Hawkins, Dalton Jones, Madeline Kanter, Mari Peterson, Lise Wallach, Marny Wheeler, and Cathy Widom. Our editor, John Wright, has been most helpful. Our reviewer, Guy Cellérier, has offered many valuable suggestions. And our typist, Mary Gill, has been superb.

The writing of portions of the book was partially supported by the Cornell Research Program in Early Childhood Education.

H.G.
S.O.

Ithaca, New York
June 1968

To JEAN PIAGET

contents

BIOGRAPHY AND BASIC IDEAS

1

1

INFANCY

26

2

THE YEARS 2 THROUGH 11:
SYMBOLISM AND PIAGET'S
EARLY WORK

72

3

THE YEARS 2 THROUGH 11:
PIAGET'S LATER WORK

117

4

ADOLESCENCE

181

5

GENETIC EPISTEMOLOGY AND
THE IMPLICATIONS OF PIAGET'S
FINDINGS FOR EDUCATION

207

6

INDEX

233

Piaget's theory of intellectual development
AN INTRODUCTION

1

biography and basic ideas

We shall begin by reviewing Jean Piaget's life in order to give the reader an idea of the influences affecting his work and of the wide scope of his activities; then we will discuss in a preliminary way some basic ideas and themes which underlie his theory of intellectual development.

BIOGRAPHY

Jean Piaget [1] was born on August 9, 1896, in the small university town of Neuchâtel, Switzerland. His father was a historian who specialized in medieval literature, and his mother was a dynamic, intelligent, and religious woman. Piaget showed an early interest in nature; he enjoyed the observation of birds, fish, and animals in their natural habitat. At school, too, his leanings were toward the biological sciences. But his was no ordinary schoolboy enthusiasm: when he was only 11 years old, a

1. Piaget has written short autobiographies in several volumes. One, although outdated, appears in English: J. Piaget, "Autobiography," in E. G. Boring, et al., eds., *History of Psychology in Autobiography*, Vol. IV. (Worcester, Mass.: Clark University Press, 1952), pp. 237–56. A more recent account of his life appears in French: *Jean Piaget et les Sciences Sociales*, Cahiers Vilfredo Pareto, No. 10 (Geneva: Librairie Droz, 1966).

natural history magazine published his first article, describing an albino sparrow seen in the park. Soon he was able to help the director of the natural history museum of Neuchâtel, where his task was to assist in the classification of the museum's zoology collection. At this time, he began to study molluscs and, from 15 to 18 years of age, published a series of articles on these shellfish. One of the papers, written when Piaget was only 15 years old, resulted in the offer of the post of curator of the mollusc collection at the Geneva natural history museum. Piaget had to decline the position in order to complete his high school studies.

As an adolescent he spent a vacation with his godfather, Samuel Cornut, a Swiss scholar, who was to have a considerable influence on his intellectual development. Cornut felt that Piaget's horizons were too restricted in the direction of the biological sciences and decided to introduce the young man to philosophy, particularly to the work of Bergson. Consequently, Piaget who, until then, had given his main attention to the study of biology and the natural behavior of organisms, now turned his thoughts to other pursuits. His readings broadened to include philosophy, religion, and logic. Contact with these subjects led eventually to a special interest in epistemology, the branch of philosophy concerned with the study of knowledge. He became curious to discover the answers to some of the basic questions of the discipline: What is knowledge? How is it acquired? Can one gain an objective understanding of external reality, or is one's knowledge of the world colored and distorted by internal factors? Although fascinated by these issues, Piaget felt that their solution could not be provided solely by philosophy. In comparing the attributes of philosophy and science, Piaget's conclusion was that "an idea is only an idea, while a fact is only a fact." [2] In other words, he was convinced that the philosophical approach was too speculative, and the scientific approach was sometimes too factual. What was needed was a linkage between the two.

We see, then, that during his adolescence Piaget concentrated on two major intellectual pursuits: biology and epistemology. There was, of course, a great gap between the two disciplines. One was concerned with life and the other with knowledge. One employed scientific methods and the other used speculation. Piaget began to wonder whether it might not be possible to bridge the gap between the two disciplines; to find some way of integrating his biological and epistemological interests. How could one investigate the very fascinating problems of knowledge, and at the same time utilize the scientific framework of biology?

Although interested in epistemological questions, Piaget put his

2. *Sagesse et Illusions de la Philosophie* (Paris: Presses Universitaires de France, 1965), p. 16.

major efforts into the study of biology. In 1916 he completed his undergraduate studies in natural sciences at the university of his home town, Neuchâtel. Only two years later, at the age of 21, he submitted to the same university his thesis on the molluscs of the Valais region of Switzerland, and received the degree of Doctor of Philosophy.

After finishing his formal studies, Piaget decided to explore psychology. He left Neuchâtel for Zurich to work in two psychological laboratories and at Bleuler's psychiatric clinic. He now discovered psychoanalysis and the ideas of Freud, Jung, and others, and in 1920 published an article on the relations between psychoanalysis and child psychology. The following year he left Zurich for Paris where he spent two years at the Sorbonne University studying abnormal psychology as well as logic, epistemology, and the philosophy of science. His encounter with philosophy once more convinced him that it was necessary to supplement pure speculation with the scientific approach.

It was during his stay in Paris that an opportunity arose which was to shape the direction of his future work. In 1920 he accepted a post with Dr. Theophile Simon in the Binet Laboratory in Paris. (With Alfred Binet, Simon had earlier constructed the first successful intelligence test.) Piaget's task was to develop a standardized French version of certain English reasoning tests. In a standardized test the wording of the questions and their order of presentation are precisely defined, and the examiner must not deviate from the pre-established procedure. The aim of a standardized test is to present each subject with the same problems so that the subsequent differences in performance can be attributed not to variations in the questions, but to differences in the subjects' intelligence (or other traits being measured).

At first, Piaget was not very enthusiastic about the work. Standardizing a test can be a very mechanical and tedious process. But then three major events occurred. First, although in intelligence testing, attention is usually focussed on the child's ability to produce correct responses, Piaget discovered that, on the contrary, the child's *incorrect* answers were far more fascinating. When questioning the children, Piaget found that the same wrong answers occurred frequently in children of about the same age. Moreover, there were different kinds of common wrong answers at different ages. Piaget puzzled on the meaning of these mistakes. He came to the conclusion that older children were not just "brighter" than younger ones; instead, the thought of younger children was *qualitatively different* from that of older ones. In other words, Piaget came to reject a quantitative definition of intelligence—a definition based on the number of correct responses on a test. The real problem of intelligence, Piaget felt, was to discover the different methods of thinking used by children of various ages.

Second, Piaget sought a different method for the study of intelligence. He immediately precluded the standardized test procedure. Such an approach, he felt, was too rigid: for example, it might lead to a considerable loss of information if the child did not understand the questions. Consequently, he sought a less structured method which would give him more freedom to question the child. His solution was to apply to the task his previous experience in abnormal psychology: he adapted the psychiatric method to research into children's thought. The new method was extremely flexible. It involved letting the child's answers (and not some preconceived plan) determine the course of questioning. If the child said something interesting, then it would immediately be pursued, without regard for a standardized procedure. The aim of this method was to follow the child's own line of thought, without imposing any direction on it.

At about the same time as his work in the Binet Laboratory, Piaget was also studying abnormal children at the Salpetrière hospital in Paris. He felt, like Freud, that knowledge of abnormal functioning might provide insight into the normal working of the mind. Piaget therefore applied the "clinical method" developed at the Binet Laboratory to his study of abnormal children. However, he found that the method was not adequate since abnormal children's verbal abilities were deficient. Consequently, for these children he added an important procedure: the child was required not only to answer questions, but also to manipulate certain materials. Unfortunately, Piaget did not immediately apply the supplemented clinical method—free verbal questioning plus materials for manipulation—to the testing of normal children. It was only after the exclusively verbal procedure proved inadequate that Piaget later made use of his experience at Salpetrière.

Third, while using the clinical method to study children's thought, Piaget was reading extensively in logic. It occurred to him that abstract logic might be relevant in several ways to children's thinking. He noticed, for instance, that children younger than about 11 years were unable to carry out certain elementary logical operations. The possibility of extensively investigating this apparent deficiency immediately presented itself. Also, Piaget felt that thought processes form an integrated structure (not a conglomeration of isolated units), whose basic properties can be described in logical terms. For example, the logical operations involved in deduction seemed to correspond to certain mental structures in older children. He set himself the goal of discovering how closely thought approximates logic. This was a unique conception of the psychology of intelligence.

The years at the Binet Laboratory were very fruitful. Piaget published several accounts of his psychological research on children. But more importantly, the stay in Paris taught Piaget that the problem of intelligence must be defined in terms of discovering children's ways of thinking; that the clinical method is useful for the study of thought; and that logic, rather than the imprecise natural language, might be an efficient way of describing thought. Furthermore, Piaget had now discovered a way in which he might integrate his biological and epistemological interests. As he saw it, the first step was to pursue the psychology of human intelligence. As a psychologist, he could study the individual's knowledge of the world: that is, his attempts to comprehend reality. This kind of psychology, in other words, would be directed at epistemological issues, and also, it would be biologically oriented. For Piaget, this meant several things. First, psychological theory might make use of biological concepts. For instance, intelligence could be viewed in terms of an organism's adaptation to its environment. Second, psychology might focus on the process of individual growth. He believed that a full understanding of human knowledge could be gained only through the study of its formation and evolution in childhood. How could one comprehend the final product without knowing how it developed? For these reasons, then, Piaget decided to engage first in the psychological study of the child's understanding of reality. His initial intention was to spend a few years in experimental studies of the child's intelligence, then turn to a second project, namely the application of his psychological discoveries to the theoretical problems of epistemology. He felt that he could clarify epistemological issues once he had developed an understanding of the individual's cognitive growth. As we shall see, Piaget spent more than a "few years" at his first task. It was only after some 30 years of psychological study that Piaget was able to turn his attention to theoretical questions of epistemology.

In 1921, the Director of the Jean-Jacques Rousseau Institute in Geneva, Edouard Claparède, who had been impressed by Piaget's early articles on children, offered him the post of Director of Research at the Institute. Piaget accepted the offer which gave him an excellent opportunity to carry on his study of child thought. The outcome of his research was a series of articles and the publication, from 1923 to 1932, of his first five books on children. The first one, *Language and Thought in the Child* [3] provides naturalistic and experimental observations on the child's use of language. Piaget found, for instance, that the young child's speech is substantially uncommunicative, and that this tendency decreases gradually as the child grows older. *Judgment and Reasoning in the Child* [4] deals

---

3. *Le Langage et la Pensée chez l'Enfant* (Neuchâtel: Delachaux & Niestlé, 1923); *The Language and Thought of the Child*, trans. M. Gabain (London: Routledge & Kegan Paul Ltd., 1926).
4. *Le Jugement et le Raisonnement chez l'Enfant* (Neuchâtel: Delachaux & Niestlé, 1924); *Judgment and Reasoning in the Child*, trans. M. Warden (New York: Harcourt, Brace & World, Inc., 1926).

with the changes in certain types of reasoning from early to late childhood. *The Child's Conception of the World* [5] used the exclusively verbal clinical method to provide data on how the child views the world around him, on what he believes to be the origins of dreams, of trees, the sun and the moon. In *The Child's Conception of Physical Causality* [6] Piaget describes the child's ideas on the causes of certain natural phenomena, such as the movement of the clouds and of rivers, the problem of shadows, or the displacement of water when an object is immersed. Finally, *The Moral Judgment of the Child* [7] provides information on the development of moral behavior and judgment. Here Piaget maintains that children show two types of moral judgment: the young child holds to a predominantly authoritarian moral code, whereas the older child develops a morality of social concern and cooperation.

Contact with psychoanalysis is evident in the early works: Piaget's theories make use of Freudian ideas and are sometimes even stated in Freudian terms. The books also give a brief indication of what Piaget was later to expand upon: a view of intellectual development as consisting of a series of stages. Through his research Piaget was becoming increasingly aware of the differences between the child's and the adult's thought processes. He realized that the child is not merely a miniature replica of the adult: not only does the child think less efficiently than the adult, but he also thinks differently. Thus, Piaget became convinced that it was necessary to conceive of intellectual development in terms of an evolution through qualitatively different stages of thought.

Piaget also attempted to discover the causes of this intellectual evolution. His first interpretation was that intellectual development resulted particularly from social factors, like language and contact with parents and peers. Later, after his study of infancy, where the role of language is negligible, but where on the contrary the child's own activity is paramount, he changed his interpretation of the nature of intellectual development; he de-emphasized the influence of social factors and stressed action as the source of thought.

Much to Piaget's astonishment, the first five books, which he himself calls his "adolescent" works, gained him considerable fame, particularly among child psychologists. Piaget, who had never in his life passed an ex-

5. *La Représentation du Monde chez l'Enfant* (Paris: Librairie F. Alcan, 1926); *The Child's Conception of the World*, trans. J. and A. Tomlinson (New York: Harcourt, Brace & World, Inc., 1929).

6. *La Causalité Physique chez l'Enfant* (Paris: Librairie F. Alcan, 1927); *The Child's Conception of Physical Causality*, trans. M. Gabain (Totowa, N. J.: Littlefield, Adams, and Co., 1960).

7. *Le Jugement Moral chez l'Enfant* (Paris: Librairie F. Alcan, 1932); *The Moral Judgment of the Child*, trans. M. Gabain (New York: Harcourt, Brace & World, Inc., 1932).

amination in psychology, suddenly became an authority on the subject. The stir caused by the books disturbed him somewhat since he considered them to be only preliminary and tentative, and not an expression of his definitive views on the nature of intelligence. He was well aware of the books' deficiencies. Nevertheless, he agreed to publish the volumes, partly because he felt they might lead others to further research which might eventually result in a fuller understanding of child thought.

In the United States, the books were at first received enthusiastically, and during the twenties and thirties Piaget's work was highly regarded in this country. Then followed a period, lasting until the middle fifties, when his views, as expressed in the early books, came under much criticism. But with the publication in the early fifties of English translations of several of Piaget's later books, interest in his work revived.

During the period from 1920 to 1930, Piaget's time was fully oc-cupied. He performed a great deal of research and at the same time also taught various courses in psychology, sociology and scientific thought at Geneva and Neuchâtel. His three children were born during these years: a daughter in 1925, a second daughter in 1927, and a son in 1931. Piaget and his wife, one of his former students, became close observers of their chil-dren's behavior. The results of their study, which covered the "sensori-motor period" from birth until about 2 years, were published in two volumes: *The Origins of Intelligence in the Child* [8] and *The Construction of Reality in the Child*.[9] Piaget's study of infancy convinced him that thought derived from the child's action, and not from his language. This increased emphasis on action led Piaget to modify his testing technique for older children. He remembered his past experience at the Salpetrière hospital and his solution to the difficulties encountered in trying to apply an exclusively verbal method to abnormal children. Consequently, he made the manipulation of concrete materials an essential aspect of the clinical method, in the case of children of all ages. The emphasis was no longer on language alone, but on manipulation supplemented by lan-guage.

From 1929 to 1939 Piaget's professional life became even more ac-tive. He was appointed Professor of the History of Scientific Thought at Geneva University. He became Assistant Director, and shortly afterwards Co-Director, of the Jean-Jacques Rousseau Institute, which he helped to reorganize when it became attached to Geneva University. He taught

8. *La Naissance de l'Intelligence chez l'Enfant* (Neuchâtel: Delachaux & Niestlé, 1936); *The Origins of Intelligence in Children*, trans. M. Cook (New York: International University Press, 1952).
9. *La Construction du Réel chez l'Enfant* (Neuchâtel: Delachaux & Niestlé, 1936); *The Construction of Reality in the Child*, trans. M. Cook (New York: Basic Books, Inc., Publ., 1954).

experimental psychology at Lausanne University. Also, Piaget became involved in international affairs and accepted the chairmanship of the International Bureau of Education, later to become affiliated with UNESCO.

Piaget's experiences led to several changes in his thinking. The studies of infancy influenced him to modify his techniques of research, and to place emphasis on the role of the child's activity in the formation of thought. Also, his teaching opened up new areas for research and experiment. The course on the history of scientific thought directed him toward the study of the child's understanding of certain scientific notions. With two important collaborators, Bärbel Inhelder and Alina Szeminska, he set out to explore this field, and in 1941 published two books on their research. The first, written with B. Inhelder was *Le Développement des Quantités Physiques chez l'Enfant.*[10] It shows how the child gradually comes to recognize that certain physical attributes of an object, like its substance or weight, do not vary when the object merely changes shape. Surprisingly, young children fail to *conserve* these invariants. The second book, written with the aid of A. Szeminska was *The Child's Conception of Number.*[11] Here Piaget describes the evolution of the child's efforts to master the notion of number.

The next book, published in 1942, *Classes, Relations et Nombres,*[12] deals with the correspondence between certain operations of formal logic and mental operations. Piaget uses logic to describe the mental operations available to the child from 7 to 11 in the stage of "concrete operations." The book is thus a fulfillment of Piaget's early intention at the Binet Laboratory in Paris to use a formal language for psychological purposes.

Piaget then became interested in the perceptual research of the "Gestalt" psychologists. His lack of agreement with some of their theories, however, led him and his collaborators to a lengthy series of experiments into the nature of perception. At first the experiments of the Gestalt psychologists were replicated. Later the studies were extended to cover not only perception as an isolated process, but also its relation to intelligence. For some 20 years, from 1943 onwards, Piaget and his associates produced a number of articles and monographs on perception. The culmination was the publication in 1961 of his book, *Les Mécanismes Perceptifs,*[13] which describes perceptual structures and processes and relates them to intellectual ones.

In the early forties, Albert Einstein suggested to Piaget that it might

10. Jean Piaget and Bärbel Inhelder, *Le Développement des Quantités Physiques chez l'Enfant* (Neuchâtel: Delachaux & Niestlé, 1941).
11. Jean Piaget and Alina Szeminska, *La Genèse du Nombre chez l'Enfant* (Neuchâtel: Delachaux & Niestlé, 1941); *The Child's Conception of Number,* trans. C. Gattegno and F. M. Hodgson (London: Routledge & Kegan Paul Ltd., 1952).
12. *Classes, Relations et Nombres* (Paris: Librairie Philosophique J. Vrin, 1942).
13. *Les Mécanismes Perceptifs* (Paris: Presses Universitaires de France, 1961).

be of interest to epistemology if he were to investigate the child's under-standing of time, velocity, and movement. Piaget followed the suggestion and in 1946 published two books on these matters: *Le Développement de la Notion de Temps chez l'Enfant*,[14] and *Les Notions de Mouvement et de Vitesse chez l'Enfant*.[15] In the same year, 1946, Piaget also published his book on symbolic thought, *Play, Dreams and Imitation*,[16] which con-tains observations on his own children, from 2 to 4 years of age.

After the Second World War, appreciation of Piaget's work began to spread throughout the world. He received honorary degrees from several universities including Harvard, the Sorbonne in Paris, Brussels, and the University of Brazil. In the United States, however, Piaget was honored but not fully understood; only his first five books had been translated. Dur-ing the forties, he continued his activities in the International Bureau of Education and was appointed head of the Swiss delegation to UNESCO. In 1947 Piaget published a small volume entitled *The Psychology of Intelli-gence*.[17] The book is a collection of lectures Piaget had given in 1942 to the College de France in Paris, and sets out, for the first time at any length, an overview of Piaget's theory of mental development.

During this time, Piaget continued his research into the various as-pects of cognition. From the experiments on perception grew the study of two closely allied fields: the child's understanding of space and geometry. In collaboration with Inhelder and Szeminska, he published in 1948 *The Child's Conception of Space*,[18] and *The Child's Conception of Geome-try*.[19] In 1949 Piaget wrote *Traité de Logique*,[20] a book dealing with the basic operations involved in logic. The book is the first full summary of his logical system: it expands upon the logical models already used in previous research, and introduces additional logical models which he was later to apply to adolescent thought.

14. *Le Développement de la Notion de Temps chez l'Enfant* (Paris: Presses Univer-sitaires de France, 1946).
15. *Les Notions de Mouvement et de Vitesse chez l'Enfant* (Paris: Presses Univer-sitaires de France, 1946).
16. *La Formation du Symbole chez l'Enfant* (Neuchâtel: Delachaux & Niestlé, 1946); *Play, Dreams, and Imitation in Childhood*, trans. C. Gattegno and F. M. Hodgson (New York: W. W. Norton & Co., Inc., 1951).
17. *La Psychologie de l'Intelligence* (Paris: Librairie Armand Colin, 1947); *The Psychology of Intelligence*, trans. M. Percy and D. E. Berlyne (London: Rout-ledge & Kegan Paul Ltd., 1950).
18. Jean Piaget and Bärbel Inhelder, *La Représentation de l'Espace chez l'Enfant* (Paris: Presses Universitaires de France, 1948); *The Child's Conception of Space*, trans. F. J. Langdon and J. L. Lunzer (London: Routledge & Kegan Paul Ltd., 1956).
19. Jean Piaget, Bärbel Inhelder, and Alina Szeminska, *La Géometrie Spontanée de l'Enfant* (Paris: Presses Universitaires de France, 1948); *The Child's Concep-tion of Geometry*, trans. E. A. Lunzer (London: Routledge & Kegan Paul Ltd., 1960).
20. *Traité de Logique* (Paris: Librairie Armand Colin, 1949).

From about 1920 to 1950, Piaget had been engaged in experimental work with children in an attempt to understand the evolution of human intelligence. Now he felt prepared to apply the results of his psychological research to the epistemological problems which had originally motivated his interest in psychology. In 1950 he published a three volume series on "genetic epistemology" entitled *Introduction a l'Épistémologie Géné-tique.*[21] The books cover various aspects of knowledge, including mathematics, physics, psychology, sociology, biology, and logic. Piaget analyzes these facets of knowledge in terms of the relation between the individual and his environment; that is, between the knower and the known. He tries to determine whether this relationship is affected by the type of knowledge involved; for instance, whether mathematical knowledge involves a different kind of interaction with the environment from that of physical knowledge. Piaget also draws a parallel between the historical and individual development of knowledge, and he finds that the evolution of individual thought sometimes follows the same progression as the history of scientific thought.

Next Piaget turned to the study of chance and the elementary concepts of probability. In 1951, he and Inhelder published a book entitled *La Genèse de l'Idée du Hasard chez l'Enfant,*[22] which deals with the child's understanding of random events in his environment. In 1952 Piaget was appointed Professor of Genetic Psychology at the University of Paris (Sorbonne), where he remained until 1962. At the same time he continued to teach at Geneva University and to head the Jean-Jacques Rousseau Institute. He also pursued his research into both perception and logical thought. In 1952 he published a book called *Essai sur les Transformations des Opérations Logiques* [23] dealing with propositional logic and various logical structures, like the group and lattice, which he used as models for adolescent and adult thought. After having studied the period of early and middle childhood, Piaget turned to the product of this earlier intellectual development, the thought of the adolescent and the adult. In 1955 Piaget and Inhelder published a book on this subject, *The Growth of Logical Thinking from Childhood to Adolescence,*[24] which compared,

21. *Introduction à l'Épistemologie Génétique,* Vol. I, *La Pensée Mathématique,* Vol. II, *La Pensée Physique,* Vol. III, *La Pensée Biologique, la Pensée Psychologique et la Pensée Sociologique* (Paris: Presses Universitaires de France, 1950).
22. Jean Piaget and Bärbel Inhelder, *La Genèse de l'Idée du Hasard chez l'Enfant* (Paris: Presses Universitaires de France, 1951).
23. *Essai sur les Transformations des Opérations Logiques. Les 256 Opérations Terniaires de la Logique Bivalente des Propositions* (Paris: Presses Universitaires de France, 1952).
24. Jean Piaget and Bärbel Inhelder, *De la Logique de l'Enfant à la Logique de l'Adolescent* (Paris: Presses Universitaires de France, 1955); *The Growth of Logical Thinking from Childhood to Adolescence,* trans. A. Parsons and S. Seagrin (New York: Basic Books, Inc., Publ., 1958).

again in logical terms, the thought processes of the adolescent with those of the younger child.

The year 1956 was important for Piaget, for he was able to initiate a project that he had been contemplating for some time. With his broad scope of interests, including biology, zoology, logic, mathematics, psychology, philosophy, and epistemology, Piaget had always dreamed of the possibility of an interdisciplinary approach to basic problems of cognition. The idea had initially encountered a certain amount of scepticism, but Piaget finally managed to establish an institution where such interdisciplinary cooperation was possible. An international Center for Genetic Epistemology was created within the Faculty of Science of Geneva University. The aim of the Center was to gather together each year a number of eminent scholars in various fields—biologists, psychologists, mathematicians and others—who would combine their efforts to study a given problem. Each person would treat the problem from the point of view of his specialty, but the research was to be coordinated through regular discussions. At the end of the year, a symposium would be held, where the researchers' conclusions would be discussed. The deliberation of each symposium would be published in a series of monographs, entitled, *Studies in Genetic Epistemology*. Over the past ten years, there have already been published 14 of these volumes, dealing with a variety of subjects such as the notion of causality, the learning processes, and mathematical thinking.

In 1959 Piaget published *The Early Growth of Logic in the Child*.[25] The book again uses logical models to describe the mental operations of the child from 7 to 11 years. It treats in particular his methods of classifying and of ordering objects. In 1964 a small book containing six short essays on various psychological topics was published [26] and the following year, 1965, Piaget published *Sagesse et Illusions de la Philosophie*. In this book he discusses the essential differences between philosophy, which leads to subjective "wisdom," and science, which leads to objective knowledge. He also explains why he turned away from his early preference for the former towards the latter. In the same year, 1965, he also published a book of four sociological studies entitled *Études Sociologiques*,[27] which is a collection of some of the lectures he had given in his courses on sociology.

The titles of Piaget's books indicate that the contents deal in general with highly specialized aspects of thinking or cognition. Each book treats

25. Jean Piaget and Bärbel Inhelder, *La Gènese des Structures Logiques Élémentaires* (Neuchâtel: Delachaux & Niestlé, 1959); *The Early Growth of Logic in the Child*, trans. E. A. Lunzer and D. Papert (London: Routledge & Kegan Paul Ltd., 1964).

26. *Six Études de Psychologie* (Geneva: Editions Gonthier, 1964); *Six Psychological Studies*, trans. A. Tenzer and D. Elkind (New York: Random House, Inc., 1967).

27. *Études Sociologiques* (Geneva: Librairie Droz, 1965).

a particular topic, like geometry or number, in a more or less identical manner. That is, the notion is studied from its origins in the child to the point, usually in adolescence, where it reaches a mature status. Although such an approach is of interest to psychologists and educators, difficulties are presented for the person who wishes only to get a general understanding of Piaget's overall system. In 1966, therefore, recognizing the need for a short introductory book on his system, Piaget and Inhelder published a short book entitled *La Psychologie de l'Enfant*,[28] which was intended for the general public. The book gives a brief summary of Piaget's theory of intellectual development and also deals with related matters like perception. In the same year, 1966, these two authors also published a book on mental imagery, *L'Image Mentale chez l'Enfant*,[29] which describes the development of mental images and relates it to the growth of intelligence. In 1967 he published *Biologie et Connaissance*,[30] which deals with the relations between biological factors and the cognitive processes. Piaget and Inhelder's most recent book, *Mémoire et Intelligence*,[31] deals with the memory processes of the child. Introducing a new approach to the study of memory, Piaget examines closely the relations existing between memory and the development of intellectual functioning. He finds, for example, that memory does not always deteriorate over time; it can also improve, as a result of the development of certain related intellectual skills.

The evolution of Piaget's interests is clearly illustrated by the titles and contents of his books and other publications. From his early work in biology, particularly the study of molluscs, he gradually turned to the psychological development of the child. His intention was to find a link between the biological study of life and the philosophical study of knowledge. His first few books on children's thought were exploratory, setting forth his preliminary theory of intellectual development. Later, however, he began to state his theories in terms of a formal language: logic. The subject matter of his books also began to change; he became attracted to study of the child's understanding of scientific and mathematical notions. Once he achieved a good measure of understanding of the child's intellectual processes, Piaget then attempted to bring his psychological theories to bear on the study of knowledge in general. He returned, after more than 30 years of psychological research, to his original interest, theoretical problems in epistemology. It is quite remarkable that, though more than 70 years old, Piaget today pursues his professional work as actively as in the

28. Jean Piaget and Bärbel Inhelder, *La Psychologie de l'Enfant* (Paris: Presses Universitaires de France, Collection "Que Sais-je?" 1966).
29. Jean Piaget and Bärbel Inhelder, *L'Image Mentale chez l'Enfant* (Paris: Presses Universitaires de France, 1966).
30. *Biologie et Connaissance* (Bussière, France: Éditions Gallimard, 1967).
31. Jean Piaget and Bärbel Inhelder, *Mémoire et Intelligence* (Paris: Presses Universitaires de France, 1968).

past. He continues to produce new theories and research and is currently writing another book on the development of the notion of causality.

BASIC IDEAS

In the present section, we will introduce several basic ideas which have shaped Piaget's approach to the study of intellectual development. A scientist usually employs a theoretical framework to guide his experimentation and theorizing. The framework is not a detailed theory but a point of view or a set of attitudes which orient the scientist's activities. A psychologist, for example, may be basically committed both to Freudian ideas and to the personality test approach, and these attitudes will then be likely to give direction to his research and analysis. For example, these ideas may influence him to choose to study the familial causes of neurosis rather than the physical bases of the disorder. Such an orientation would almost certainly lead him to investigate the matter by giving paper and pencil tests which might lead to different results from those which could be obtained by the direct observation of the child in his home. This is not to deny, of course, that scientists do change their opinions as a result of conflicting research evidence. However, it is nevertheless true that orienting attitudes can be influential; the scientist does not begin his work without any preconceptions.

Piaget's orienting attitudes, stated quite explicitly, have to do with the nature of intelligence and with its structure and functions.

Intelligence

First, how does Piaget define the nature of intelligence? The reader should be aware that Piaget had almost complete freedom in this regard. Previous to the 1920's, when he began his investigations, there had been little research or theorizing on intelligence. The mental testing approach was in evidence, as exemplified by the Binet-Simon IQ test; and there were also scattered experimental investigations of intellectual processes like memory in the adult. However, neither of these approaches had been developed extensively, and psychologists had hardly agreed, and do not concur even today, on the proper subject matter for the psychology of intelligence. Does intelligence refer to rote memory, to creativity, to IQ test performance, to the child's reasoning, or to other matters? Because Piaget began his studies during a pioneering era he was free to conceive of intelligence in terms of his unique perspective. He was careful not to begin by proposing too rigid or precise a definition of intelligence. Piaget did not want to fall into the trap of too narrowly circumscribing the subject matter when so little was known about it. To lay down an overly restrictive definition at the outset would have been to curtail investigation and impede discovery. In fact, the major aim of Piaget's research was to discover what actually constitutes intelligence.

Desiring to avoid premature restrictions, Piaget offered several definitions of intelligence, all couched in general terms. These definitions reflect Piaget's biological orientation. For example, ". . . intelligence is a particular instance of biológical adaptation . . ." [32] This states quite clearly that human intelligence is one kind of biological achievement, which allows the individual to interact effectively with the environment at a psychological level. Another definition states that intelligence "is the form of equilibrium toward which all the [cognitive] structures . . . tend." [33] The use of the term "equilibrium," borrowed from physics, implies a balance, a harmonious adjustment between at least two factors; in this case between the person's mental actions (the cognitive structures) and his environment. Although the environment may disturb the equilibrium, the individual can perform mental actions to restore the balance. The definition also states that equilibrium is not immediately achieved: the cognitive structures only gradually "tend" towards equilibrium. It is of special interest to the biologist to study this evolution and the dynamic processes underlying it. Piaget's primary goal, then, could be defined as the study of children's gradual attainment of increasingly effective intellectual structures. Another definition stresses that intelligence is "a system of living and acting operations." [34] Piaget is interested in mental activity, in what the individual *does* in his interaction with the world. Piaget believes that knowledge is not given to a passive observer; rather, knowledge of reality must be discovered and constructed by the activity of the child. As we shall see later, this position is at odds with the essentially passive-mechanistic view held by American behavorists.

Thus far, we have seen that intelligence involves biological adaptation, equilibrium between the individual and the environment, gradual evolution, and mental activity. These definitions are quite general. It is also instructive to take note of what the definitions do *not* stress. They do not emphasize individual differences in intelligence. While such an emphasis would be quite consonant with a biological approach, Piaget is not concerned with whether one person is more intelligent or more clever than another, or why. Piaget, of course, recognizes that differences in intellectual ability do exist, but he is not particularly interested in this analysis; instead, he seeks to abstract from the various idiosyncratic manifestations of be-

32. *Origins of Intelligence*, pp. 3–4.
33. *Psychology of Intelligence*, p. 6.
34. *Ibid.*, p. 7.

havior a description of the general form of thought. Piaget's theories do not describe the average level of cognitive functioning; rather they depict the optimum capability of thought at a given period in development.

It is important to note that the definitions place little emphasis on the emotions. However, Piaget recognizes that the emotions influence thought, and in fact, he repeatedly states that no act of intelligence is complete without emotions. They represent the energetic or motivational aspect of intellectual activity. Nevertheless, Piaget's empirical investigations and detailed theories substantially ignore the emotions in favor of the structure of intellect.

Piaget has chosen one of several available strategies with which to investigate the psychology of intelligence. He de-emphasizes individual differences and the effects of emotions on thought, and instead focusses on the optimum level of functioning. Many psychologists, particularly English and American, have concentrated on individual differences by means of the test approach in order to investigate intellectual activity. Others have attempted from the outset to consider the influence of the emotions, especially anxiety, on intellectual performance. Which strategy is best? The answer seems to be that all are of interest. All view the problem of intelligence from different angles and deal with somewhat different issues. Since a man cannot study everything, he usually settles on one approach if he is to accomplish anything at all. As we shall see in the pages to follow, Piaget's approach seems to have amply demonstrated its merits.

In addition to proposing general definitions, Piaget has structured the psychology of intelligence by the selection of the particular subject matter he has investigated. As we saw in the biographical review, Piaget's early works were concerned with such matters as verbal communication and moral judgment. With the passage of time Piaget has come to stress the child's understanding of various scientific and mathematical ideas like velocity and one-to-one correspondence. This emphasis reflects Piaget's focus on epistemological problems. To understand Piaget's conception of intelligence, therefore, we must not only consider his definitions, but the nature of his research activities. The latter, especially in recent years, reveal rather unique epistemological concerns.

In conclusion, we have seen how Piaget's two major interests—biology and epistemology—have shaped his approach to the psychology of intelligence. The biological concern resulted in definitions of intelligence in general terms of growth, stages, adaptation, equilibrium, and similar factors. The epistemological focus has resulted in the empirical investigation of the child's understanding of space, time, causality, and similar notions.

In essence, Piaget looks at intelligence in terms of content, structure, and function. We will consider aspects of these in the following sections.

Content

One simple aspect of thought is its manifest content. This refers to what the individual is thinking about, what interests him at the moment, or the terms in which he contemplates a given problem. For instance, suppose a mechanic is asked what makes a car go. He gives an answer in terms of the explosion of gas, the movement of pistons, the transfer of power from one point to another. These statements reflect the contents of his thought. If a young child were posed the same question, his response would be quite different. Ignorant of the workings of the motor, he might suppose that the car's movement results from all the horses inside. Obviously, the content of his thought is quite different from that of the adult.

During the early portion of his career, Piaget's research focussed on the contents of the child's thought. *The Child's Conception of the World* and *The Child's Conception of Physical Causality*, both written in the 1920's, paid particular attention to the child's views of the physical world. The clinical method was used to obtain the child's answers to such questions as, where do shadows come from, what causes rivers to flow, or the clouds to move? Despite these initial investigations, Piaget felt that the study of content was only a minor goal for the psychology of intelligence. While descriptions of content may have some interest, they do not get at the heart of the matter; they do not explain why thought takes the form it does. For Piaget, therefore, the primary goal of the psychology of intelligence is not the mere description of the content of thought but the basic processes underlying and determining the content. Piaget has therefore devoted the greater part of his career in psychology to the study of the structures and functions of intelligence.

Hereditary Structures

It should come as no surprise that Piaget's theoretical framework deals with the role of biological factors in the development of intelligence. These factors operate in several ways: one of them is defined as the *hereditary transmission of physical structures*. Different species are, of course, endowed by heredity with different physical structures. The nervous system, for example, varies considerably from worm to man. It is immediately obvious that the inherited physical structures both permit certain intellectual achievements and prohibit others. The human eye is one example of a physical structure. It is constructed in such a way that human beings are able to perceive three dimensional space. It is conceivable, however, to think of eyes created that would perceive two dimensional space, and the existence of such a physical structure would undoubtedly affect intelligence.

Another type of structure transmitted by heredity is the *automatic behavioral reaction*. For example, from birth members of many species possess various *reflexes*. When a specified event in the environment (a *stimulus*) occurs, the organism automatically responds with a particular behavior. No learning or training or other experience with the environment is usually necessary for the reflex response to occur. Moreover, all members of the species, unless they are in some way defective, possess the reflex. The basis for this automatic behavior is an inherited physical mechanism. When the stimulus occurs it activates this mechanism which produces the response. One example of this behavior is the sucking reflex which is necessary for survival. When any object (the stimulus) touches an infant's lips, the automatic response is to suck. The newborn does not need to be taught to suck. A further example is the ability to cry. The newborn's physical structure is such that when hungry he automatically signals his discomfort with a wail. Often the reflexes are adaptive: they help the organism in its interaction with the environment.

Piaget feels that in the case of human intelligence, reflexes and other automatic patterns of behavior play only a minor role. It is only the infant, and more specifically the newborn, whose behavior is heavily dependent on the elementary behavioral structures of the type described. Piaget's research has shown that after the first few days of life, the reflexes are modified by the infant's experience and are transformed into a new type of mechanism—the psychological structure—which is not directly and simply provided by heredity. As we shall see, psychological structures form the basis for intellectual activity and are the product of a complex interaction between biological and experiential factors.

General Principles of Functioning

We have seen that heredity affects intelligence in two ways. Inherited physical structures set broad limits on intellectual functioning. Inherited behavioral reactions have an influence during the first few days of human life but afterward are extensively modified as the infant interacts with his environment. Piaget's theoretical framework postulates that biological factors affect intelligence in a third way: all species inherit two basic tendencies or "invariant functions": *adaptation* and *organization*.

Let us first consider organization. This term refers to the tendency for all species to systematize or organize their processes into coherent systems which may be either physical or psychological. In the former case, fish possess a number of structures which allow functioning in the water—for example, gills, a particular circulatory system, and temperature mechanisms. All these structures interact and are coordinated into an efficient system. This coordination is the result of the organization tendency. It should be emphasized that organization refers not to gills or the circulatory structure in particular, but to the tendency observed in all life to integrate their structures into a composite system (or higher-order structure).

At a psychological level, too, the tendency to organize is present. In his interaction with the world, the individual tends to integrate his psychological structures into coherent systems. For example, the very young infant has available the separate behavioral structures of either looking at objects or of grasping them. He does not initially combine the two. After a period of development, he organizes these two separate structures into a higher-order structure which enables him to grasp something at the same time he looks at it. Organization, then, is the tendency common to all forms of life to integrate structures, which may be physical or psychological, into higher-order systems or structures.

The second general principle of functioning is *adaptation*. All organisms are born with a tendency to adapt to the environment. The ways in which adaptation occurs differ from species to species, from individual to individual within a species, or from stage to stage within any one individual. Nevertheless, the tendency to adapt in some way or another is an invariant function and therefore considered an aspect of biology. Adaptation may be considered in terms of two complementary processes: *assimilation* and *accommodation*.

We will illustrate these processes first by means of a simple physiological example; namely, digestion. When a person eats something his digestive system reacts to the substances incorporated. In order to deal with the foreign substance, the muscles of the stomach contract in various ways, certain organs release acids, and so on. Putting the matter in general terms, we may say that the person's physical structures (the stomach and related organs) *accommodated* to the environmental event (the food). In other words, the process of accommodation describes the individual's tendency to change in response to environmental demands. The functional invariant of *assimilation* is the complementary process by which the individual deals with an environmental event in terms of his current structures. In the case of digestion the acids transform the food into a form which the body can use. Thus the individual not only modifies his structures in reaction to external demands (accommodation), he also uses his structures to incorporate elements of the external world (assimilation).

For Piaget intellectual adaptation is also an interaction, or an exchange, between a person and his environment and involves the same two processes—assimilation and accommodation—as are found in biology. On the one hand the person incorporates or assimilates features of external reality into his own psychological structures; on the other hand he modifies or accommodates his psychological structures to meet the pressures of the environment. Consider an example of adaptation in infancy. Suppose an infant of 4 months is presented with a rattle. He has never before had the opportunity to play with rattles or similar toys. The rattle, then, is a feature of the environment to which he needs to adapt. His subsequent behavior reveals the tendencies of assimilation and accommodation. The infant tries to grasp the rattle. In order to do this successfully he must accommodate in more ways than are immediately apparent. First, he must accommodate his visual activities to perceive the rattle correctly; then he must reach out and accommodate his movements to the distance between himself and the rattle; in grasping the rattle he must adjust his fingers to its shape; in lifting the rattle he must accommodate his muscular exertion to its weight. In sum, the grasping of the rattle involves a series of acts of accommodation, or modifications of the infant's behavioral structures to suit the demands of the environment.

Grasping the rattle also involves assimilation. In the past the infant has already grasped things; for him, grasping is a well-formed structure of behavior. When he sees the rattle for the first time he tries to deal with the novel object by incorporating it into a habitual pattern of behavior. In a sense he tries to transform the novel object into something that he is familiar with; namely, a thing to be grasped. We can say, therefore, that he assimilates the object into his framework.

Adaptation, then, is a basic tendency of the organism and consists of the two processes of assimilation and accommodation. How do the two relate to one another? First, it is clear that they are complementary processes. Assimilation involves the person's dealing with the environment in terms of his structures, while accommodation involves the transformation of his structures in response to the environment. Moreover, the processes are simultaneously present in every act. When the infant grasps the rattle his fingers accommodate to its shape; at the same time he is assimilating the rattle into his framework, the grasping structure.

In sum, Piaget postulates that there are two general principles of functioning which affect intelligence: *organization* and *adaptation* (assimilation and accommodation). These are biological factors in the sense that they are common to all species. While organization and adaptation are inherited, they are not structures (like reflexes) but *tendencies*. The particular ways in which an organism adapts and organizes its processes depend also on its environment, and its learning history. In Piaget's view, the human being does not inherit particular intellectual reactions; rather, he does inherit a tendency to organize his intellectual processes, and to adapt to his environment, in some way.

Psychological Structures

We have seen that man tends to organize his behavior and thought and to adapt to the environment. These tendencies result in a number of psychological structures which take different forms at different ages. The child progresses through a series of stages each characterized by different psychological structures before he attains adult intelligence. From birth to about 2 years the infant is unable to think; he can only perform overt action. For example, if a toy falls apart he cannot first think how it might best be put together again; instead, he might immediately act on the toy and try to reassemble it. His activities, however, are not random, but display order and coherence. Almost immediately after birth the infant shows organized behavior. As we have seen, some of these patterns of action, like the reflex, are due mainly to hereditary factors. However, specific heredity cannot explain all of the orderliness in the infant's behavior. For example, the two-month old infant usually sucks his thumb or a finger. When put in the crib he regularly brings his hand to the mouth in a relatively quick and efficient way. In the common language we would probably say that he has acquired the "habit" of thumb-sucking. The word "habit" implies a regularity, a coherence, in the infant's actions. It is clear that thumb-sucking is not based entirely on inherited physical structures. While there is a reflex to suck any object touching the lips, there is no innate tendency to bring the hand to the mouth; this activity must be learned. In Piaget's theory, such an organized pattern of behavior is termed a *scheme*.[35] The concept of scheme is used in a very broad way. It can refer to the reflexes and other kinds of innate behavior already discussed. It is in this way that Piaget speaks of the "sucking scheme." But the vast majority of schemes are not innate; instead they are in some way based on experience as in the case of the thumb-sucking scheme.

Thus far we have spoken of the scheme only as a pattern of behavior, or as an action which displays coherence and order. However, there are a number of additional aspects of the scheme. First, it involves activity on the part of the child; the concept is used to describe things he *does*. Most often, use of the term in this way presents no difficulties. Occasionally, however, scheme is used to describe actions which are not immediately obvious. For example, Piaget speaks of the "looking scheme." The use of "scheme" here is quite deliberate since he means to imply that vision is

---

35. Piaget's French term *scheme* has usually been translated into English as *schema* (plural, *schemata*). We do not follow this practice since Piaget has lately been using the French word *schema* for another purpose. Also, the reader should be aware that scheme need not refer only to behavior; there are mental schemes too.

an active process; the child's eyes move as they actively *search* the environment. Second, scheme refers to the basic structure underlying the child's overt actions. Scheme is used to designate the essence of the child's behavior. Let us take thumb-sucking as an example. If we examine the infant's behavior in detail, we will see that no two acts of thumb-sucking performed by one child are precisely the same. On one occasion the activity starts when the thumb is 10 inches from the mouth; on another when it is 11 inches away. At one time the thumb travels in almost a straight line to the mouth; at another time its trajectory is quite irregular. In short, if we describe behavior in sufficient detail, we find that there are no two identical actions. There is no one act of thumb-sucking, but many; in fact as many as the number of times the child brings the thumb to the mouth. At first glance this situation might seem to pose insurmountable difficulties for the psychologist. How can he describe and explain behavior if each act is different from every other? Fortunately, the difficulty is only apparent, since most psychologists are not really interested in the fine details of behavior. What is important, especially for Piaget, is the structure of behavior; that is, an abstraction of the features common to a wide variety of acts which differ in detail. In the case of thumb-sucking, whether or not the act starts from a distance of 10 or 11 inches is of no significance. What is crucial is that the infant has acquired a regular way of getting the thumb into the mouth. This "regular way" is an abstraction furnished by the psychologist. The infant puts his hand into his mouth in many particular ways, no two being identical, and the psychologist detects in these specific actions a certain regularity which he then calls a scheme.

Let us now consider another type of psychological structure: that of the classifying *operations* of the older child from about 7 to 11 years. Suppose an examiner presents him with a collection of red and blue beads mixed together. Confronted with this situation the older child first thinks of the objects as being members of classes. There is the class of red beads and the class of blue ones. Further, unlike the younger child, he realizes that the class of red beads is included in a larger class, that of beads in general. Another way of putting the matter is to say that he groups the red beads into one class and conceives of it as being a part of a hierarchy of classes. The class immediately "above" the red beads (that is, the more inclusive class) is that of beads-in-general. Of course, the class of beads-in-general may also be located in a classification hierarchy. The class of solid objects will contain the class of beads.

Obviously the older child's operational schemes are quite different from the infant's behavioral schemes. The latter involve patterns of behavior because the infant acts overtly on the world. Although the older child's schemes also involve acting on the world, this is done intellectually. He considers, for example, the relatively abstract problem of whether given classes are contained in others. Piaget describes this aspect of the older child's thought in terms of the operations of classification. What is important for Piaget is not that the child can answer questions about beads (that, of course, is trivial), but that his activities reveal the existence of a basic structure; namely, the operations of putting things together, of placing them in classes, of forming hierarchies of classes, and so on. Classification, then, is composed of a series of intellectual activities which constitute a psychological structure. Of course, the child does not realize that he has such a structure and may not even know what the word "classification" means. The classification structure and "schemes" both describe an observer's conception of the basic processes underlying the child's activities; the child himself is certainly not aware of these structures.

The Description of Structures

If we accept that Piaget's theoretical framework is based on the concept of psychological structures, how can we go about describing them? One way to describe them is by using common language. We can say that the child classifies objects or that his moral judgment is "objective," and so forth. Sometimes the common language adequately conveys meaning, but sometimes it does not. Unfortunately, there are occasions when an ordinary word means different things to different people. When this occurs the scientist is in danger of being misunderstood. Consequently, the sciences have tended to develop various formal languages in order to guarantee precise communication. The physicist does not say that objects "fall very fast" or "pick up speed as they go along." Instead, he writes a formula in which each term is precisely defined and in which the relations among the terms are completely specified by the formal language of mathematics. If the reader of the formula knows what the terms mean and understands the requisite mathematics, then the physicist's meaning can be accurately transmitted without the danger of misinterpretation.

Piaget feels that psychology too should attempt to use formal languages in describing the structures underlying thought. Psychological words in particular are quite ambiguous. While the theorists may intend a particular meaning for words like "habit," or "thought," or "classification," it is extremely probable that these terms will signify to others a wide variety of alternative interpretations. Consequently, Piaget has attempted to use formal languages—particularly terms of logic and of mathematics—to describe the structures underlying the child's activities. In later chapters we shall consider in detail both the formal description of the structures and Piaget's rationale for using it.

Functions, Structures, and Equilibrium

We cannot emphasize sufficiently the extent to which Piaget believes that the functional invariants—organization and adaptation (assimilation and accommodation)—and the psychological structures are inextricably intertwined. As we have seen, assimilation and accommodation, although complementary, nevertheless occur simultaneously. A balance between the two is necessary for adaptation. Moreover, adaptation is not separate from organization. In the process of organizing his activities the individual assimilates novel events into pre-existing structures, and at the same time he accommodates pre-existing structures to meet the demands of the new situation. Furthermore, the functional invariants (organization and adaptation) are closely related to the structures of intelligence.

As a result of the tendencies toward adaptation and organziation, new structures are continually being created out of the old ones which will be employed to assist the individual in his interaction with the world. Looking at the matter in another way, structures are necessary for adaptation and organization. One could neither adapt to the environment nor organize one's processes if there were no basic structures available at the outset. On the other hand, the very existence of a structure, which by Piaget's definition is an organized totality, entails the necessity for organization and adaptation. There are, however, important differences between the invariant functions and the structures. As the individual progresses through the life span, the functions will remain the same but the structures will vary, and appear in a fairly regular sequence. Another way of saying this is that intellectual development proceeds through a series of *stages* with each stage characterized by a different kind of psychological structure. An individual of any age must adapt to the environment and must organize his responses continually, but the instruments by which he accomplishes this—the psychological structures—will change from one age level to another. For example, both the infant and adult will organize and adapt; but the resulting psychological structures are quite different for the two periods.

Piaget further proposes that organisms tend toward equilibrium with the environment. The organism—whether a human being or some other form of life—tends to organize structures into coherent and stable patterns. His ways of dealing with the world tend toward a certain balance. He tries to develop structures which are effective in his interaction with reality. This means that when a new event occurs he can apply to it the lessons of the past (or assimilate the events into already existing structures), and he will easily modify his current patterns of behavior to respond to the requirements of the new situation. With increasing experience he acquires more and more structures and therefore adapts more readily to an increasing number of situations.

SUMMARY AND CONCLUSIONS

Early in his life Piaget developed two major intellectual interests: biology, the study of life, and epistemology, the study of knowledge. After devoting a number of years to each of these disciplines, Piaget sought a way to integrate them. In the course of his work at the Binet Laboratory in Paris, he came to the conclusion that psychology might provide the link between biology and epistemology. Piaget decided to spend a few years on the study of the evolution of knowledge in the child and then to apply the fruits of this research to the solution of the theoretical problems which initially motivated him. Fortunately for child psychology the few years became many, and in their course Piaget has produced over 30 volumes reporting his investigations into such matters as the child's moral judgment, the infant's patterns of behavior, and the adolescent's solution of scientific problems. Only in the 1950's was Piaget able to return to theoretical issues in epistemology. Today, even at the age of more than 70 years, Piaget continues his contributions to psychology, as he has recently published works on mental imagery, memory, and other matters.

Piaget's research and theory have been guided by a framework which can be defined as a set of orienting attitudes. His definition of intelligence is not restrictive, but states that intelligence involves biological adaptation, equilibrium between the individual and his environment, and a set of mental operations which permit this balance. Piaget's research activities also have increasingly come to focus on the growth of the child's understanding of the basic concepts of science, mathematics, and similar disciplines. Piaget is less interested in studying the contents of the child's thought than the basic processes underlying it.

The individual inherits physical structures which set broad limits on his intellectual functioning. He also inherits a few automatic behavioral reactions or reflexes which have their greatest influence on functioning in the first few days of life. These reflexes are rapidly transformed into structures which incorporate the results of experience. The third kind of inheritance—the general principles of functioning—is another biological aspect of intelligence. One general principle of functioning is organization; all species have the tendency to organize their processes.

A second aspect of general functioning is adaptation which may be further subdivided into assimilation and accommodation. Accommodation refers to the organism's tendency to modify its structures according to the pressures of the environment, while assimilation involves using current structures which can deal with the environment. The result of the principles of functioning is a series of psychological structures which differ qualitatively from one another throughout a person's lifetime. For example, the infant employs behavioral schemes or patterns of action, while the child from about 7 to 11 uses mental operations. What is important for Piaget is not the child's behavior in all its detail but the structure underlying his activities. For the purpose of clarity Piaget has made an attempt to describe these structures in terms of formal languages—logic and mathematics. The general tendencies—adaptation and organization—and the structures are all related to one another.

Assimilation and accommodation are complementary, whereas organization and adaptation are interwoven. For instance, one assimilates an environmental event into a structure, and one accommodates a structure to the demands of the environment. Eventually the organism tends toward equilibrium. He aims toward a balance between his structures and the requirements of his world. In this balance the structures are sufficiently developed so that he need exert little effort either to accommodate them to reality or to assimilate events into them.

Piaget's framework is quite general, and at this point the reader must find it hard to evaluate. In the following pages we will see the fruitfulness of Piaget's orienting attitudes. We will review, for example, the evolution of the psychological structures underlying the child's intelligence; we will examine the ways in which assimilation and accommodation affect the child's interaction with the world; and we will consider Piaget's theory of equilibrium.

2

infancy

Piaget's theory divides intellectual development into four major periods: sensorimotor (birth to 2 years); preoperational (2 years to 7 years); concrete operational (7 years to 11 years); and formal operational (11 years and above). This chapter treats the first of these periods, the sensorimotor which occurs during infancy.

The account of infancy is novel and sometimes surprising. The surprises usually take one of two forms: cases where, according to Piaget, the infant is capable of much more sophisticated and elaborate forms of behavior than we would have expected; and, conversely, cases where the infant appears unexpectedly to be deficient. Consider an example of the first case.

The untrained observer of an infant in the first few months of life usually reports several impressions. The baby, who is much smaller than anticipated, appears weak and fragile, and extraordinarily passive. He does not seem to *do* much of anything. The newborn spends most of his time in sleep, and usually wakes only to be fed. Even during the feeding, he does not seem very alert, and sometimes, in fact, falls asleep during the meal. Since the infant seems to show little reaction to people or things, our observer may even suspect that the newborn does not *see* the world clearly, if at all. Apparently such an infant is capable of learning almost nothing.

Piaget's view offers a strong contrast to this conception of the new-born as a predominantly helpless and inactive creature, for he character-izes the newborn as active and as an initiator of behavior. The infant quickly learns to distinguish among various features of the immediate environment and to modify his behavior in accordance with their demands. In fact, his activity reveals the *origins of intelligence.*

One of the first questions we should ask about these surprising find-ings (or indeed about *any* findings) is, how does he know? What are the methods which allow Piaget to penetrate beyond the commonly held assumptions and to propose a new and startling view of infancy? The question is particularly germane in the case of Piaget since he is methodo-logically unorthodox, at least by current standards.

METHOD

In the course of his psychological investigations, Piaget has employed a variety of methods. The assumption has been that methods must be tailored to meet the requirements of different problems and age groups. In the case of infancy, the methodology employed is partly naturalistic and partly informal-experimental.

For much of the time, Piaget carefully observed the behavior of his own three children—Lucienne, Laurent, and Jacqueline—as it occurred naturally. For instance, he would sit by the crib and make careful notes of the child's play; or he would direct his attention to the child's eye movements and try to determine the direction of the child's gaze. In these instances Piaget did not make use of specific scientific instruments or experimental apparatus. He did not use another observer to check the reliability of the observations. In general, the intention was to employ careful observation, unaided by instrumentation, to learn as much as possi-ble about the behavior of the child in his natural habitat. The procedure is obviously different from the usual experimental approach in which the child's behavior or physiological reactions are observed, often with special instruments, under carefully controlled conditions in the laboratory. But Piaget's approach is hardly unique or scientifically taboo. Naturalistic methods are used in zoology, for example, by those interested in the be-havior of animals in their natural surroundings. It has been used, too, in child psychology, by the "baby biographers" who observed their own chil-dren and who included such notable figures as Charles Darwin.

Piaget's procedure has its unique advantages and disadvantages. The latter have often been stressed at the expense of the former. For example, Piaget based his conclusions on a sample of only three children, hardly a sufficient number to ensure the generality of the results. Piaget and his wife made all the observations themselves. Although his wife was a trained psychologist, it is the general feeling that parents are, at least sometimes, notoriously poor evaluators of their own children's performance. Also, when naturalistic observation is used, it is impossible to identify cause-and-effect relations with certainty. While some event may have seemed to be the cause, other uncontrolled events may in fact have been involved too. Further, the standard statistical tests were not used, although today they are usually seen as indispensable tools of research.

Despite these clear deficiencies, Piaget's methods offer a number of equally clear advantages. First and foremost, Piaget is an exceedingly sensitive observer of children. Some people, probably regardless of formal training, have this ability and some people do not; Piaget does. The acuity of Piaget's observations is confirmed by their generally successful replication by independent investigators.[1] Second, Piaget's intimate contact with his subjects allowed him to *discover* phenomena which might have gone unobserved or unnoticed in the laboratory. The controlled experiment tends to focus the investigator's attention on a limited class of behavior which he finds of interest, and indeed, often makes it impossible for other kinds of behavior to occur or be noticed. These other events, of course, may be of greater interest than that which the experimenter is studying. Third, Piaget's great familiarity with his children often gave him the insight to resolve certain delicate issues of interpretation. If, for example, one of his children was unable to wind up a toy, Piaget's extensive knowledge of the child was likely to give good grounds for deciding whether the failure was due to lack of interest, or fatigue, or real inability. An experimenter, on the other hand, since he does not know his subjects well, often is unable to make such reasonable decisions.

Fourth, Piaget was able to observe his subjects over a long period of time. Such longitudinal studies are rare in psychology and provide a perspective which is notably absent from most experimental designs. Fifth, Piaget feels that at the initial stages of research use of statistics may be premature. One's aim at the outset is to explore and describe. The intention is to discover and identify the significant processes and problems which at a later stage of investigation may be subject to rigorous statistical test. Sixth, Piaget attempts to compensate for the obvious deficiencies of the naturalistic procedure by performing informal experiments. If, for example, observation suggests that the child cannot deal with certain kinds of obstacles, Piaget may intervene in the natural course of events by imposing these obstacles on the child and then observe the results. These experiments are, of course, informal, since a very small number of

1. For example, see Thérèse Gouin Décarie, *Intelligence and Affectivity in Early Childhood*, trans. E. P. Brandt and L. W. Brandt (New York: International Universities Press, Inc., 1965).

subjects—three at most—is involved, and since the controls are often incomplete. Nevertheless, Piaget is very sensitive to the limitations of naturalistic observation and tries to supplement it as fully as is practical with experimental techniques.

The result of these investigations is an account of infancy in terms of six "sensorimotor" stages. It should be emphasized that the age limits of each stage are only approximate, and subject to wide individual variations. Piaget stresses the flexibility of the age norms which are probably influenced by individual differences in physical and social environment, physiological factors, and so on. What is important is the regular order of succession of the stages, regardless of the particular ages at which they appear.

STAGE 1: BIRTH TO 1 MONTH

The newborn is not a completely helpless creature. He arrives in the world with certain abilities which are provided by heredity. (In fact, over the past several years research has shown that the newborn is far more skilled—visually, for example—than was ever supposed.[2]) One innate skill that the newborn possesses is the sucking reflex. When his lips are touched, the newborn in all cultures responds automatically with unlearned sucking movements. In describing the newborn's behavior, Piaget's central themes are, first, that the sucking reflex, and others too, are not simply activated by external stimuli; instead, the newborn often initiates activity himself. Second, although the physical structure of the infant provides ready-made mechanisms, like the sucking reflex which functions from birth and which is of obvious utility, these furnish only a basis for future development. Even in the first month of life experience plays an important role in modifying and supplementing the inherited mechanisms.

Consider the following observation.

During the second day also Laurent again begins to make sucking-movements between meals. . . . His lips open and close as if to receive a real nippleful but without having an object. This behavior subsequently became more frequent. . . .[3]

The observation may at first seem quite pedestrian. But let us review it. Why did Laurent suck between meals? There are several possible interpretations. Sometimes reflex activity may be said to be involved. That is, an "external excitant" or "unconditioned stimulus," like a finger, may auto-

2. For example, see R. L. Fantz, "The Origin of Form Perception," *Scientific American*, CCIV (1961), pp. 66–72.
3. *Origins of Intelligence*, pp. 25–26.

matically set off the reflex of sucking. But in the case of Laurent a reflex interpretation seems untenable since no external excitant appears to have been involved. Another explanation might attribute Laurent's sucking to hunger; but this interpretation too seems implausible since Laurent's sucking sometimes occurred soon after his last feeding (when, presumably, he was not hungry), and not just immediately preceding the next feeding (when he probably was hungry). A third possibility, also rejected by Piaget, involves two steps: (a) We assume that in the past the child's nutritive sucking had been associated with pleasure; that is, when he sucks he gets milk which reduces his hunger pangs and is therefore pleasurable. (b) Because of this previous association between sucking and pleasure, it gradually occurs that sucking alone in the absence of milk acquires the power to elicit feelings of pleasure in the infant. Consequently, it may be that in the observation cited Laurent sucked because sucking itself had become rewarding through its past association with pleasure. But this explanation too seems implausible since the extent of the association between pleasure and sucking was limited to such a short period of time.

Since these various explanations—external excitant, hunger, and association with pleasure—do not seem able to account for non-nutritive sucking, Piaget invokes one form of assimilation to explain the results. Recall that in Chapter One we defined assimilation as a *functional invariant*, a tendency common to all forms of life. In its most general form assimilation involves the organism's tendency to deal with environmental events in terms of current structures. Piaget has further proposed that assimilation takes three particular forms. In the present instance, the principle of *functional assimilation* applies. (The other two types are *recognitory assimilation* and *generalizing assimilation*, which we will discuss later.) The principle of functional assimilation asserts that when an organism has a structure available, there is a basic tendency to exercise the structure; that is, to make it function. This is particularly true when the structure is not well formed or is incomplete in some way. Also, the principle applies whether the structure is innate, as in the case of the sucking reflex, or learned, as in other instances we will review shortly. When applied to the present observation, the principle of functional assimilation asserts that Laurent's non-nutritive sucking simply represents the tendency of the sucking reflex to exercise itself or to function. This simple behavioral scheme is not yet well formed and requires exercise in order to consolidate itself. In other words, Laurent did not suck because he was hungry, or because an external excitant set off the reflex, or because he had associated the sucking with pleasure. He sucked because there is a tendency for available schemes like sucking to function.

A closely related tendency is *generalizing assimilation*. Since schemes need exercise and repetition, they also require objects to be used in satisfying this need. The sucking scheme, therefore, tends to extend itself, to *generalize,* to a variety of objects. While the newborn at first sucks only the nipple, or perhaps a finger that accidently comes into contact with his lips, he later exercises his sucking on new objects like his blanket or various toys. Thus, Piaget stresses activity on the part of the infant. The sucking reflex is not simply activated by a series of excitants; rather the child, in seeking to exercise his scheme (functional assimilation), actively searches out objects which will allow it to function. The objects serve as nourishment, or "aliments," for the need to suck.

The first two principles—functional and generalizing assimilation—are energetic: they get the newborn's behavior started. In the course of his activities, he has the occasion to learn about the environment. The reflex of sucking becomes "differentiated." Consider this observation concerning Laurent:

At 0;0(20) [*zero years, zero months, and 20 days*] *he bites the breast which is given him 5 cm. from the nipple. For a moment he sucks the skin which he then lets go in order to move his mouth about 2 cm. As soon as he begins sucking again he stops. . . . When his search subsequently leads him accidently to touch the nipple with the mucosa of the upper lip (his mouth being wide open), he at once adjusts his lips and begins to suck.*[4]

From this and other similar observations, Piaget concludes that the infant in the first month of life shows a primitive recognition called *recognitory assimilation.* When the infant is not too hungry, he may suck anything—the fingers, the blanket, etc.—to exercise his scheme. But when hunger is strong, the infant shows selectivity or discrimination in choosing objects to suck. While he rejects the skin surrounding the nipple, he seizes immediately upon the nipple itself and does this so rapidly that we may reasonably call the behavior a crude form of recognition. One caution here: Piaget does not propose that the infant "recognizes" the nipple in the same sense that an adult does. (We will see later that the infant's concept of objects is immature.) In the present case the infant merely shows that when it is necessary he can perceive the difference between the nipple and other things.

How does the infant learn to recognize the nipple? Learning must be involved since the newborn does not immediately display this kind of recognition; experience is certainly required for it to develop. Piaget's position is that in the course of exercising and generalizing his sucking scheme the infant comes into contact with a variety of stimulation. Some of the stimulation is visual (the sight of the breast, etc.). Some is tactual-kinesthetic (touches on the lips, the feeling of swallowing milk, etc.). And some stimulation is postural (the infant is generally lying down in a certain

4. *Ibid.,* p. 26.

position). As the infant accumulates this experience, he comes to differentiate among many aspects. He finds that some areas of the breast look different from others; some feel different from others; and that one area yields milk while others do not. The infant's recognition of the nipple then is a discrimination of this conglomeration of cues. The infant comes to make this discrimination through repetitious experience which is the result of functional and generalizing assimilation. Then, when the infant is hungry he shows evidence of his previous perceptual learning. He chooses that area which has produced milk in the past and rejects other areas. To put the matter in another way, the infant learns about the world in the course of his explorations; when properly motivated he manifests this learning by the performance of certain distinctive reactions.

Finally, an even more complicated kind of learning occurs during the first stage. The principle of accommodation—of modification of the scheme to suit the demands of the environment—is also operative, and one result is that the infant learns to search for the nipple in an increasingly effective manner. Consider these observations:

At first, when put to the breast, Laurent does not show particularly systematic search for the nipple. He obviously has not had sufficient experience either to recognize the nipple or locate it. But on

. . . *The third day Laurent makes new progress in his adjustment to the breast. All he needs in order to grope with open mouth toward final success is to have touched the breast or the surrounding teguments with his lips. But he hunts on the wrong side as well as on the right side. . . . As soon as his cheek comes into contact with the breast, Laurent at 0;0(12) applies himself to seeking until he finds drink. His search takes its bearings: immediately from the correct side, that is to say, the side where he experienced contact. . . .*[5] *At 0;0(26) Laurent . . . feels the nipple in the middle of his right cheek. But as he tries to grasp it, it is withdrawn 10 cm. He then turns his head in the right direction and searches. . . . This time he goes on to touch the nipple, first with his nose and then with the region between his nostrils and lips. . . . He raises his head in order to grasp the nipple.*[6]

We quote these observations in some detail to document the extent of the infant's learning during the first month. Not only does he learn to recognize the nipple, but he also learns where to look for it. Thus, in response to the requirements of the situation, he accommodates—he develops new patterns of action, which result in fairly systematic search. How are these patterns of behavior learned? At the outset the child's head

5. *Ibid.*, p. 26.
6. *Ibid.*, p. 29.

movements are "desultory," that is, essentially without order in relation to the nipple. By chance, some of the movements lead to grasping the nipple and some are unsuccessful. As time goes on, the infant learns through this process of trial and error that a turn of the head in the direction of the touch on the cheek provided by the nipple leads to the reward of swallowing milk. With increased experience the infant becomes relatively proficient and flexible in this search; now he can proceed not only in a sideways direction toward the cheek, but in an upward or downward direction as well. This last observation is important since some head movements at birth are reflexive. When the infant is touched on the cheek near the mouth, he automatically turns his head in that direction. The sideways movement is the "rooting reflex." Consequently, a learning explanation may not be required for the sideways movement, but does seem necessary for the upward and downward motions.

Such, then, is the first stage. The apparently primitive behavior of the infant in the first month of life in fact involves considerable complexity, and the extent of the learning achieved is not immediately obvious. The result is that the hereditary sucking scheme becomes progressively modified and elaborated as a function of experience. At the end of stage 1, sucking is no longer an automatic pattern of behavior provided by heredity. In accordance with the principle of *organization*, the sucking scheme has become elaborated and has developed into a fairly complex psychological structure which now incorporates the results of the infant's experiences.

While stage 1 involves significant learning, there are also limitations on the infant's accomplishments. Learning is confined to the sphere of the reflexes and does not go far beyond them; the effects of experience are centered about the mechanisms provided by heredity. We shall see how the infant in stage 2 begins to overcome these limitations.

At the time it was proposed, Piaget's view of infancy was novel in several respects. The two most influential theories of the day—Freud's personality psychology and Hull's experimental psychology—both emphasized that the organism seeks *escape* from stimulation and excitation. All motives are seen as analogous to the sexual or hunger drives; when these drives intensify, the organism takes actions to reduce them and to return to a quiescent state. Piaget's emphasis, on the other hand, is that even in the first few days of life the infant often *seeks stimulation*. When he is capable of activity, he tends to perform it (functional assimilation); when he has available a structure, he tends to generalize it to new objects (generalizing assimilation). In Piaget's view, all behavior cannot be explained by the infant's reacting to a noxious state of affairs; instead, he sometimes actively *seeks* the stimulation which his behavior provides. It seems fair to say that recent psychological research has shown that the Hullian and

Freudian concepts are not fully adequate, and that alternative views de-signed to explain the individual's preference for activity and stimulation must be developed.

STAGE 2: 1 TO 4 MONTHS

In the second stage of sensorimotor development the infant acquires certain habits, which, although fairly simple and centered about his own body, nevertheless surpass the acquisitions of the first stage. Now the historical development of sucking, for example, extends beyond the feeding situation.

Primary circular reaction

Piaget's theory involves the notion of *primary circular reaction*. The infant's behavior by chance leads to an advantageous or interesting result; he immediately attempts to reinstate or rediscover the effective behavior; after a process of trial and error, he succeeds in doing so. Thereafter, the behavior and the result may be repeated; they have become "habits." Consider these examples:

At 0;1(1) Laurent is held by his nurse in an almost vertical position. . . . He is very hungry. . . . Twice, when his hand was laid on his right cheek, Laurent turned his head and tried to grasp his fingers with his mouth. The first time he failed and succeeded the second. But the movements of his arms are not coordinated with those of his head; the hand escapes while the mouth tries to maintain contact. . . .

At 0;1(3) . . . after a meal . . . his arms, instead of gesticulating aimlessly, constantly move toward his mouth . . . it has occurred to me several times that the chance contact of hand and mouth set in motion the directing of the latter toward the former and that then (but only then), the hand tries to return to the mouth. . . . [Later, though] it is no longer the mouth that seeks the hand, but the hand which reaches for the mouth. Thirteen times in succession I have been able to observe the hand go back into the mouth. There is no longer any doubt that coordination exists. . . . At 0;1(4) . . . his right hand may be seen approaching his mouth. . . . But as only the index finger was grasped, the hand fell out again. Shortly after it returned. This time the thumb was in the mouth . . . I then re-move the hand and place it near his waist. . . . After a few minutes the lips move and the hand approaches them again. This time there is a series of setbacks. . . . [But finally] the hand enters the mouth, the thumb alone is retained and sucking continues. I again remove the hand. Again lip movements cease, new attempts ensue, success results for the ninth and tenth time, after which the experiment is interrupted.[7]

These observations nicely illustrate Piaget's dual role of observer and experimenter. Note how Piaget as patient observer, records that the infant spontaneously places the hand in the mouth 13 times in succession. Then, Piaget as experimenter, intervenes in the natural course of events by placing the infant's hand near his waist in order to determine whether, under these modified conditions, the infant is able to direct the hand to the mouth.

The observations also display the gradual and steady development of thumb-sucking. First the infant cannot consistently get his hand into his mouth; then he slowly learns to do so; next he learns to suck the thumb alone, not the whole hand; and finally, after a long and continuous process of learning, he is able to perform the entire sequence of actions with rapidity.

Piaget's explanation of thumb-sucking again involves principles of assimilation and of accommodation. However, the sequence begins with an unplanned or unintentional occurrence. Recall that another person initially placed Laurent's hand on his cheek; he did not do so himself. After the hand was put there, Laurent took the initiative by attempting to grasp the hand with the mouth. This action was, of course, a previously learned scheme: Laurent had earlier acquired behavior patterns enabling him to search for the nipple. Other observations not described above reveal that in some cases the initial behavior is a chance occurrence, and not caused by the intervention of another person. In either event, the unplanned behavior leads to a result which has value for the infant. In the case of Laurent the hand in the mouth enables the sucking scheme to function. This is rewarding since, according to the principle of functional assimilation, the sucking scheme needs to function. In other words, a fortuitous occurrence has given the infant a chance to exercise one of his previously established schemes, and this activity, in itself, is a satisfying event. But Laurent's movements are not yet fully coordinated; it occurs that the hand falls from the mouth and interrupts the functioning of the sucking scheme. The child then desires to reinstate the pleasurable activity and resume sucking the thumb. This desire, stemming from the interruption, then *directs* the child's behavior. Laurent actively tries to insert the hand in the mouth. In two senses, then, is the infant's learning active: his desire sets in motion the sequence of events, and he initiates behavior to fulfill his desire.

The principle of accommodation is now operative. The child modifies the previously aimless movements of his hand to make them effective in

7. *Ibid.*, pp. 51–53.

bringing it to the mouth. Initially Laurent is on the wrong track; he tries to bring the mouth to the hand. It is only after some failure that he reverses the procedure. The learning is slow and seems to involve two factors —muscular adjustments and direction by the proper cues. The infant must learn to make certain precise muscular movements which are new to him, and the infant must learn to bring these movements under the direction of the proper cues. When touching the blanket, the hand must be moved in certain ways; when touching the cheek, it must be moved in other ways. The infant learns that certain cues and certain movements are useful while others are not. The useful ones, of course, are those which lead to placing the hand in the mouth. Thus, success "confirms" some of the movements and cues, while failure eliminates other attempts at accommodation. Yet the observations show that the infant's learning is not complete. He apparently finds it more satisfying to suck the thumb than the other fingers, and through a process of learning similar to that described above becomes able to place the thumb alone in the mouth. Further, his behavior shows that he distinguishes (recognitory assimilation) the thumb from the rest of the hand. The result of all this learning is finally a smoothly organized and directed series of movements, a new scheme or structure, which can be exercised repeatedly.

In summary, the primary circular reaction involves an action on the part of the infant which fortuitously leads to an event which has value for him and which is centered about his own body. The infant then learns to repeat the behavior in order to reinstate the event. The culmination of the process is an organized scheme.

Primitive Anticipations

While the newborn in the feeding situation sucks only when his lips are in contact with the breast, the older infant shows a different pattern of behavior. This observation concerns Laurent at the beginning of the second month.

. . . *as soon as he is in a position to eat (in his mother's arms or on the bed, etc.) his hands lose interest, leave his mouth, and it becomes obvious that the child no longer seeks anything but the breast, that is to say, contact with food . . . at the end of the month, Laurent only tries to nurse when he is in his mother's arms and no longer when on the dressing table. . . .*[8]

. . . *between 0;3(15) and 0;4 . . . [when Laurent] is put in my arms in position for nursing, he looks at me and then searches all around . . .*

8. *Ibid.*, p. 58.

but he does not attempt to nurse. When I place him in his mother's arms without his touching the breast, he looks at her and immediately opens his mouth wide. . . .[9]

The infant initially sucks, then, only when the nipple is inserted in his mouth. The nipple is an external excitant which automatically elicits sucking. After a period of experience with feeding, he makes sucking-like movements *before* the external excitant can operate. During the second month, Laurent shows sucking as soon as he is placed in his mother's arms or on the bed. Later, Laurent's sucking-like movements are aroused only by being in the mother's arms. One way of looking at these facts is to say that, while at first only the nipple served as a cue or signal for sucking, later the infant's being in the mother's arms replaced the nipple as a signal for sucking. Another way of phrasing the matter is to maintain that the infant seems to show a primitive *anticipation* of feeding, and that this expectancy, as time goes on, is evoked by fewer and more appropriate events than formerly. In either event, the phenomenon is similar to what has been called "classical conditioning," although Piaget's explanation of the facts differs from the traditional one.

Piaget emphasizes that the association between sucking and the various signals (e.g., position in the mother's arms) that precede it is not acquired in a mechanical way. What happens is this: the sucking scheme comes to consist of more than sucking alone. It also involves a set of postural kinesthetic cues. That is, when the infant nurses in the first few months he is almost invariably held in the same position, and the internal body sensations associated with this position become a part of the act of sucking. The body sensations and the movements of the lips form a whole. Then, when the infant is placed in the position for nursing and the postural and kinesthetic sensations are activated the whole cycle of the sucking act is released. Because the two aspects of the cycle—bodily sensations and lip movements—form a whole, the occurrence of one aspect usually evokes the other. Piaget feels that this process does not involve mere "passive recording" on the part of the child, since the infant himself *enlarges* his initially limited scheme of sucking to include other components such as bodily cues. Furthermore, the association cannot be maintained if it is not consistently "confirmed" by the environment. That is, for postural cues to provoke the child's anticipatory sucking, the sucking must ordinarily be followed by drinking milk. Thus, the association between postural cues and sucking derives its meaning only from a larger set of relationships existing between the scheme of sucking and its satisfaction. The reflex must have a chance to function effectively (to drink milk) before any associations can be formed. Thus, the sequence *bodily cues* ⟶ *sucking* ⟶

9. *Ibid.*, p. 60.

satisfaction of need forms a whole, and to isolate the first two terms in this sequence and call them a conditioned reflex omits much that is relevant.

Curiosity

In the discussion of the second stage Piaget introduces a motivational principle of great importance. The following is a preliminary observation in connection with the problem of vision:

Laurent at 0;0(24) watches the back of my hand which is motionless, with such attention and so marked protrusion of the lips that I expect him to suck it. But it is only visual interest. . . . At 0;0(25) he spends nearly an hour in his cradle without crying, his eyes wide open. . . . He stares at a piece of fringe on his cradle. . . .[10]

Why does the infant attend to these mundane features of the environment? He is not rewarded for doing so and is not in any other way encouraged to direct his attention to an object like the fringe of the cradle. Again, Piaget invokes the principle of functional assimilation to account for these facts. The eyes are structures, given by specific heredity, and require exercise. In the present instance exercise means looking at things, and the things looked at are necessary for the functioning of the eyes.

Thusfar, the principle of functional assimilation has been applied to the case of vision in much the same way as it was used to explain some features of sucking: both schemes need to function. One result of repetitious looking at things is that they become familiar to the infant. Through a process of perceptual learning, the infant becomes acquainted with his environment. He comes to recognize things. These observations are made next:

At 0;1(15) he systematically explores the hood of his bassinet which I shook slightly. He begins by the edge, then little by little looks backward at the lowest part of the roof. . . . Four days later he resumes this exploration in the opposite direction. . . . Subsequently, he constantly resumes examining the cradle but, during the third month, he only looks at the toys hanging from the hood or at the hood itself when an unwonted movement excites his curiosity or when he discovers a particular new point (a pleat in the material, etc.).[11]

Notice how at first the infant thoroughly examines the cradle until he is apparently familiar with it. Then, during the third month his attention becomes more selective than was previously the case. He no longer seems to explore the cradle and instead directs his attention to novel objects

10. *Ibid.*, p. 64.
11. *Ibid.*, p. 68.

or movements connected with the cradle. For example, he stares at toys hanging from the hood or at a previously unnoticed pleat in the material.

Piaget's explanation of the infant's curiosity involves an extension—really a further specification—of the principle of generalizing assimilation. The infant's looking scheme, according to Piaget, tends to extend the range of objects it "uses." But the infant does not simply look at more and more things. His visual preferences become selective. The infant's attention is directed at events which are *moderately novel*: ". . . one observes that the subject looks neither at what is too familiar, because he is in a way surfeited with it, nor at what is too new because this does not correspond to anything in his [schemes]. . . ." [12] This motivational principle may appear deceptively simple and trite. In reality, however, it represents a point of view which is radically different from previous (and some current) theories and is only now receiving the attention it deserves. First, like the principle of assimilation, the moderate novelty principle is strongly at odds with theories which stress avoidance of stimulation as the only kind of motivation. On the contrary, according to Piaget's view, the child actively seeks out new stimulation—he is not forced to look at novel objects. Second, the moderate novelty principle is different from other motivational theories in that it is a relativistic concept. That which catches an individual's curiosity is not entirely the physical nature of the event. It is not the object *per se* that attracts attention; instead curiosity is a function of the *relation* between the new object and the individual's previous experience. A given toy may elicit interest in one child and boredom in another. Presumably the first child has had experience with toys moderately different from the one in question; the second child may either have had experience with toys *highly* similiar to the new one, or else he may have had no experience with toys, in which case the new object presumably "does not correspond to anything in his [schemes]." In sum, the novelty principle asserts that what determines curiosity is not the physical nature of the object, but rather the degree to which the object is discrepant from what the individual is familiar with, which, of course, depends entirely on the individual's experience.

Imitation

An important aspect of the infant's behavior is imitation. Piaget considers imitation, like all other behaviors, as yet another expression of the infant's endeavors to comprehend reality and interact effectively with his world. Consequently, the development of imitation is seen to progress concurrently with other aspects of the infant's behavior.

12. *Ibid.*, p. 68.

During stage 2, as we have seen, the reflexes are modified to become habits or primary circular reactions. This extension of the child's hereditary schemes leads to a rudimentary and sporadic form of imitation. At this stage the child imitates only actions which he has himself previously performed. Since his repertory of actions is still restricted, imitation is confined to elementary vocal and visual movements, and to grasping (prehension). Here is an example of the imitation of this stage:

At 0;1(21), Lucienne spontaneously uttered the sound rra, but did not react at once when I reproduced it. At 0;1(24), however, when I made a prolonged aa, she twice uttered a similar sound, although she had previously been silent for a quarter of an hour.

At 0;1(25) she was watching me while I said "a ha, ha, rra," etc. I noticed certain movements of her mouth, movements not of suction but of vocalization. She succeeded once or twice in producing some rather vague sounds, and although there was no imitation in the strict sense, there was obvious vocal contagion.

At 0;3(5) I noted a differentiation in the sounds of her laughter. I imitated them. She reacted by reproducing them quite clearly, but only when she had already uttered them immediately before.

At 0;3(24) she imitated aa, and vaguely arr in similar conditions, i.e., when there was mutual imitation.[13]

The early forms of vocal imitation are characterized by two major features. First, there is the phenomenon of "vocal contagion." A person called a "model" makes a sound, and the infant tries to reproduce it. Limited abilities, however, prevent the infant from perfect reproduction of the sounds. Nevertheless, stimulated by the model's sounds the infant continues to produce vocalizations of many kinds having little relation to the model's sounds. "Vocal contagion" refers, then, to the model's stimulation of diffuse vocal activity in the infant.

Second, there is "mutual imitation." If the model reproduces a sound which the infant is currently engaged in producing, the child is stimulated to repeat the same sound. If the model again imitates the child, there is set in motion a pattern of alternating imitation by infant and model which continues until one or the other tires or loses interest. This pattern of behavior does *not* occur if the model makes a sound which is new for the infant.

Piaget explains both the contagion and mutual imitation phenomena by reference to the principle of functional assimilation. You may recall that the child has a tendency to repeat schemes which have already been established. In the case of vocal contagion the principle of functional assimilation is applied in the following way. When the model makes a

13. *Play, Dreams, and Imitation in Childhood*, p. 10.

sound the infant does not distinguish it from his own; it is as if the infant had made the sound. Because of the process of functional assimilation, the infant tends to repeat the activity (believed to be his own) which has already been set in motion; that is, the infant carries on the activity of making sounds in general.

In the case of mutual imitation a similar explanation is advanced. When the infant produces a sound the model's imitation merely stimulates the process of functional assimilation. The infant's imitation is in a way illusory; he does not so much *reproduce* the model's behavior as merely continue his own. Note that in both cases—contagion and mutual imitation—the infant repeats behavior of which he is already capable. The infant cannot yet reproduce novel activities of a model.

Categories of Reality

Thus far, we have described the inception of several aspects of the infant's behavior. In particular, we have noted the contribution of experience toward the elaboration of the infant's activity, and the ways in which he extends his behavior beyond the feeding situation. As the infant begins to manipulate the objects which surround him, he gradually develops a practical "understanding" of external reality. In playing with toys, blankets, his own body, and that of adults, he learns something about the properties of these things and about the relations between them. And as the infant's skills increase in number and scope, so does he acquire an increasingly complex practical knowledge of certain features of his environment.

During the sensorimotor period, the infant elaborates several basic dimensions of reality, especially the primitive notions of the *permanent object, space, time,* and *causality*. At first, these basic dimensions of reality are closely related to the infant's bodily actions, to the movements of his arms, fingers, legs, and eyes. The infant's initial "understanding" of the world is based entirely on what Piaget calls the "plane of action." Only later, after a gradual process of development, does the infant become able to elaborate the categories of reality on the "plane of thought." One of Piaget's central themes is that concrete action precedes and makes possible the use of intellect. Thus, the acquisitions of the sensorimotor period form the foundations of the individual's mental development. We will discuss only one of these categories, the concept of the permanent object. The other notions follow a similar development.

Object Concept (Stages 1 and 2)

To understand the development of what Piaget calls the *object concept*, it is important to keep in mind one essential point. An "object," according to Piaget, is something which the individual conceives of as having a reality of its own, and as extending beyond his immediate perception. For example, a man who has hung his coat in a closet knows several hours later that, in all likelihood, the coat is still there. Although he cannot see or touch the coat, he knows that it remains behind the closet door. The object, therefore, involves more than the direct perception of external reality; the object is conceived to exist independently of a person's perception of it. Strange as it may sound, the infant is at first incapable of this apparently simple notion, and it is only after a long process of development that he elaborates the cognitive skills necessary for a mature object concept.

During stage 1 the infant's reactions are evoked only by immediately present sensory events which may be internal or external. Feeling the pangs of hunger, the infant cries; experiencing a touch on the lips, he sucks. The same holds in the case of visual perception. If the mother's face suddenly appears in his visual field, the infant stares at it. But when the face is just as suddenly withdrawn the infant immediately stops looking and resumes other activities. It is clear that he has no conception that the face continues to exist when he loses visual contact with it. Instead, the infant merely perceives a series of images or *pictures*, as Piaget calls them, which appear and then disappear.

Certain behavioral patterns which appear in stage 2 are a first step toward the acquisition of the object concept. The infant coordinates various perceptual schemes which, until then, had been used in unrelated ways. Consider the coordination of vision and hearing. In stage 1, if a sound had occurred near a newborn, he would have shown evidence (for example, a startle) of having heard it, but he would have made no effort to bring the source of the sound into his sight. In stage 2, however, the infant will try to turn toward the sound he hears in order to see what produced it. At first his efforts will be very clumsy, but with practice they will gradually improve and become more successful. Because of this coordination of vision and hearing, external reality will no longer be apprehended by a single sensory organ at any one time, but may now be experienced through two or more senses simultaneously. The result is that after a time the infant will establish a relation between what he hears and sees. He finds that certain sounds, like the voice, usually emanate from certain sources, like the mouth. The infant begins to discover a coherence in his world. Instead of merely perceiving isolated and unrelated aspects of reality, he learns that sights and sounds (and other kinds of percepts too) often go together in regular ways. This coordination of basic schemes, since it introduces a measure of coherence to the infant's world, is a vital first step toward acquisition of the object concept.

Another accomplishment of stage 2 concerns *passive expectation.* The clearest example involves vision. At this stage the infant can follow a moving object with his eyes. Or as Piaget says, the infant accommodates his looking scheme to the moving thing. The interesting observation here is that once the object leaves the visual field, the infant continues to stare at the spot where the thing disappeared. One might almost be tempted to state that he already has the object concept and is hoping for the thing to return. But this interpretation, Piaget feels, is fallacious, since the infant does not actively *search* for the vanished object as he will do in later stages. Instead, the stage 2 infant merely pursues an action (looking) which has been interrupted. If after a short while the thing does not reappear, the infant discontinues his passive watching and turns his attention to other elements of his surroundings. But this passive expectation, which does not go beyond the simple repetition of the already activated looking scheme, is the first step toward the later active search for the missing object and hence toward acquisition of the object concept.

In summary, the first two stages are characterized by a passive attitude toward objects which disappear from the infant's immediate perception. In stage 1, the infant immediately turns his attention to those things he can still see; in stage 2, he merely repeats earlier actions (looking) which occurred when the object was present. While the second reaction represents an advance over the first, both indicate the lack of the mature object concept.

STAGE 3: 4 TO 10 MONTHS

Secondary Circular Reactions

In stage 2, the primary circular reaction is always centered about the infant's own body. He learned, for example, to bring his thumb to his mouth. In stage 3, the infant's horizons expand. He begins to crawl and manipulate things extensively. The circular reactions of this stage are called "secondary," since they now involve events or objects in the external environment. The secondary circular reactions describe the infant's new-found ability to develop schemes which reproduce interesting events which were initially discovered by chance in the external environment. The following excerpt is a lengthy record of such a reaction and illustrates Piaget's skill and caution as an observer:

Laurent, from the middle of the third month, revealed global reactions of pleasure, while looking at the toys hanging from the hood of his bassinet. . . . He babbles, arches himself, beats the air with his arms, moves his legs, etc. . . . At 0;2(17) I observe that when his movements induce those of the toys, he stops to contemplate them, far from grasping that it is he who produces them. . . . On the other hand at 0;2(24) I made the following experiment. . . . As Laurent was striking his chest and shaking his hands which were bandaged and held by strings attached to the handle of the bassinet (to prevent him from sucking), I had the idea of using the thing, and I attached the strings to the celluloid balls hanging from the hood. Laurent naturally shook the balls by chance and looked at them at once (the rattle made a noise inside them). As the shaking was repeated more and more frequently Laurent arched himself, waved his arms and legs—in short, he revealed increasing pleasure and through this maintained the interesting result. But nothing yet authorizes us to speak of circular reaction. . . .

The next day, at 0;2(25) I connect his right hand to the celluloid balls. . . . The left hand is free. At first the arm movements are inadequate and the rattle does not move. Then the movements become more extensive . . . and the rattle moves. . . . There seems to be conscious coordination but both arms move equally and it is not yet possible to be sure that this is not a mere pleasure reaction. The next day, same reactions.

At 0;2(27), on the other hand, conscious coordination seems definite, for the following four reasons: (1) Laurent was surprised and frightened by the first shake of the rattle which was unexpected. On the other hand, since the second or third shake, he swung his right arm (connected to the rattle) with regularity, whereas the left remained almost motionless. . . . (2) Laurent's eye blinks beforehand as soon as his hand moves and before the rattle moves, as though the child knew he was going to shake it. (3) When Laurent temporarily gives up the game and joins his hands for a moment, the right hand (connected to the rattle) alone resumes the movement while the left stays motionless. (4) The regular shakes . . . reveal a certain skill; the movement is regular.

At 0;3(10) I attached a string to the left arm after six days of experiments with the right. The first shake is given by chance: fright, curiosity, etc. Then, at once, there is coordinated circular reaction: this time the right arm is outstretched and barely mobile while the left swings. . . . This time it is therefore possible to speak definitely of secondary circular reaction.[14]

One intepretation of the infant's behavior is that a secondary circular reaction is involved. The infant, lying in his crib, by chance makes an arm movement which causes the string attached to his hand to move and rattle the toys. Laurent does not, of course, have this goal in mind from the outset. The movement and rattling are interesting to the infant,

14. *Origins of Intelligence,* pp. 160–62.

and he desires to continue them. Over a period of time, he learns the arm movements necessary to reproduce the interesting result. At this point, his behavior is intentional.

But another interpretation is possible, and it is particularly fascinating to observe how Piaget attempts to rule it out. The alternative explanation asserts that the infant's arm movements are not intended to produce the interesting result. Instead, just the reverse is true: the interesting event causes arm movements in the infant. In other words, the infant initially moves his arm by accident. The balls move and make the infant happy. As part of his joy the infant shows physical excitement which again, by accident, produces the shaking of the balls; this in turn starts the cycle over again and is the *cause* of the infant's hand movements.

The observations show that Piaget was quite cautious in his interpretations. He did not accept the first explanation (secondary circular reaction) until the facts made it abundantly clear that the alternative explanation was not plausible. For example, Piaget observed that Laurent seemed to anticipate the result before it occurred; consequently, the result could not be an accident. In fact, the sequence of observations shows why Piaget's observational procedure is not necessarily inferior to the formal experimental method; the advantages of detailed knowledge of the child's history are obvious, and many of the observations perform the same function as control groups in ordinary experiments.

The explanation of the infant's learning of secondary circular reactions involves many of the principles that were invoked earlier. First, the infant's accidental movement produces an external result which is moderately novel and which therefore interests him. Second, the infant perceives that his actions are related to the external result. Piaget asserts that if the infant does not perceive the connection, no further learning is possible. Third, once the interest and the connection between act and result are established, the infant desires to repeat the interesting event. In other words, after the infant looks at and listens to the toys rattling (or, in more technical language, assimilates the interesting event into the visual and auditory schemes), he wants to reinstate the interesting events and assimilate them once again into his schemes of looking and listening. This, of course, is the familiar principle of functional assimilation: once a scheme (in this case viewing and hearing the toys) is able to function, it tends to repeat itself. After this point, the infant's goal of restoring the interesting events motivates and directs his actions.

Thus far, the infant has perceived an interesting result, has recognized that it is connected to his actions, and desires to repeat the result. The fourth step involves accommodation; he needs to learn the hand movements necessary for consistent reproduction of the result. Part of the process involves rediscovering the movements which were previously effective. While Piaget does not make the matter entirely explicit, it is clear from his observations that a directed trial and error process is involved. The infant's behavior is directed in the sense that the desire to reproduce the interesting result guides his actions and in the sense that he attempts only behaviors which are clearly relevant: he does not kick his feet, but limits his efforts to arm movements. Within these constraints the process involves trial and error since the infant does not know at first precisely which arm movements are effective. He has to try them out to see which meet with success and which with failure. It is also clear from the observations, and again not explicit in Piaget's explanation, that the infant does not simply rediscover old movements. This may be his original objective and accomplishment, but with practice he develops movements which are more precise, skilled, and effective than those which originally and accidentally obtained the goal.

The result of this activity is a secondary circular reaction which is a far more complex structure than anything the infant had developed earlier. Now the infant is interested in the external environment and is able to develop behaviors which serve as a primitive means for obtaining some ends. However, the secondary circular reaction has two deficiencies. First, it is not fully intentional as the infant does not have a goal in mind from the outset; rather, the goal has been discovered by accident, and it is only after this chance event has occurred that the goal guides behavior and gives it thereby a purposive character. A second deficiency is that the behavior is essentially conservative. The infant's aim is to reproduce, to duplicate some behavior which produced interesting results in the past. He does not attempt to invent new behaviors. These two deficiencies lead Piaget to maintain that the secondary circular reaction does not yet constitute *intelligent* behavior.

Primitive Classes

One of the most interesting aspects of Piaget's theory has to do with the infant's formation of classes or meanings. Their development, according to Piaget, begins very early in life. The following observations illustrate the matter:

At 0;6(12) Lucienne perceives from a distance two celluloid parrots attached to a chandelier and which she had sometimes had in her bassinet. As soon as she sees them, she definitely but briefly shakes her legs without trying to act upon them from a distance. . . . So too, at 0;6(19) it suffices that she catches sight of her dolls from a distance for her to outline the movements of swinging them with her hand.

From 0;7(27) certain too familiar situations no longer set in motion secondary circular reactions, but simply outlines of schemes. Thus when seeing a doll which she has actually swung many times, Lucienne limits herself to opening and closing her hands or shaking her legs, but very briefly and without real effort.[15]

In essence, Piaget has observed that when the infant comes into contact with some familiar object he does not apply to it the secondary circular reaction which normally would be employed. Instead, Lucienne exhibits an abbreviated form of the behavior, and does not seem to intend to produce the usual result. The abbreviated action does not seem mechanical, like a conditioned response. Further, the infant is "perfectly serious" and repeats the action on a number of different occasions.

Piaget's interpretation is that the abbreviated acts are special cases of recognitory assimilation. If you will recall, in earlier stages the infant's overt behavior showed that he distinguished between various objects; for example, when hungry he sucked the nipple but rejected a pacifier. Thus, the infant's behavior is said to involve recognitory assimilation when he is selective in applying his schemes to various aspects of the environment.

The case of abbreviated movements involves this selectivity too. Lucienne, for example, kicks in response to toys which she has swung, but not in response to other toys. However, the present instance involves more than selectivity. The infant's behavior is abbreviated; she does not choose to display the entire scheme when it would be quite feasible to do so. Piaget interprets the abbreviation as a behavioral precursor of *classification* or *meaning*. Lucienne, of course, does not have an abstract conception of the parrot. She cannot verbalize its properties or identify it as an instance of the class of animal toys. But the abbreviated behavior shows that Lucienne makes a beginning attempt at classification of the object. The brief kicking, for instance, is the first step toward thinking the thought, "That's the parrot; that's something to be swung." Her "understanding" is of course quite primitive and does not yet operate on a mental level. Nevertheless, she has made progress over stages 1 and 2, since she displays behavior which indicates that the first steps toward internalization of action are occurring. The abbreviated scheme is the first approximation to thought.

Piaget proposes a technical terminology for describing these events. He designates as a *signifier* an object,[16] event, etc., which stands for something else, the child's reaction to the object or event is the *signified*. In

15. *Ibid.*, pp. 186–87.
16. Strictly speaking, we should say that the object is the pattern of physical energies impinging on the infant's sensory apparatus. As mentioned previously, the "object" is a permanent object for us, but not necessarily for the infant.

the present case the signifier is the parrot, and the signified is the child's brief kicking. The signifier is the "thing," and the signified is what it means to the infant. With development, the signifier may be no longer a thing but a word, and the signified may be not a behavior but an act of intellectual understanding.

Primitive Relations

As we shall see later, in Chapter Four, classification is considered a vital aspect of the child's thought and is investigated in great detail. Similarly, we shall see in the same chapter that the notion of *relation* occupies a prominent place in Piaget's theories. And relations, too, have primitive behavioral origins which arise in the course of the first several stages. Here is an example:

In the evening of 0;3(13) Laurent by chance strikes the chain while sucking his fingers . . . he grasps it and slowly displaces it while looking at the rattles. He then begins to swing it very gently which first produces a slight movement of the hanging rattles and an as yet faint sound inside them. Laurent then definitely increases by degrees his own movements: he shakes the chain more and more vigorously and laughs uproariously at the result obtained.—On seeing the child's expression it is impossible not to deem this gradation intentional.[17]

In other words, the infant seems to see the difference between a slight movement on his part and a strong one; similarly, he can discriminate between a loud and a soft rattle. He can put two sounds or two movements into relationship with each other. Furthermore, the infant seems to see that the intensity of his movements is directly related to the intensity of sounds made by the rattle. These perceptions of differences in intensity are the origins of quantitative thought. We shall see later in stage 4 how these relationships are developed.

Imitation

In stage 3 the infant's attempts at imitation become increasingly systematic. Through the secondary circular reactions the infant acquires increasingly extensive experience of the environment. His schemes increase in number and range with the result that the child is more capable than formerly of behavior which matches that of a model. Since the child can now assimilate more models, there is greater opportunity for imitation. It is still the case, however, that the child continues to imitate only what is

17. *Origins of Intelligence*, p. 185.

familiar—only actions which he already can do—and cannot yet reproduce novel actions. This conservative feature of imitation is analogous to that displayed by the secondary circular reactions.

Object Concept

In stage 2 we saw that the infant made no attempt to search for a vanished object. Stage 3, on the other hand, is characterized by the acquisition of four new behavior patterns which represent considerable progress in the formation of the object concept.

First, there is visual anticipation of the future positions of objects. If, for example, an object drops very quickly and the infant cannot see all of the movement, he can nevertheless anticipate the final resting place of the object. At first the infant does this best if he himself has dropped the object. Later, he can anticipate the position of an object dropped by someone else. Consider the following illustration:

At 0;6(3) Laurent, lying down, holds in his hand a box five centimeters in diameter. When it escapes him he looks for it in the right direction (beside him). I then grasp the box and drop it myself, vertically, and too fast for him to be able to follow the trajectory. His eyes search for it at once on the sofa on which he is lying. I manage to eliminate any sound or shock and I perform the experiment at his right and at his left; the result is always positive.[18]

Here we see that the infant no longer continues passive viewing of the place where he saw the object vanish, as he did in the previous stage, but he now visually searches for it in a new location. This behavior shows that the infant anticipates that the object's movement will continue even though he himself is unable to see it. In this sense the infant confers on the object a preliminary sort of intrinsic permanence which, however, remains subjective since it is closely related to his own actions. He searches for the object chiefly if he himself has caused its disappearance.

A second achievement of this stage is what Piaget calls *interrupted prehension*. This is the tactual equivalent to the above mentioned behavior of visual accommodation to rapid movements. In other words, if the infant has already set in motion certain movements of the hand or fingers with the purpose of grasping an object and then loses it or does not succeed in grasping it, he will search for the object by continuing the movements.

As in the case of visual accommodation the infant attributes only a subjective permanence to the object. The object exists only in relation to

18. *The Construction of Reality in the Child*, pp. 14–15.

the action he was performing when it vanished or slipped out of his grasp. The infant originates no new movements to retrieve the lost object, but merely repeats his past gestures of holding or attempting to hold the object. Also, if no movements toward the object had been initiated in the first place, the infant makes no active attempt to search for a disappearing object.

Third, we can observe during this stage a behavior which is called *deferred circular reaction*. In this case a circular reaction involving an object is interrupted and resumed spontaneously by the infant at a later time. The resumption of the actions on an object implies that the infant expects it to continue to be available. For example:

At 0;8(30) Lucienne is busy scratching a powder box placed next to her on her left, but abandons that game when she sees me appear on her right. She drops the box and plays with me for a moment, babbles, etc. Then she suddenly stops looking at me and turns at once in the correct position to grasp the box; obviously she does not doubt that this will be at her disposal in the very place where she used it before.[19]

This is an important step forward, since such behavior is not merely a continuation of previous movements when an object is lost from sight or touch. Here the action has been completely interrupted and replaced by another quite different pattern of behavior. Yet at a later point, not too far removed in time, the infant, of his own accord, returns to the place where he had been playing and expects what he had been playing with to be there still. This shows that the infant attributes at least some permanence to the object. Despite this accomplishment, the infant's object concept is not yet fully developed. By contrast with advances to be made in the future, the infant's behavior in the present stage is still too closely associated with a practical situation and previous activities, and does not yet involve an entirely mature object concept.

In a fourth reaction typical of the present stage the infant can now recognize an invisible object even when he is able to see only certain parts of it. If the infant is shown a toy which (while he watches) is completely covered by a cloth, he makes no attempt to search for the toy. If, however, certain parts are left visible the infant tries to lift the cloth to discover the rest of the toy. But even this ability is curiously limited; he is able to recognize the whole only when some portions are visible. For example, one of Piaget's children was able to recognize his bottle only if either end was visible and the middle hidden. If only the middle portion were shown, he was not able to recognize the bottle and made no attempt to suck on it.

The recognition of partly hidden objects occurs only after the child has acquired sufficient skill in manipulating things. The manipulation of

19. *Ibid.*, p. 25.

a variety of toys and other objects enables the infant to explore visually the things he holds in his hands. By varying the distances and angles of these things, bringing them closer to his eyes, turning them around, and moving them from side to side, he will gradually gain a better knowledge of their shape and their other properties. This sort of knowledge, of course, is necessary for such activity as the recognition of partly hidden objects and thus contributes toward the development of a genuine object concept.

In brief, the four previous types of behavior of the present stage: (1) visual anticipation of rapid movements; (2) interrupted prehension; (3) deferred circular reactions; and (4) reconstruction of an invisible whole from a visible fraction, all present similar limitations and shortcomings with respect to the object concept. These behaviors all indicate that at this stage the object does not have a fully independent or individual existence but is closely related to the infant's own action. When the object disappears the infant is content to repeat actions that were being performed at the time of disappearance. His attempts to rediscover the lost object consist only of a repetition of the past actions associated with the object. No novel behavior is introduced.

STAGE 4: 10 to 12 MONTHS

Coordination of Secondary Schemes

The following observations show how the child after initial failure develops the behavior patterns characteristic of stage 4:

. . . *at 0;6(0) I present Laurent with a matchbox, extending my hand laterally to make an obstacle to his prehension. Laurent tries to pass over my hand, or to the side, but he does not attempt to displace it. As each time I prevent his passage, he ends by storming at the box while waving his hand. . . . Same reactions at 0;6(8), 0;6(10), 0;6(21), etc.*

Finally, at 0;7(13) Laurent reacts quite differently almost from the beginning of the experiment. I present a box of matches above my hand, but behind it, so that he cannot reach it without setting the obstacle aside. But Laurent after trying to take no notice of it, suddenly tries to hit my hand as though to remove or lower it; I let him do it to me and he grasps the box. I recommence to bar his passage, but using as a screen a sufficiently supple cushion to keep the impress of the child's gestures. Laurent tries to reach the box, and bothered by the obstacle, he at once strikes it, definitely lowering it until the way is clear. . . .

Moreover, one notes that the intermediate act serving as means (removing the obstacle) is borrowed from a familiar scheme; the scheme of striking. We recall that Laurent from 0;4(7) and above all from 0;4(19) has the habit of hitting hanging objects in order to swing them and finally from 0;5(2) of striking the objects. . . . Now, this is the usual scheme of which Laurent makes use at the present time, no longer in the capacity of an end in itself (of a final scheme) but as a means (a transitional or mobile scheme). . . .[20]

The interpretation of Laurent's behavior utilizes many of the principles discussed in connection with stage 3. There are, however, some important differences. One difference is that Laurent has the goal in mind from the outset. If you will recall, in stage 3 the infant *accidentally* discovers a goal and only then pursues it. In stage 4, on the other hand, Laurent initially perceives the presented object as a familiar goal. The infant has already developed schemes for dealing with the goal and immediately tries to assimilate it into them. Or in simpler language, the infant already knows what to do with the object and wants to do it. The directional force affecting his behavior—his desire to achieve the goal—is, of course, once again a matter of functional assimilation. Once the scheme of the goal—grabbing the matchbox—is activated, it needs to function.

But an obstacle arises (the father's hand or the cushion) which prevents the child from attaining the goal. Now we can see the second feature which distinguishes behavior in stage 4 from that in stage 3. The infant is now required to develop new means for removing the obstacle so that he can achieve his ends. Unlike stage 3, it is not now simply a matter of *rediscovering* some behavior which earlier led (accidentally) to the goal. The infant must show some degree of originality in order to remove the obstacle. But his originality is of a very limited sort. Instead of *inventing* new means for dealing with the obstacle, Laurent attempts to utilize as means schemes which have been developed in connection with other situations. That is, he generalizes patterns of previously learned behavior to the new problem (generalizing assimilation). In the course of this generalization the older schemes may be somewhat, but not fundamentally, modified. Also, he may try out several schemes, but in the end retains only the one which works by removing the obstacle. Accommodation is once again dependent on practical success. The result is a coordination of two secondary schemes, each of which had been learned earlier, and each of which is only slightly modified for the present occasion. One scheme serves as the means and the other as the ends. The child's originality rests not in inventing two separate schemes but in combining in a novel way two previously learned patterns of behavior.

Several features of this coordination are emphasized by Piaget. First, it is still essentially conservative. The infant's aim is to treat the goal

20. *Origins of Intelligence*, pp. 217–18.

object in the same way as previously. Once the obstacle is removed, the infant applies a *familiar* scheme. Second, the infant's behavior at this stage is for the first time truly intentional and therefore intelligent. Piaget's criteria for the existence of intention are three in number: (a) The infant has the goal in mind from the beginning and does not discover it accidentally as was the case in stage 3; (b) An obstacle arises which prevents direct attainment of the goal and necessitates some kind of indirect approach; (c) To overcome the obstacle, he employs a scheme (means) which is different from that employed in the case of the goal (ends).

A third feature of this coordination emphasized by Piaget is that the behavior under discussion is mobile. The novel coordination between two schemes not previously associated is made possible by the infant's relatively new ability to detach his schemes from their usual contents. In other words, the scheme used as means is generalized or transferred from the situation in which it was originally learned. This flexibility in the application of schemes is what constitutes mobility.

Relations

In stage 3 we discussed the very first manifestations of relations in the infant. With the coordination of schemes in stage 4 the infant becomes capable of establishing more complex relationships.

Let us recall, for example, Laurent's coordination of secondary schemes: removing an obstacle in order to attain a goal. When Laurent does this, it is as if he "understands" that the obstacle stands in a certain relationship to the goal. The obstacle is *in front of* the goal and it must be removed *before* the goal can be attained. In other words, just as an abbreviated performance of one scheme is a primitive indication of a class, so the *coordination* of two schemes implies a behavioral analogue of the understanding of relations.

Let us take another example:

. . . *at 0;9(17), Laurent lifts a cushion in order to look for a cigar case. When the object is entirely hidden the child lifts the screen with hesitation, but when one end of the case appears Laurent removes the cushion with one hand and with the other tries to extricate the objective. The act of lifting the screen is therefore entirely separate from that of grasping the desired object and constitutes an autonomous "means," no doubt derived from earlier and analogous acts.*[21]

Thus the sequence is a clear case of secondary circular reaction.

21. *Ibid.*, p. 222.

Laurent has learned how to get the goal. But has he not also learned something of the relation between obstacle and goal? Laurent's behavior may be interpreted as showing a concrete understanding of certain relations: the cushion is *on top of* the cigar box which in turn is *under* the pillow. We emphasize once again that the child's "understanding" of relations is not abstract like the adult's; instead, it is entirely contained in his means-end behavior.

Perhaps the most remarkable feature of relations is that even in the first few stages they involve an element of quantity. For example:

At 0;9(4) Laurent imitates the sounds which he knows how to make spontaneously. I say "papa" to him, he replies papa or baba. When I say "papa-papa" he replies apapa or bababa. When I say "papapapapapapa" he replies papapapa, etc. There exists a global evaluation of the number of syllables: the quantity corresponding to 2 is in any case distinguished from 3, 4, or 5. . . .

At 0;10(4) Laurent repeats pa when I say "pa," papa for "papa" and papapa *for a number of 4 or more than 4.*[22]

Thus the infant shows a primitive appreciation of number; he can discriminate among different numbers of syllables.

Anticipation

If you will, recall that in connection with the abbreviated schemes of stage 3, we discussed the development of the operations of classification and the relation between the signifier and the signified. For example, when Lucienne briefly shakes her legs at the hanging parrots, the sight of the toys is the signifier and the abbreviated motion is the signified—the primitive meaning of the parrots for the child. In the present stage, the system of meanings is used in the service of anticipation. (This occurs also in stage 3, but in rudimentary form.) Here is an example concerning Jacqueline:

At 0;9(16) . . . she likes the grape juice in a glass, but not the soup in a bowl. She watches her mother's activity. When the spoon comes out of the glass she opens her mouth wide, whereas when it comes from the bowl, her mouth remains closed. . . . At 0;9(18) Jacqueline no longer needs to look at the spoon. She notes by the sound whether the spoonful comes from the glass or from the bowl and obstinately closes her mouth in the latter case. . . .

Lucienne has revealed most of the same reactions. Thus at 0;8(23)

22. *Ibid.*, p. 241.

she also closes her mouth to the spoonful coming from the bowl (of soup) and opens it to those coming from the glass (of fruit juice).[23]

How can we interpret these reactions? First, note that they are *anticipatory*. The infant does not avoid the soup when it is in her mouth, but before it gets there. Apparently the sight of the soup or even its distinctive sound is a signifier, and the signified is the unpleasant taste of the soup. In other words, the infant sees or hears the soup, and its meaning for her is an unpleasant experience. She then closes her mouth not in response to the actual taste of the soup, but to the meaning that soup has for her before it enters her mouth. Furthermore, the infant in this stage does not form only anticipations which are connected with his own actions. For example, Jacqueline once cried when she saw someone who was sitting next to her get up. Apparently for Jacqueline the sight of the person getting up was a signifier of his expected imminent departure (the signified), and it was to this signified (the expectation of departure) that she reacts.

How do these anticipations develop? Formerly Jacqueline had observed that the signifier—in this case the person getting up—was followed by another event, his departure. She had consequently perceived a connection between the two events, so that now the signifier gives rise to an anticipation concerning the event to follow.

Imitation

Considerable progress in imitation occurs during stage 4. The infant can now establish relationships between the movements of a model and the corresponding movements of invisible parts of his own body. Also, he begins to imitate new actions of models.

Consider this example of the first case:

. . . *at 0;8(4) Jacqueline began by making a slight noise with her saliva as a result of the friction of her lips against her teeth, and I had imitated this sound at the outset.*[24] *[On the same day] Jacqueline was moving her lips as she bit her jaws. I did the same thing and she stopped and watched me attentively. When I stopped she began again. I imitated her. She again stopped and so it went on. . . .*[25]

Here we see that Jacqueline establishes a connection between what she sees in the model (the movement of his lips) and what she cannot see on herself, but can only feel, her own lip movements. How does she

23. *Ibid.*, p. 249.
24. *Play, Dreams, and Imitation*, p. 31.
25. *Ibid.*, p. 30.

manage to do this? At first she makes a sound with her saliva which is imitated by Piaget. Jacqueline repeats this sound and at the same time carefully watches the movements of the model's mouth. Now while she is reproducing the sound of the saliva and watching Piaget's mouth, she becomes aware of certain tactile-kinesthetic feelings. The sound becomes associated on the one hand with these feelings, and on the other with the sight of the model's lip movements. Thus, the sound is a common denominator linking the visual and kinesthetic cues. Later the sound is no longer necessary, and she becomes able to imitate mouth movements without either the model or herself having to produce the sound first.

The following is an example of the imitation of new actions of a model:

At 0;9(12) I alternately bent and straightened my finger, and she [Jacqueline] opened and closed her hand. At 0;9(16) she reacted to the same model several times in succession by waving her hand, but as soon as she stopped trying to imitate me she raised her finger correctly. When I resumed she again began to wave goodbye.

At 0;9(19) I tried the same experiment. She imitated me, but used her whole hand which she straightened and bent without taking her eyes off my finger.

. . . Finally at 0;9(22) she succeeded in isolating and imitating correctly the movement of the forefinger.[26]

Here Piaget initiates a new movement in front of the child. Jacqueline, contrary to her reactions of the preceding stage, no longer ignores the new movement, but tries to imitate it. Two restrictions on the initial imitation of novel behavior are apparent in the above example. In the first place, the infant imitates only movements which are similar to those he is already able to perform. For instance, bending and straightening the finger is not too different from bending and straightening the hand. The infant is consequently interested in imitating such behavior since he can assimilate it to some known scheme. Furthermore, imitation is only very approximate at this point. The infant rarely succeeds in reproducing the correct movement on the first trial. He gradually improves his technique with practice, and by a succession of adjustments accommodates his schemes to the novel movement.

Object Concept

The behavior of the stage 4 infant toward objects shows a marked progress on that of the previous stage and is a result of the infant's im-

26. *Ibid.,* pp. 46–47.

proved manipulatory skills. Since he is now better able to coordinate his hand and eye movements, he can explore objects more adequately than before. By holding an object while he brings it closer to or further from his eyes, or by turning it around in his hand, he becomes aware that the object remains the same even though many visual changes have taken place. This discovery leads to the attribution of qualities of permanence and substance to objects. As a result, when an object vanishes the infant tries to find it again by active search for it. He no longer attempts to rediscover the object by merely prolonging or repeating the actions which were underway when the object disappeared. Instead, the infant now initiates new movements and actions which indicate that the object has become detached from its previous subjective relationship with the infant's own activity.

In certain conditions, however, the object concept continues to retain some of its subjective qualities. This phenomenon may be seen clearly from the following observation:

At 0;10(18) Jacqueline is seated on a mattress without anything to disturb or distract her (no coverlets, etc.). I take her parrot from her hands and hide it twice in succession under the mattress, on her left, in A. Both times Jacqueline looks for the object immediately and grabs it. Then I take it from her hands and move it very slowly before her eyes to the corresponding place on her right, under the mattress, in B. Jacqueline watches this movement but at the moment when the parrot disappears in B she turns to her left and looks where it was before, in A.[27]

Jacqueline presents the reaction typical of this stage. In certain situations the infant is unable to take into account the number or complexity of the movements of an object, and he attempts to look for the object in the place where he had previously succeeded in discovering it. In other words, if the situation is too complex, he tends to attribute to the object a sort of absolute or privileged position which is that associated with previously successful discoveries. If, on the other hand, the object simply disappears in one spot, the infant will search for it in the right place.

In stage 4, then, the infant attributes to the object the qualities of substance and permanence. In straightforward situations the object has become detached from the infant's actions and is now an objective entity. Should its movements become too complicated for the infant to follow, however, the object once again takes on certain subjective properties and becomes related to the infant's past actions, especially those which had proved successful in discovering the object previously.

27. *Construction of Reality,* p. 51.

STAGE 5: 12 TO 18 MONTHS

Tertiary Circular Reaction

In stage 5 behavior loses its conservative emphasis, and the child, who has now begun to walk, begins to search for novelty. Here is an observation on Laurent:

> . . . at 0;10(2) *Laurent discovered in "exploring" a case of soap, the possibility of throwing this object and letting it fall. Now, what interested him at first was not the objective phenomenon of the fall—that is to say the object's trajectory—but the very act of letting go. He therefore limited himself, at the beginning, merely to reproducing the result observed fortuitously.*
>
> . . . at 0;10(10) . . . *Laurent manipulates a small piece of bread. . . . Now, in contradistinction to what has happened on the preceding days, he pays no attention to the act of letting go whereas he watches with great interest the body in motion . . . [The falling bread].*
>
> At 0;10(11) *Laurent is lying on his back. . . . He grasps in succession a celluloid swan, a box, etc., stretches out his arm and lets them fall. He distinctly varies the positions of the fall. Sometimes he stretches out his arm vertically, sometimes he holds it obliquely, in front or behind his eyes, etc. When the object falls in a new position (for example on his pillow), he lets it fall two or three more times on the same place, as though to study the spatial relation; then he modifies the situation. At a certain moment the swan falls near his mouth; now he does not suck it (even though this object habitually serves this purpose), but drops it three times more while merely making the gesture of opening his mouth.*[28]

The striking thing about these observations is Laurent's curiosity about the objects in his world. Laurent does not focus interest on himself or on those properties of an object which aid in attaining some goal; instead, he seems curious about the object as an object, and he seems desirous of learning all he can about its nature. This interest in novelty for its own sake is called a tertiary circular reaction.

Piaget's explanation begins with noting that the infant often discovers the initial result by chance. For example, in the process of playing with his soap dish Laurent accidentally dropped it and observed the fall. Moreover, the initial chance event interests the infant, and this interest can be explained in terms of the moderate novelty principle described

28. *Origins of Intelligence*, pp. 268–69.

earlier. The infant, of course, desires to *reproduce* the interesting event, and this behavior involves the principle of functional assimilation. Consequently, Laurent repeats the original act and drops the case of soap several times in succession.

Thus far the infant's behavior is no different from that of stage 3: an interesting result accidentally occurs, and the infant attempts to find a means by which to conserve it. However, at this point two distinctive features of the tertiary reaction manifest themselves. First, instead of continuing simple and rigid repetition of the interesting event, Laurent initiates behavioral changes which produce variations in the event itself. Laurent drops the bread and then the toys from different heights or from different positions. Second, he acts as if he now has interest in the new actions of the objects themselves and searches for novelties—for the unexpected. He seems to treat the unanticipated trajectories of the toys as something to be understood.

The explanation of the tertiary circular reaction involves several steps. (a) At first the infant tries to assimilate the new objects into his usual scheme of dropping. He finds, however, that the habitual scheme does not work very well as he meets with resistance. That is, the infant tries to drop the piece of bread in the same way he dropped the soap once, then he tries to drop the swan in the same way he dropped the bread. Since all of these objects do not fall in the same way, he meets with a resistance which is imposed by the reality of the objects themselves. Laurent finds that his available scheme of dropping does not apply in the same way to all of the objects. Each object has properties of its own which must be taken into account.

(b) The infant becomes interested in these resistances. Piaget points out that at this stage of his development the infant is more capable of appreciating novelty. If you will recall, the "interesting" was defined as that which is moderately different from that which the infant recognizes as familiar. Consequently, the more things the infant is familiar with and the more schemes he has, the more objects and events he is able to recognize as novel and interesting. The newborn's world is largely restricted to sucking; events outside the oral sphere (as most events are) cannot be interesting for him because he lacks schemes relevant to them. But the infant at stage 5 has developed skills which permit him to contact increasingly larger segments of the world; consequently, there is much that he will find interesting. In summary, the more complex the system of schemes, the more the infant will be attracted to novelty. He will then be interested in the resistances which he encounters from applying his old schemes to new events.

(c) He is interested in the properties of objects from another point of view, too. At this stage the infant has begun to attribute permanence to objects and recognizes that they have an existence independent of his own. In fact, objects are even "centers of forces," with powers and properties of their own. This new objectification of the world also contributes to the infant's desire to explore.

Once the infant recognizes and has interest in the potential novelties of a situation, he begins to accommodate. He "gropes" or uses a kind of trial and error procedure to discover the properties of the objects. The infant's groping does not involve completely random responses; rather each of his explorations guides the next. The results of one "experiment" lead to new experiments. For instance, Laurent may release the swan from points which are increasingly high above his head and observe the extent to which the swan bounces when it hits the bed. The infant, of course, does not know beforehand what will happen; he modifies his behavior to find out. By exploring the object and accommodating his own behavior to it, the infant may eventually become able to master the object—to assimilate it without difficulty into his (modified) schemes. In this way he begins to explore and understand novel aspects of his world.

Discovery of New Means

The infant's tendency toward experimentation allows him to discover new means for attaining a goal. Consider the following observation on Lucienne at 1;0(5). Piaget presents her with this problem. On a table is a large box turned upside down. The box is so arranged that it moves only by pivoting around its center point. On the box, away from the infant's reach is an attractive toy, a bottle.

Lucienne at first tries to grasp the box, but she goes about it as though the handkerchief were still involved. [Pulling a handkerchief was a scheme which Piaget had previously observed in the child.] She tries to pinch it between two fingers, in the center, and tries this for a moment without being able to grasp it. Then, with a rapid and unhesitating movement she pushes it at a point on its right edge. . . . She then notes the sliding of the box and makes it pivot without trying to lift it; as the box revolves, she succeeds in grasping the bottle.[29]

In order to get the object, Lucienne at first attempted to apply an already available scheme; pinching the box like a handkerchief. Then, however, she "groped," and accommodated her behavior in a trial and error sort of way. The result was discovery of a new means. Lucienne struck the box, and this action was successful in bringing the toy close. But while her behavior was to some extent characterized by groping, or

29. *Ibid.*, p. 287.

trial and error, her actions were nevertheless *directed* in two senses. First, her accommodations were directed by the goal: Lucienne wanted to get the bottle and was trying out various means for this purpose. The means were hardly randomly selected; she did not, for instance, try to obtain the toy by taking off her socks. Second, Lucienne interpreted the groping by means of her already available schemes. That is, after Lucienne by chance hit the box and saw it move, she was able, through her past experience, to "understand" the meaning of her action. She interpreted the hitting as another method for displacing objects. Thus the child's groping is directed both by the goal and by earlier schemes which enable her to understand what is happening. Therefore, learning is not explained solely by contact with the environment; that is, by experience with a world that simply forces the infant's behavior to take certain forms. The infant himself makes an important contribution too as he interprets and gives meaning to the data of experience.

Imitation

At stage 5 the child becomes capable of the systematic imitation of new models. In the previous stage he had begun to imitate new models which were not too different from his own spontaneous actions, but he was rarely correct on the first trial. In the present stage the child becomes more systematic in his techniques of imitation. Here is an example:

At 0;11(20) she [Jacqueline] watched me with interest when I touched my forehead with my forefinger. She then put her right forefinger on her left eye, moved it over her eyebrow, then rubbed the left side of her forehead with the back of her hand, but as if she were looking for something else. She reached her ear, but came back toward her eye. . . .

At 0;11(28) J., confronted with the same model continued merely to rub her eye and eyebrows. But afterwards, when I seized a lock of my hair and moved it about on my temple, she succeeded for the first time in imitating me. She suddenly took her hand from her eyebrow, which she was touching, felt above it, found her hair and took hold of it, quite deliberately.

At 0;11(30) she at once pulled her hair when I pulled mine. She also touched her head when I did so, but when I rubbed my forehead she gave up. . . . It is noteworthy that when she pulled her hair she sometimes turned her head suddenly in an attempt to see it. This movement is a clear indication of an effort to discover the connection between tactual and visual perception. . . .

At 1;0(16), J. discovered her forehead. When I touched the middle of mine, she first rubbed her eye, then felt above it and touched her hair, after which she brought her hand down a little and finally put her finger on her forehead. On the following day she at once succeeded in imitating this gesture, and even found approximately the right spots indicated by the model.[30]

Two observations are of interest concerning these examples. First, they clearly show that the infant is more adept than he formerly was at the immediate imitation of new actions of models. The infant tries to control his movements in a systematic way. For example, Jacqueline tries to look at her hair when she pulls it. Second, these examples illustrate some general processes of imitation. The chief aim of imitation is to reproduce the act of a model. When the model's actions are new, as in the present case, accommodation is required. That is, the infant must modify his movements to make them like the model's. Thus, accommodation has priority over assimilation. In the case of intelligent behavior, on the other hand, the processes of assimilation and accommodation are in balance. The infant attempts both to modify his behavior in response to the demands of the environment (accommodation) and to understand this environment in terms of his own schemes (assimilation).

Object Concept

In stage 5 the infant is finally able to follow correctly a visible sequence of an object's movements. He now understands positional relationships between the object and other elements of the environment. Therefore, even if the object disappears successively in a number of places the infant will search for it in the place where it was last seen. The infant does not, as in stage 4, look for the object in the place where he had previously been successful in discovering it. Thus, the object is no longer connected with a practical situation (the infant's past successes), but has acquired a permanence of its own. At this stage, though, the infant can understand only visible movements of the object. If he is unable to see all the displacements and must therefore infer that some are invisible, he reverts to an earlier reaction—looking for the object where he had been successful in finding it in the past. The reason for the failure is that when invisible movements of the object are involved, the infant must *infer* relationships of position, and he is not yet capable of inference. Consider the following illustration:

At 1;1(18) Lucienne is seated on a bed, between shawl A and cloth B. I hide a safety pin in my hand and my hand under the shawl. I remove my hand closed and empty. Lucienne opens it at once and looks for the pin. Not finding it, she searches under the shawl and finds it. . . .

30. *Play, Dreams, and Imitation,* pp. 55–56.

But with a beret, things become complicated. I put my watch in the beret and the beret under pillow A (on the right); Lucienne lifts the pillow, takes the beret, and removes the watch from it. Then I place the beret, again containing the watch, under cushion B on the left; Lucienne looks for it in B but, as it is hidden too far down for her to find it at once, she returns to A.

Then, twice, I raise cushion B so that Lucienne sees the beret obviously containing the object; both times she resumes looking in B but, not finding the watch right away, returns to A! She searches even longer in A than in B after having seen the object in B! [31]

Here we see that the object seems to be endowed with a dual nature. On the one hand, if the infant is able to follow the object's movements perceptually, he believes in its permanence and continued existence. If, however, he cannot follow the movements visually but must imagine them, the infant no longer endows the object with the property of permanence. The object reverts to its earlier status of being associated with a previously successful scheme.

STAGE 6: 18 MONTHS TO 2 YEARS

Beginning of Thought

In the course of his five stages of development, the infant has most certainly made great progress. The newborn displays simple patterns of learning which are limited to the sphere of his hereditary mechanisms; the infant in stage 5 has a genuine interest in the things of his environment, explores them, and even has the ability to *invent* new ways of dealing with the world. But the infant's achievement to this point is as nothing compared with his next development. Before stage 6 he was not capable of thought or language and so was largely limited to the immediate data of experience. Stage 6, however, forms the transition to the next period of development in which the infant is able to use mental symbols and words to refer to absent objects. This period of symbolic thought will begin to free the infant from the concrete here and now and introduce him to the world of possibilities. We shall discuss symbolic thought in detail in Chapter Three; at present we will limit ourselves to a brief description of the beginnings of thought, as illustrated by these observations:

Piaget is playing with Lucienne, at 1;4(0), and hides an attractive watch chain inside an empty match box.

31. *Construction of Reality,* pp. 76–77.

*I put the chain back into the box and reduce the opening to 3 mm.
It is understood that Lucienne is not aware of the functioning of the opening and closing of the match box and has not seen me prepare the experiment. She only possesses two preceding schemes: turning the box over in
order to empty it of its contents, and sliding her fingers into the slit to
make the chain come out. It is of course this last procedure that she tries
first: she puts her finger inside and gropes to reach the chain, but fails
completely. A pause follows during which Lucienne manifests a very curious reaction. . . .*

*She looks at the slit with great attention; then, several times in suc-
cession, she opens and shuts her mouth, at first slightly, then wider and
wider!*

*[Then] . . . Lucienne unhesitatingly puts her finger in the slit, and
instead of trying as before to reach the chain, she pulls so as to enlarge
the opening. She succeeds and grasps the chain.*[32]

This observation reveals an important advance in the child's capabilities. Lucienne was confronted with a situation for which a new solution
was required. To get the chain out of the box she tried methods which had
in the past been successful in similar situations. But these schemes were
not adequate for the new problem. What would the stage 5 child do in
these circumstances? He would experiment with various new means until
one of the inventions was successful. His behavior would show groping.

But Lucienne does not do this. Instead, she pauses and looks at the
box intensely. Her chief overt behavior at this time is only an opening and
closing of the mouth. After this delay, she immediately solves the problem.
What does the opening and closing of the mouth signify? Piaget interprets
it as showing that she tries to think about ways of solving the problem.
Lucienne is not yet very profficient at thought; she is not yet capable of
representing the situation to herself fully in mental terms. Consequently,
she "thinks out" the problem partly by way of movements of the mouth.
Even though her thought is not yet fully internalized, it involves a considerable short cut over the groping of stage 5. Now Lucienne need not
act out her attempted solution for she is at least partially able to employ
a more economical procedure: to *think*. Thus, Lucienne is on the threshold
of a new period of intellectual development in which the acquisition of
the symbolic function permits the growth of true mental activity.

Imitation

The notable achievement of stage 6 is the appearance of the capacity
to represent mentally an object or action which is not perceptually present.

32. *Origins of Intelligence*, pp. 337–38.

The capacity for such *representation* has repercussions on the progress of imitation, and contributes to the appearance of two new reactions during stage 6. In the first place, the infant when faced with new models no longer needs to perform overtly his trial attempts at imitation; instead, he now tries out the various movements mentally. When he has made the necessary mental adjustments, he can then perform the correct action. Since the process is largely mental, the stage 6 infant can imitate more quickly than the one who must first try out all the movements. The internalization of the trial and error process consequently leads to what appears to be an immediate imitation of models.

Another feature of the present stage is that the infant becomes capable of imitating for the first time a model which is no longer present. This *deferred imitation* is due to the fact that he can imagine the model even though it is absent. That is, the infant is capable of evoking (representing) the absent model in some internal symbolic form, for example, by means of a visual image. Consider the following example of deferred imitation:

At 1;4(3) Jacqueline had a visit from a little boy of 1;6 whom she used to see from time to time, and who, in the course of the afternoon got into a terrible temper. He screamed as he tried to get out of a playpen and pushed it backward, stamping his feet. Jacqueline stood watching him in amazement, never having witnessed such a scene before. The next day, she herself screamed in her playpen and tried to move it, stamping her foot lightly several times in succession.[33]

The internalization of the action is quite clear. The infant does not reproduce the scene at the time of its occurrence, but at some later period. Therefore, representation was required for the child to preserve the original scene in order for it to be evoked at a later time.

Object Concept

Finally, at stage 6 the concept of the permanent object is fully elaborated. Not only does the infant take into account visible displacements of the object; he can also reconstruct correctly a series of invisible displacements. For example:

At 1;7(23) Jacqueline is seated opposite three object-screens, A, B and C (a beret, a handkerchief, and her jacket) aligned equidistant from each other. I hide a small pencil in my hand saying "Coucou, the pencil." [The child had previously found it under A] I hold out my closed hand to her, put it under A, then under B, then under C (leaving the pencil

33. *Play, Dreams, and Imitation*, p. 63.

under C); at each step I again extend my closed hand, repeating, "Coucou, the pencil." Jacqueline then searches for the pencil directly in C, finds it and laughs.[34]

Jacqueline has seen the pencil disappear only once and into Piaget's hand. She does not, however, look into his hand to find the pencil, but under the last object where he had placed his hand. This reaction indicates that she believes that the pencil continued to exist within the hand during the whole sequence of displacements, and that she has inferred that the invisible object was displaced from A to B to C. In other words, Jacqueline has formed a mental image of the pencil and can follow the image through a series of complex displacements.

SUMMARY AND CONCLUSIONS

The infant's development in the sensorimotor period is a truly remarkable achievement. In *stage 1*, the newborn depends heavily on his reflexes for interaction with the environment. The environment, however, does not simply turn on and off these tools provided by heredity. The infant, even in the first month of life, profits from experience and actively modifies the reflex schemes. He learns, for example, to recognize the nipple and to search for it.

In *stage 2*, the infant shows behavior patterns which are removed from the feeding situation. (a) He develops the primary circular reactions. For example, he develops the motor coordinations necessary for bringing the hand to the mouth. (b) He learns in a primitive way to anticipate future events. When placed in the appropriate position, the infant anticipates nursing by initiating sucking movements. (c) The first signs of curiosity appear. The infant shows an interest in moderately novel events. (d) The infant sometimes repeats the behavior of models. This is a very primitive kind of imitation, since it occurs only when the model performs an action highly similar to a scheme available to the infant. It is as if the infant did not distinguish the model's acts from his own; therefore, the apparent imitation is merely the infant's repetition of behavior which he believes to be his own. (e) The infant lacks a mature object concept, but develops several patterns of behavior which are preliminary steps in the right direction. He coordinates the previously independent schemes of looking and hearing, among others. He shows passive expectancy by watching for a brief time the spot where an object has disappeared.

In *stage 3*, the infant's behavior and interest extend beyond his own body, and he makes more extensive, but still immature, contact with the

34. *Construction of Reality*, pp. 79–80.

external environment. (a) The infant develops secondary circular reactions. By chance, he discovers an interesting environmental event and attempts to rediscover the actions which produced it. (b) The infant shows preliminary indications of classification or meaning. Presented with a familiar object, he sometimes reacts by showing mere abbreviations of the actions it usually elicits. This behavior appears to be a precursor of mental recognition and understanding of the object. (c) The infant's imitation is now more systematic and precise. He is fairly successful at imitation of models, but only when familiar patterns of behavior are involved. (d) The infant makes considerable progress toward attainment of the object concept. If he himself has caused an object's disappearance, he attempts a visual or tactual search. This search only involves continuation of behavior (like looking or grasping) which is already underway. To this extent the object concept remains subjective—intimately bound to his own behavior.

In *stage 4*, the infant's behavior is increasingly systematic and well organized. (a) He is able to coordinate secondary schemes. He has a goal in mind from the outset, and he uses one scheme as a means for attaining the goal and a second scheme for dealing with the goal. This behavior is purposive and therefore intelligent. (b) By interacting with his environment, the infant learns something about relations of objects. In removing an obstacle to a goal, for instance, the child achieves a preliminary and concrete understanding of the fact that the obstacle is *in front of* the goal and must be removed *before* the goal can be attained. (c) The infant's increasing understanding of the environment is apparent by his ability to anticipate events which do not depend on his own actions. At this period he expects people to act in certain ways; he begins to recognize that they are "centers of forces" independent of himself. (d) The infant begins to imitate the novel behavior of models, but he is not yet strikingly successful. Also he imitates actions—like sticking out the tongue—which he cannot see himself perform. (e) The infant's object concept is almost fully developed. He employs a variety of behavior to search for vanished objects. He clearly attributes to things a degree of substance and permanence; he begins to conceive of objects as autonomous and as independent of his own subjective state. Nevertheless, he is not yet successful at following a complex series of displacements of an object.

Stage 5 is the climax of the sensorimotor period. (a) The infant shows an active interest in producing new behavior and novel events. Before this stage, the child's behavior was essentially conservative. He tried to rediscover old actions which happened to lead to interesting results. (b) When confronted with an obstacle he attempts to develop new means for dealing with it, and he does not rely solely on schemes which were successful previously. (c) The infant is now increasingly adept at imitating new actions of models. He attempts, for instance, to produce sounds he has never uttered before. (d) The infant has reached a further stage in the sensorimotor development of the object concept. He can now comprehend a complex series of displacements and search for the object in the proper place.

Stage 6 forms the transition to symbolic thought. (a) In our preliminary overview we saw that the infant attempted to *think* about a problem; to develop solutions on a mental rather than a physical level. (b) Similarly, he could now imitate a model even though the latter may not be present. It is apparent that after he observes a model the infant forms a mental representation of it, so that the later imitation is based not on a physically present model, but on a mentally present one. (c) The infant now can reconstruct a series of invisible displacements of an object because of his new abilities in representation.

In the most general sense, development reveals a process of *decentration*. The infant begins life in an undifferentiated state. He does not separate self from environment or wish from reality. He is *centered* about the self. For example, we have seen how the infant in the first few stages does not have a mature object concept. A thing ceases to exist when it passes outside his immediate perception. Furthermore, for the infant the world is merely a series of unstable and unconnected "pictures." Neither self nor external environment exist as autonomous entities. In the course of development the infant advances from this "adualistic" or undifferentiated state to one of greater separation of self and environment. He *decenters* from the self. In the case of the object concept, for example, the infant now conceives of things existing independently. Objects now are centers of forces and have properties which do not depend on his will. This greater understanding of the external world is at the same time an increased comprehension of the self. The realization of the separateness of things necessarily involves the simultaneous apprehension of the existence of self. In other words, the person who believes that his wishes influence the movements of things, does not understand either self or things; the person who believes that the two are separate has a greater understanding of both.

Piaget stresses several points concerning development in the sensorimotor period. First, the age norms are only approximate. As we noted earlier it is impossible to give precise age norms when only three children provide the data for study. More importantly, Piaget fully recognizes that the timing of the stages depends on a host of factors which vary among children. Development is a function of complex interaction between many factors, among which may be the nature of the social environment, the infant's rate of physical maturation, and so on. Given these complexities, it is clear that infants' progress through the stages will show many individual differences. For instance, Piaget cites the example of Jacqueline who was born in the winter. Because she was bundled up in the carriage to protect her against the cold, she did not have as much opportunity as did the other children, born in warmer weather, to develop coordination between hand and eye. From this finding Piaget concluded that the sensorimotor stages may not appear at precisely defined times in the infant's life.

Second, Piaget insists, however, that the ordering of the stages is invariant. A child must pass through stage 3 before stage 4, and the reverse cannot occur. Also, a child cannot skip a stage entirely. The reasons for Piaget's assertion are both empirical and theoretical. First, Piaget's observations showed that his three children followed the sequence of development in the order described. Second, each stage is both a culmination of the one preceding and a preparation for the one to follow. Since each stage lays the groundwork for the following stage, it is hard to see, on rational grounds alone, how the order of any two stages can be reversed.

Third, Piaget emphasizes that development is a gradual and continuous process. One does not find sudden transformations in an infant's behavior so that one day he is characterized by stage 3 and the next by stage 4 activities. Development takes time, and because of this one seldom sees "pure" examples of the behaviors which Piaget uses to describe a stage. Piaget's stages are, in fact, ideal types which are abstracted from the continuum of the infant's development. While these abstractions are very useful and convenient, Piaget is careful to remind us that in the normal course of events the infant's behavior takes many forms intermediary between those described by the stages. Also development is not always consistent across all spheres of behavior. The "stage 4 child" is again only an abstraction. In fact, one sees children whose object concept may be characterized by stage 4, while at the same time their level of imitation is stage 3, and so on.

Fourth, Piaget stresses that the behaviors characteristic of a given stage do not disappear when the infant attains the next stage. Instead, even as new abilities are added the child retains the old ones. For example, the stage 5 infant confronted with an obstacle and trying to remove it may first apply schemes which have been successful in other situations (stage 4 behavior), and only then may he attempt to invent new means (stage 5 behavior).

In conclusion we would like to make a few general comments about Piaget's theory of infancy and clarify some aspects of his theory that are often misunderstood. First, Piaget's position on the role of the environment is subtle, and consequently, often misinterpreted. He feels that it is obvious that the environment exerts effects on the infant, but acceptance of this proposition hardly solves any problems. The problem then becomes to discover *how* the environment operates. Piaget feels that the environment does not mold behavior by simply imposing itself on a passive subject, evoking the infant's response and rewarding it. Instead, Piaget's central theme is that the infant is *active*; that is, he seeks contact with the environment. His curiosity does not let him wait for environmental events to happen; rather he searches them out and seeks increased levels of stimulation and excitation. When some environmental event occurs, the infant does not register it passively, but instead he interprets it. It is this interpretation, not the event itself, which affects his behavior. Suppose we have two infants, one who is capable of anticipations concerning adults and one who is not. Both witness an adult who rises and puts on a coat. One infant cries and the other remains calm. "Experience"—seeing the adult get up and put on the coat—has affected the infants differently. The explanation is that one infant expected him to leave and the other did not. The infants interpreted the events in different ways. We might even say that there existed two different "realities," each one constructed by the infants. The infants assimilated the perceived event into their differing expectations concerning adult behavior. This assimilation or interpretation gave the event meaning and produced the subsequent behaviors. So the infants did not passively register a mere "copy" of reality; instead, they interpreted, constructed, and assimilated, or, in short, gave meaning to the events. Experience, then, does not exert effects *on* an infant, but instead, exerts effects *with* an infant; that is, the child modifies raw experience as much as it changes him.

Second, Piaget is sometimes misunderstood concerning his views of the roles of maturation and learning. It should be abundantly clear that Piaget is not a simple maturationist. He does not believe that the infant's development unfolds solely as a result of some kind of physical maturation. Piaget's position is that maturation has a role, but it certainly is not the only factor in development. As we have seen, he believes that the effects of the environment are quite important, and to this extent Piaget is in agreement with the environmentalists. But, as has been noted, Piaget's account of learning is quite subtle and is in many ways at variance with other theories of learning. For example, he introduces novel motivational principles, such as assimilation and the moderate novelty principle, and emphasizes the infant's interpretation of the raw data of sensory experience. In short, Piaget is neither a maturationist nor an environmentalist, at least not in the dominant behaviorist tradition. His position incorporates elements of both traditions, and, in addition, elaborates on them in highly original ways. He thinks of himself as an "interactionist," for his theory stresses that intellectual development results from an interplay between internal and external factors.

As we shall see in Chapter Four, Piaget has elaborated and supplemented his account of experience and maturation since his first writing of the books on infancy. The later theory of "equilibration" expands on the role of experience, and in addition introduces the concept of internal cognitive change.

Third, the nature of Piaget's stages is occasionally misunderstood. Piaget is sometimes compared with Gesell who offered an account of infancy in terms of stages of development. Gesell's stages were merely listings of specific *behaviors* which occurred at different ages. For example, the infant is found to crawl at such and such an age, to walk at another, to run at another, and so on. While such information may be valuable, it is clear that Gesell's stages merely list the empirical phenomena and have no theoretical content whatsoever. By contrast Piaget's stages are a theoretical taxonomy. Take, for example, stage 4 which is concerned with the coordination of secondary schemes. Piaget's theory proposes that in this stage the infant can coordinate two previously disparate patterns of behavior in order to attain a preconceived goal. This statement—the theory of this stage—is an abstraction which transcends the details of any specific behaviors which merely illustrate the stage. The statement is intended to allow us to understand what the infant does regardless of the particular behaviors involved. Piaget's stages are therefore theoretical or explanatory, and as such are radically different from Gesell's.

3

the years 2 through 11: symbolism and piaget's early work

The present chapter covers two broad topics. The first to be considered is the development of cognitive processes in the child of approximately 2 to 4 years. At this time some very important advances occur in the child's thought. One such advance is the onset of the symbolic function. We will concentrate on the young child's use of mental symbols and of words, and on his symbolic play. The second topic to be considered is the development of certain characteristics of thought in the child from 4 to 12 years. We shall review Piaget's early work on this topic and cover such matters as egocentrism, communication, and moral judgment.

THE SYMBOLIC FUNCTION

The sensorimotor period involves a rapid and remarkable development of behavioral schemes. The newborn entered the world with only a limited repertory of automatic behavior patterns provided by heredity. After a period of extensive development of about two years, the child can interact quite effectively with his immediate world of things and of people. He possesses schemes enabling him to manipulate objects and use them as means for the attainment of his goals. He also experiments with things in order to achieve a practical understanding of their properties. But all of these abilities, although useful, are nevertheless concrete; that is, limited to immediately present objects. For example, while the infant may be able to use a stick to draw to him an object beyond his reach, he cannot conceive of relationships between objects that are not within his immediate scope of vision. He is able to act only on things which he can perceive directly. Toward the end of the second year the child begins to develop novel cognitive, or mental processes.

One important aspect in the development of cognition is the appearance of the *symbolic function*. This refers to the fact that from 2 to 4 years the child begins to develop the ability to make something—a mental symbol, a word, or an object—stand for or represent something else which is not present. For example, the child can use a mental symbol of a bicycle, or the word "bicycle," or a small schematic toy to stand for the real bicycle when it is not in immediate view. The ability to symbolize in this way makes it possible for the child to operate on new levels. At this stage he is not restricted to acting on things in the immediate environment because the symbolic function allows him to evoke the past. For example, because he has formed a mental symbol of the bicycle he is able to recall his previous experience with this toy.

The symbolic function manifests itself in several ways. During the period from 2 to 4 years the child begins to employ mental symbols, to engage in symbolic play, and to use words. Let us review each of these activities in turn.

Mental Symbols

One example of the use of mental symbols involves deferred imitation. Let us recall the example of the temper tantrum:

At 1;4(3) [Jacqueline] had a visit from a little boy of 1;6, whom she used to see from time to time, and who, in the course of the afternoon, got into a terrible temper. He screamed as he tried to get out of a play-pen and pushed it backward, stamping his feet. J. stood watching him in amazement, never having witnessed such a scene before. The next day, she herself screamed in her play-pen and tried to move it, stamping her foot lightly several times in succession.[1]

The important feature of the observation is that Jacqueline's imitation was deferred: it occurred some time after she had originally seen the boy throwing the tantrum. Her behavior did not therefore simply copy an immediately observable model. If not, on what was her behavior based? How can we explain delayed imitation? One interpretation is that when

---

1. *Play, Dreams, and Imitation*, p. 63.

Piaget observed her, Jacqueline happened to throw a tantrum for the first time, and quite independently of anything the boy had done. But the explanation is quite implausible, because her behavior was so much like the boy's. Consequently, we are forced to postulate a more complicated explanation which involves mental symbolism. The reasoning is as follows. We know that in throwing the tantrum Jacqueline did not simply copy an immediately present model. Nevertheless, her behavior was clearly similar to the boy's. Consequently, we assume that Jacqueline must have formed a mental symbol of the tantrum and then based her behavior on this symbol. In other words, Jacqueline must have had available a mental event which stood for or represented the boy's real action. The ability to symbolize in this way allowed her to copy the boy's behavior at a later time.

What is the nature of mental symbols? It is difficult to answer this question since we have no method which permits a direct "look" at the child's thought. One possibility, however, is that the child's mental symbols are, at least in part, visual images. Perhaps Jacqueline "pictured" the tantrum to herself. While visual imagery does indeed occur (and may or may not have been used by Jacqueline), Piaget reminds us that mental symbols may take other forms as well. Although sometimes a person may use visual imagery, he may at other times represent objects by their sounds, or even by an abbreviated form of their movements. Piaget also proposes that the individual may not even be conscious of his mental symbols. A child may display imitative behavior without realizing that it is based on the actions of another person. Surely, after Freud's work, it should come as no surprise that many of our thought processes are unconscious.

We have seen, then, that the mental symbol may or may not be conscious and may or may not involve visual imagery. Does the mental symbol involve language? Was Jacqueline able to imitate the tantrum because she carried in her head the *words*, "He is lifting his arms, he is shouting," etc.? Although this sort of interpretation is very popular, particularly among American psychologists, Piaget rejects it. He cites two major reasons. First, certain experiments with animals show that chimpanzees, for instance, have mental symbols which, of course, could not be based on language. If non-verbal symbolism is possible in animals, then why not in the human too? Second, observation of the child shows that behavior like deferred imitation occurs while language skills are still very primitive. It is quite unlikely that Jacqueline was at that time capable of a reasonably full verbal description of the boy's temper tantrum. Yet, her imitation was quite accurate. Since a mental symbol based on the child's crude language could not have provided a basis for such accurate imitation, the linguistic explanation must be ruled out. In fact, in order to explain

Jacqueline's deferred imitation, we must postulate her use of mental symbols. These symbols probably do not involve language to a significant degree, but we cannot confidently specify their exact nature.

A second example of mental symbolism can be seen in the child's reaction to hidden objects. If you will recall, in stage 6 of the sensorimotor period the child could reconstruct a series of invisible displacements of an object. In an observation described in Chapter Two, Piaget hid a small pencil in his hand and then placed the hand consecutively under a beret, a handkerchief, and finally under a jacket where he left the pencil. Jacqueline did not look for the pencil in her father's hand which was the last place she had seen it, and which is where the younger child searches; instead, she immediately reached under the jacket and found the pencil.

How can we explain Jacqueline's behavior? It was not random, since she had acted in essentially the same way on many occasions. Piaget assumes that Jacqueline formed a mental symbol of the pencil. When Piaget covered the pencil in his hand, Jacqueline believed in its continued existence. When the hand was placed under a succession of objects, the use of the mental symbol enabled her to follow mentally the invisible displacements. The availability of a mental symbol is thus necessary for a mature object concept.

Thus far, we have seen two kinds of behavior—deferred imitation and search—which may be interpreted as demonstrating the existence of mental symbolism in the child. We may now inquire as to the development of mental symbols.

The Formation of Mental Symbols

How does the child form mental symbols? There seems to be at least two possible answers to this difficult question. One explanation is that the ability to symbolize is an entirely new function which suddenly makes its appearance when the child is about 2 years of age. Another possibility is that symbolism has precursors in the sensorimotor period. Because he emphasizes continuity in intellectual development, Piaget adopts the second alternative. He postulates that the symbolic function is derived from imitation. Consider the following observation from the sensorimotor period:

. . . At 1;3(8) J. [Jacqueline] was playing with a clown with long feet and happened to catch the feet in the low neck of her dress. She had difficulty in getting them out, but as soon as she had done so, she tried to put them back in the same position. . . . As she did not succeed, she put her hand in front of her, bent her forefinger at a right angle to reproduce the shape of the clown's feet, described exactly the same trajectory as the

clown and thus succeeded in putting her finger into the neck of her dress. She looked at the motionless finger for a moment, then pulled at her dress, without of course being able to see what she was doing. Then, satisfied, she removed her finger and went on to something else.[2]

Here we have a case of imitation put to the service of understanding an unusual phenomenon. In the course of playing with a familiar toy, Jacqueline discovered that the clown did something unexpected and initially unexplainable. Its feet caught her dress in a way that had not occurred before. Jacqueline immediately tried to understand the cause of the unexpected event. Her method of doing so was through imitative action: she formed her finger into the shape of the clown's foot, placed the finger in the dress, and then pulled to see what would happen. She discovered that the finger got caught and therefore prevented free movement of her arm. In this way she came to understand that the shape of the clown's foot similarly restricted its removal. Another way of looking at the observation is to say that it involves a special kind of imitation: Jacqueline used her own body to represent or stand for the clown's movements. Her actions symbolized the clown's. This is not an isolated observation; Piaget finds that the child often imitates things. For example, he noted that Lucienne upon observing that her father's bicycle could be made to move back and forth performed the same motions herself. She swayed to and fro at about the speed of the bicycle.

Piaget argues that such imitation of things is the sensorimotor *forerunner* of mental symbolism. The infant's swaying back and forth is the behavioral equivalent of the older child's having a mental symbol of the bicycle. In other words, for the infant the action of swaying signifies a bicycle, whereas for the older child a mental symbol performs the same function. Toward the end of the sensorimotor period the child's imitation goes underground, figuratively speaking. Instead of imitating things on the level of overt behavior, the older child does so internally. For instance, in place of actually swaying back and forth, the older child might imitate the bicycle by making very slight and almost imperceptible movements of his muscles. Or, instead of forming the fingers in the shape of the clown's foot, the older child might tense his finger muscles so slightly that an observer would not notice. Moreover, this internal imitation is no mere oddity. The child's internal and almost undetectable movements *constitute* the mental symbol. The child's muscles perform an abbreviated imitation of swaying, and these bodily sensations symbolize for him the bicycle. When the child's finger tenses ever so slightly, this internal imitation, which is not necessarily a visual image, signifies the clown.

We have seen, then, that the sensorimotor child represents things

2. *Ibid.*, p. 65.

by acting like them. The older child, on the other hand, performs such imitation internally, and these abbreviated body movements constitute the mental symbol. Eventually he becomes so proficient at internal imitation that the movements are extremely abbreviated and, therefore, almost impossible to detect.

Several interesting points can be made concerning the formation of the mental symbol. First, Piaget's theory gives us additional insight into the nature of the child's mental symbols. We said earlier that they might involve a visual component, and that they probably do not consist of linguistic features. Now we know that mental symbols initially involve the child's actions in an important way. The mental symbol of the bicycle consists not only of a visual image, but it also may involve bodily sensations corresponding to the bicycle's movements.

Second, in referring to the symbol as consisting of internal imitation, Piaget uses the term imitation in a very broad sense in order to account for visual imagery. Consider this hypothetical example. When a person sees a table, his perception accommodates to it. His eyes must follow the table's outline, detect its color, focus to localize the table in space, and so on. In these ways, the person establishes a number of relationships concerning the table (space, color, etc.) which together form his perception of it. In other words, the environment does not simply impose on him the perception of the table. Instead, his perception derives from his own activity; from a series of intricate movements of his eyes and from complex activity in the brain and nervous system. Visual perception is an activity, just as the child's swaying is an activity. Now we may see the role of imitation. At a later time when the table is no longer present, the person may repeat in an abbreviated form the movements involved in his initial perception of the table. That is, his eyes may again move as they did when they traced the table's contour, adjusted to its distance, and so on. This internal and abbreviated imitation of the perceptual activity *constitutes* the visual image of the table. Since an image of an object is seldom as rich or as detailed as the original perception, the image merely represents or symbolizes the actual object. In brief, the mental symbol may involve visual imagery, and the latter may be considered the internal imitation of the originally perceived object.

Third, Piaget introduces a technical vocabulary for dealing with mental symbols. We have already seen that one type of symbol is the *visual image*. In addition, there may be *auditory images* and other types. The symbol is a *signifier*: it signifies or represents something to the individual. The symbol involves *accommodation*. This is so because the symbol consists of internal imitation, and imitation involves modifying one's behavior to fit that of another person, or, in broader terms, to meet the demands imposed by the social or physical environment. Finally, the symbol is *personal* and in some way *resembles* what it stands for. For one child, swaying (which resembles the bicycle's movement) may symbolize the bicycle; for another, the visual image (resembling the bicycle's appearance) may suffice. Consequently, one person's symbol may transmit to another no information about what is referred to. By contrast, consider the word (in Piaget's terminology called a *sign*). The word is social, not personal, and is arbitrarily related to the thing it stands for. "Bicycle" for example is not an idiosyncratic term: most of us agree that "bicycle" stands for the same object, and therefore use of the term transmits considerable information. Also, the word "bicycle" bears no resemblance to the real thing; if our linguistic community so decreed, we could as well substitute "elephant" for "bicycle." In summary, one type of mental symbol is the image. The mental symbol, unlike the word, is personal and resembles the thing referred to. The symbol is a signifier, referring to something, and the symbol involves imitation, and therefore accommodation.

The complexity of Piaget's terminology should not obscure the fact that the ability to form mental symbols is an achievement of great magnitude. In the sensorimotor period this capacity was lacking. If you will recall, the only signifiers were concrete attributes of things. For example, the mother's voice or footsteps signified to the infant that she would soon come. However, this primitive signifier, or "index," was linked to the infant's actually hearing the voice or footsteps. He had no mental symbol for these events; therefore, the signifier had meaning for him only when the events actually occurred. By contrast, the older child can use mental symbols to stand for absent events or things. Things no longer need to be present for the child to act on them. In this sense, the ability to symbolize eventually liberates the child from the immediate present. He can imagine things that are both spatially and temporally separate from himself. It may therefore be said that the use of mental symbols permits the child to transcend the constraints of space and time.

Meaning

Having reviewed Piaget's theory of the formation of mental symbols, we shall now deal with the process by which they acquire meaning. Let us consider an apparently simple question: what does the child's mental symbol, like swaying back and forth, refer to? We may pose the same question with regard to the word: what does "bicycle" designate? Our first response to this question is to say that both the mental symbol and the word obviously refer to the real bicycle. But according to Piaget, the matter is more complicated than that. The "signified" (what the symbol or word stand for, or their meaning) is not the real object, but rather the child's understanding or intellectual construction of the real object. To put it differently, symbols or words do not refer to things, but instead stand for one's knowledge of things. Suppose one child uses the word "bicycle." For him, a bicycle has two wheels, a seat, and handlebars. A bicycle is something that goes delightfully fast, and also, it is one kind of vehicle. For another child, however, the signified may be somewhat different. He agrees that a bicycle has two wheels, a seat and handlebars; but he has often fallen from bicycles and therefore feels that they are frightening and dangerous. Further, he has no conception of the bicycle as a vehicle. Note that for both these children the word "bicycle" evokes some common meaning: two wheels, handlebars, and so on. Both children can therefore easily identify what is a bicycle and what is not. In this sense, the word does refer to the real object. But the children also disagree as to the word's meaning; for one a bicycle is delightful and for the other it is frightening. Also, for one child it is a member of the class of bicycles which in turn is included in the larger class of vehicles. The other child, on the other hand, employs no such class hierarchy. In Piaget's terms, each child has assimilated the word "bicycle" into a different set of schemes (the signified or the meaning). Therefore, the word "bicycle," or the children's personal mental symbols for it, do not refer to the real thing but to their understanding of it.

To summarize, internal imitation (accommodation) provides the child with symbols. The child then endows these symbols and words too with meaning. He assimilates them into his mental schemes. Therefore, what the symbol or word refer to (the signified) is always personal, if not idiosyncratic, although in the case of words there is a sufficient amount of common signification for communication between persons to occur.

Symbolic Play

A further example of an activity implying use of the symbolic function is symbolic play. Here is an observation.

[At 1;3(12) Jacqueline] . . . *saw a cloth whose fringed edges vaguely recalled those of her pillow; she seized it, held a fold of it in her right hand, sucked the thumb of the same hand and lay down on her side, laughing hard. She kept her eyes open, but blinked from time to time as if she were alluding to closed eyes.*[3]

The observation involves several interesting features. First, Jacqueline acted toward the cloth in roughly the same way as she behaved toward a pillow. She put her head on it, sucked her thumb, and so on. Second,

3. *Ibid.,* p. 96.

Jacqueline's behavior revealed a certain playfulness; that is, she laughed at what she was doing. Apparently, she thought her actions quite funny.

One simple interpretation of this behavior is that the child merely confused the cloth with the pillow. But this explanation is not very plausible because it fails to explain why the child laughed. After all, Jacqueline did not ordinarily giggle upon going to bed.

Piaget interprets the behavior as a case of the playful use of concrete (not mental) symbols. It is clear from Jacqueline's laughter and from her attitude of pretense that she knew perfectly well that the cloth was not really a pillow. Her playfulness indicates that she realized that the cloth was a substitute for another thing. In other words, the cloth was a symbol or signifier, and what it signified was the pillow. The cloth, of course, was a concrete object and not a mental symbol.

How did this assignment of meaning to the cloth come about? Piaget's interpretation is that meaning is achieved in terms of assimilation. While in the past Jacqueline had performed the actions of lying down, closing the eyes, and so on only in connection with the pillow, she now extends these schemes to an object which she knows not to be a pillow. We can therefore say that Jacqueline assimilated the cloth into schemes previously applied only to the pillow. It is the process of assimilation to schemes (the signified), then, which provides the meaning for the symbol. Moreover, Jacqueline is aware of the make-believe character of her acts. Her playfulness should not make us underestimate the seriousness and importance of her accomplishment: she has achieved a primitive comprehension of the nature of symbols. Indeed, we often find that the child's "play" involves significant intellectual activity.

It is interesting to note that Piaget feels that symbolic games play an important role in the child's emotional life as well. The child from 2 to 4 years is in a very vulnerable stage of development in the sense that he is beginning to acquire a new set of ways of dealing with the world around him. He also finds that he must conform to a set of social rules, not the least of which is language. He must accept the fact that words stand for things without any apparent justification. His capacity for self-expression via language is extremely limited and rudimentary. The words available to him frequently are inadequate to express his needs and feelings. He must obey commands whose purpose he cannot understand. His natural spontaneity is being compressed into the social mould of his culture, and he is generally powerless to resist.

These feelings of inadequacy lead to frustration, and subsequently to conflict with persons around him. Symbolic play, which forms a large part of the child's activity in this stage, is an appropriate means of providing an adjustment to reality. With this form of interaction the child can assimilate the external world almost directly into his own desires and needs with scarcely any accommodation. He can therefore shape reality to his own requirements. Furthermore, in symbolic play, he can act out the conflictual situations of real life in such a way as to ensure a successful conclusion in which he comes out the winner, and not, as is usually the case in real life, the loser. In brief, symbolic play, serving a necessary cathartic purpose, is essential for the child's emotional stability and adjustment to reality.

Language

We have now seen two different manifestations of the symbolic function: the use of mental symbols and symbolic play. We will turn now to a third aspect of the symbolic function, and see how the child uses language and gives it meaning.

In the sixth stage of sensorimotor development, the child's first use of words is not symbolic. Instead it is intimately related to his ongoing actions. Consider this example concerning Laurent:

. . . at 1;5(19) "no more" meant going away, then throwing something on the ground, and was then used of something that was overturned (without disappearing). He thus said "no more" to his blocks. Later "no more" merely meant that something was at a distance from him (outside his field of prehension), and then it referred to the game of holding out an object for someone to throw back to him. At 1;6(23) he even said "no more" when he wanted something someone was holding. Finally, at 1;7 "no more" became synonymous with "begin again." [4]

Note that Laurent did not use "*no more*" in a symbolic way. He did not make the words stand for an absent thing or event as in the sentence, "There is no more water in the garden." Instead, Laurent's use of "no more" was concrete in two senses. First, he employed the words in connection with objects that were immediately present like the overturned blocks. Second, the words were used to express his immediate desires, as when he wanted something a person was holding. In addition to being tied to concrete things or actions, the child's first words are very unstable. The phrase "no more" was used to refer to going away, to something overturned, to something at a distance, etc. The meaning of words is not constant for a young child. In fact, for him, words have little socially agreed upon meaning; instead, they are quite personal, and in this respect they resemble the mental symbols of this period.

4. *Ibid.*, p. 218.

The next step in the development of language involves the use of words in a symbolic way. At about 2 years of age, the child gradually begins to use words to stand for absent things or events. For example, at 1;11(11) after returning from a trip, Jacqueline told her father about it. She said, "Robert cry, duck swim in lake, gone away." [5] These events had occurred some time previously, and Jacqueline was able to remember them. Moreover, she was capable of using words to stand for past events. Thus, through a gradual evolution, words are no longer used to refer solely to ongoing actions, desires, or immediately present events.

Now that words have generally assumed a symbolic character and refer to absent things, we may ask whether the child uses them in the same way as the adult. For example, we saw that Jacqueline used the words "duck swim in lake" to refer to events in the past. Despite the fact that the words are symbolic, does the child give them the same meaning that an adult does? Another way of putting the question is to ask whether the child's *concept* of duck, or the meaning he assigns to the word "duck," is the same as the adult's. The mere fact that the child uses the word does not necessarily imply that he gives it what we consider its ordinary meaning. Here are some observations which may clarify the issue:

> . . . *at 2;7(12), seeing L. [Lucienne] in a new bathing suit, with a cap, J. [Jacqueline] asked: "What's the baby's name?" Her mother explained that it was a bathing costume, but J. pointed to L. herself and said: "But what's the name of that?" (indicating L's face) and repeated the question several times. But as soon as L. had her dress on again, J. exclaimed very seriously: "It's Lucienne again," as if her sister had changed her identity in changing her clothes.* [6]

The observation shows that Jacqueline's concept of her sister, or the use of the word "Lucienne," is quite different from the adult's. Jacqueline's thinking attributes little individuality to her sister. There is not one Lucienne who is the same person regardless of superficial changes; instead, as a result of wearing different clothing the real Lucienne is seen as two different little girls. The child at this age fails to recognize that a person or thing remains the same, or conserves its identity, when it undergoes minor variations in appearance.

In addition to perceiving insufficient individuality, the child also shows other unusual uses of words.

Once Jacqueline was in the garden and walked on the landlord's flowers. She remarked "*Me spoil uncle Alfred's garden.*" [7] She earlier had

5. *Ibid.*, p. 222.
6. *Ibid.*, p. 224.
7. *Ibid.*, p. 224.

had contact with her uncle's garden, and in the present case used the phrase "uncle Alfred's garden" to refer to the landlord's. In other words, she used one phrase to refer to two different things. All gardens are "uncle Alfred's garden." In the case of her sister, Jacqueline saw the same individual under different guises as different individuals; in the present instance she saw different "individuals" (gardens) as the same "individual." Clearly, in neither case did Jacqueline's use of words correspond to an adult's. The concepts or meanings evoked by "Lucienne" or "uncle Alfred's garden" were quite primitive.

Reasoning

During the years 2 to 4, the child shows three different kinds of reasoning. In one type, the child is faced with a simple situation which he has experienced before. He then "reasons" about the situation very concretely in terms of what had occurred in the past. For example, at 2;4(16) Jacqueline called her father who did not answer. She concluded from this: *"Daddy didn't hear."* At about the same time Jacqueline saw her father getting hot water and reasoned: *"Daddy's getting hot water, so he's going to shave."* [8] In both cases, Jacqueline had had previous experience with her father in similar situations. Her "reasoning" about them was limited merely to simple memory of what had occurred in these situations in the past.

Piaget feels that this type of reasoning is simply an application of previous experience to a current situation and is not to be confused with the genuinely deductive reasoning of the mature person.

In a second kind of reasoning, the child's desires distort his thinking. For example, at 2;10(8) Jacqueline wanted to eat oranges. Her parents explained that this was impossible because the oranges were still green and not yet ripe. Jacqueline "seemed to accept this, but a moment later, as she was drinking her camomile tea, she said: *'Camomile isn't green, it's yellow already . . . Give me some oranges!'"* [9] Apparently Jacqueline, having a strong desire for oranges, reasoned that if the tea were yellow then the oranges must be yellow too, and therefore she could have them to eat. At this stage, the child attempts to reason in order to achieve some goal, but his thought distorts reality in accordance with desire. (As will be evident shortly, the tea observation is also an example of transduction.)

A third type of reasoning is what Piaget calls "transductive." In logic a distinction is sometimes made between deduction and induction. Deduction is usually characterized as a process of reasoning from the gen-

8. *Ibid.,* p. 231.
9. *Ibid.,* p. 231.

eral to the particular. For instance, if we assume that all men have hearts of gold, and if we are then shown a particular man, we deduce that he has a heart of gold. Induction is usually considered a method for reasoning from the particular to the general in order to establish general principles from examination of particular cases. For instance, if we have met a large number of men all of whom have hearts of gold, we might conclude that all men have hearts of gold. According to Piaget, the young child's reasoning lies in between induction and deduction. He does not go from the general to the particular (deduction), or from the particular to the general (induction), but rather from the particular to the particular without touching on the general. Transductive reasoning sees a relationship between two or more concrete (particular) items when there is none. For example, on an afternoon when Lucienne did not take a nap, she said: "*I haven't had my nap so it isn't afternoon.*" [10] In this case, Lucienne's thought proceeded from the nap (one particular) to the afternoon (the second particular) and concluded that the afternoon depended on the nap, when of course the relationship was of a different type.

Summary and Conclusions

In the period from 2 to 4 years the child achieves the capacity to form mental symbols which stand for or represent absent things or events. In order to deal with things, he no longer requires that they be immediately present; instead, he is able to create a mental substitute for the real thing. This ability frees the child from the immediate here and now. Instead of having to manipulate things, he works with their substitutes. The child forms mental symbols through imitation. The child looks at things, handles them, and acts like them, and in these ways incorporates a great deal of information about them. These actions of the child lay the foundation for mental symbolism. In fact, imitation may be considered to bridge the gap between sensorimotor and later intelligence. During the sensorimotor period the infant develops his abilities in imitative behavior. When he is proficient at imitation at a later age, he begins to imitate internally, and thereby he forms the mental symbol. In Piaget's terminology mental symbols are *signifiers*. The symbol is personal and resembles what it refers to. For example, Lucienne swayed back and forth to represent a bicycle. Once mental symbols are formed, the child gives them meaning through the process of assimilation. He assimilates them into the schemes which are already available. Therefore, what the symbol refers to (the signified) is always personal and intimately related to the child's experience. A good example of the relation between the symbol and its meaning is the child's

10. *Ibid.*, p. 232.

playful use of symbols. In a make-believe fashion, the child makes some things (symbols) stand for others. The child playfully assimilates some objects into schemes appropriate for others. Another type of signifier is the word which is also used to refer to something else. The word, however, usually does not resemble its referent, but has a conventionally agreed upon meaning in order to facilitate communication.

During this period the child begins to use words. After a preliminary stage in which words are closely related to ongoing actions and desires, the child uses language to refer to absent things and events. The child, however, does not use words in the same way that an adult does; the meaning assigned to words, or the concept associated with them, is still quite primitive. The child's concepts are in fact only pre-concepts: they are sometimes too general and sometimes too specific. The child also shows signs of his first reasoning. Sometimes it is successful, but only when it does not go far beyond mere memory for past events. At other times the reasoning may be faulty. This is either due to the tendency for wishes to distort thought, or to the transductive nature of the child's thought: he reasons from the particular to the particular.

These, then, are the beginnings of symbolic activity in the young child. His initial efforts are imperfect, and from the adult point of view involve many "errors." A long evolution is necessary before the child can achieve maturity in thought; logical thinking does not emerge fully formed in the child of 2 years.

Piaget argues that language plays a limited, but not negligible, role in the formation of the child's thought. Clearly, language does not fully shape the child's mental activities. Despite his new ability at language, the child often thinks non-verbally. He forms mental symbols which are based on imitation of things and not on their names. Language does, however, make a contribution. For example, when an adult uses a word which refers to a *class* of things, the child is given a glimpse at one facet of adult reasoning. An adult's language forces the child, to some degree, to consider the world from a new perspective. Nevertheless, it is probably fair to say that the child's thought depends less on his language than his language does on his thought. As we saw earlier the child interprets words in terms of his own personal system of meanings, and the child's meaning is not necessarily the same as the adult's. Although the culture provides the child with language, the latter does not immediately socialize the child's thought. In other words, language does not completely impose on the child the culturally desirable ways of thinking. Instead, the child distorts the language to fit his own mental structure. The child achieves mature thought only after a long process of development in which the role of language is but one contributing factor.

THE CHILD FROM 4 TO 11 YEARS
(PIAGET'S EARLY WORK)

We have now reviewed the accomplishments of the sensorimotor period (0–2 years) and the acquisition of the symbolic function (2–4 years). It is hard to emphasize sufficiently the magnitude of the child's achievements. In the space of only a few years, he has transformed himself from an organism almost totally dependent on reflex and other hereditary equipment to a person capable of symbolic thought. During the years to follow (after the age of 4), neither sensorimotor nor symbolic activities disappear. The child older than 4 years continues to develop sensorimotor schemes applicable to a wide range of objects, to improve his skills in language, and to acquire mental symbols for increasingly large portions of the world about him. But at the same time the child's development extends into a number of new areas.

The present section offers an account of intellectual growth in the child from about 4 to 11 years. Recall that Piaget's first five books cover this age span and present preliminary and tentative conceptualizations. Later works offer more elaborate and mature theorizing on the same age range. We will describe here Piaget's early views on the child from 4 to 11 years; Chapter Four reviews the later work. As we shall see, Piaget's early work, although preliminary, is still quite fascinating and, according to some criteria, rates among the best work that he has accomplished.

The Use of Language

Piaget's early work begins with a consideration of children's use of language.[11] At the outset he poses a fundamental question: what is the function of the child's language? Our first response is probably that the purpose of language is communication. The child, like the adult, most likely uses language to express his thoughts to others; that is, to transmit information. But a little reflection should suffice to convince us that even in the adult, language is not entirely communicative. Adults when alone often talk to themselves on a mental level. Occasionally they even speak aloud when no one else is present. Therefore, our initial hypothesis about the purpose of language is not always true.

If this is so, then several questions immediately arise. How much of

11. Remember that this work was carried out before the investigations of the 2 to 4-year-old child's use of words which is discussed above; consequently, the early work does not employ the concepts of signifier and signified.

language—particularly children's language—is communicative and how much is not? What is the non-communicative variety like? And when it is not communicative, what purpose does children's language serve? To answer these and other questions Piaget carried out a series of investigations. He began by observing two 6-year-old boys for about a month in their class at school. The children, who were from the poorer sections of Geneva, attended a progressive class. The students could draw or make what they liked, could work individually at "games" of mathematics and reading, had the freedom to talk or play together, and could go without permission from one room to another. As the two boys pursued their activities, Piaget and another observer took down in full detail the children's speech as well as the context in which it occurred. Piaget attempted to avoid interfering with the children's activities and tried not to influence their behavior in any way. The intention, of course, was to obtain a full record of the child's use of language in his natural school environment. If you will recall, Piaget used such naturalistic observation in his studies of infancy and the period from 2 to 4 years. Several of the advantages and disadvantages of this method have already been discussed in Chapter Two. One question that was not considered is whether or not Piaget is correct in assuming that the children's behavior is not affected by the presence of an observer. Do children act and speak differently when watched by an adult? Unfortunately, there is little empirical evidence on this issue. At the moment we can only use our informal experience in similar situations to hazard a guess that after a short period of time young children generally learn to ignore adult observers and seem to behave quite naturally.

After recording the two children's speech, Piaget attempted to categorize each sentence spoken by each child. He discovered several varieties of both communicative and non-communicative language. Non-communicative or "egocentric" speech may be divided into three types. One type is *repetition*, which involves the child's mimicking something he has just heard; for example, "Jac says to Ez: '*Look, Ez, your pants are showing.*' Pie, who is in another part of the room, [and was one of the two children Piaget observed] immediately repeats: '*Look, my pants are showing, and my shirt too.*' " [12] The statement clearly involved copying another's speech since Pie was in fact quite properly dressed. Thus Pie's utterance was a clear case of repetition and did not serve a communicative function. Very often too the child is not aware that he is merely repeating what another person has said, but believes that his statement is an original one. According to Piaget's records, repetition made up about 1 or 2 per cent of the total number of statements.

A second kind of egocentric speech is the *monologue*. This type

---

12. *Language and Thought*, p. 35.

occurs when the child is alone and yet talks aloud, often at great length. For example, "Lev sits down at his table alone: *'I want to do that drawing there . . . I want to draw something, I do. I shall need a big piece of paper to do that.'* " [13] Since no one else was present apart from the observer who, by this time presumably no longer disturbed the child, Lev's statement clearly did not involve communication. In the case of Pie, monologue constituted 5 per cent of his speech, and for Lev the figure was 15 per cent.

Perhaps the most interesting kind of egocentric speech is the *collective* monologue. This occurs when two or more children are together and one of them speaks a soliloquy to which the others do not listen. The speaker may intend to interest the others in his remarks and may in fact believe that the others are listening. But the egocentric nature of the monologue prevents the others from understanding him even if they wanted to. Despite the fact that the speaker is in a group, his statements are not communicative; he is merely talking to himself aloud. For example, when sitting with some other children and apparently playing with toys or drawing, Lev said: "*I say, I've got a gun to kill him with. I say, I am the captain on horseback. I say, I've got a horse and a gun as well.*" [14] Note that Lev's continual use of the phrase "I say" seems to indicate that he wanted the others to listen to him, and that he intended to transmit information. But at the same time, Lev's statement is unclear: we do not know whom he intended to kill with the gun; who was the captain on horseback, and so on. Moreover, Lev's remarks were unrelated to anyone else's and did not succeed in making the other children listen. In fact, each child, although apparently working with and speaking to the others, offered soliloquies like Lev's. There was no "give and take" among members of the group or any continuity in the discussion; each child spoke about what interested him at the moment, and this involved mostly his own activities. The collective monologue is therefore neither truly social nor communicative as it is merely the simultaneous occurrence of at least two monologues. According to Piaget's calculations, the collective monologue involved 23 per cent of Lev's speech and 30 per cent of Pie's. Egocentric speech as a whole—repetition, monologue, and collective monologue—represents 39 per cent of Lev's and 37 per cent of Pie's total number of sentences.

The remainder of the children's speech is communicative or "socialized." In this case the child takes into consideration the point of view of the listener and attempts to transmit information to him. For example, he tells another child certain simple facts, like how to operate a toy. Or

13. *Ibid.*, p. 37.
14. *Ibid.*, p. 41.

he criticizes another child, or asks him questions, or in other ways interacts with him. While serving a communicative function, such speech nevertheless shows certain deficiencies. The children do not attempt to explain events to one another, and they do not speak in terms of the causes of events. Also, children do not try to give proof or logical justification for what they have proposed. The reason is that they do not consider the possibility that the listener may have a contrary opinion.

After establishing these facts in the case of Lev and Pie, Piaget then went on to study a larger group of 20 children varying in age from 4 to 7 years. Again, the method was naturalistic and involved the recording of the children's spontaneous remarks. In general, the findings replicated the data on Lev and Pie. A significant proportion of speech was egocentric, and this proportion was especially large in the speech of the youngest children about age 4.

These, then, are the results of Piaget's naturalistic observations. There seems to be a decline in egocentrism and an increase in communication as the child gets older. The child's language, especially in the early portion of the years from 4 to 5 or 6 years, does not entirely serve the function of communication. Often, the child does not assume the point of view of the listener; he talks of himself, to himself, and by himself.

How can we explain the non-communicative nature of the child's speech? What purposes does it serve? Piaget offers a number of interesting hypotheses which he regarded as tentative and not conclusive. Let us consider verbal repetition where the child simply mimics what others say or repeats phrases of his own. Piaget's interpretation is that repetition is "simply the joy of repeating for its own sake . . . the pleasure of using words . . . for the sake of playing with them." [15] You will no doubt observe that this explanation is another version of the principle of functional assimilation—the tendency to repeat schemes and to exercise them. In the present case the child mimics both his own words and those of others, just as earlier in the sensorimotor period he repeated patterns of behavior. Consequently, repetition is not motivated by the desire to communicate, but by the need to exercise verbal schemes.

But repetition comprises only a small portion of the child's speech. Let us now turn to the monologue which involves a substantial proportion of the total number of statements. Piaget offers two hypotheses concerning the monologue which are not mutually exclusive. One hypothesis is that the monologue serves the purpose of wish-fulfillment. When the child's actions are not successful in producing an intended result, he uses words to achieve his goal. If, for example, he would like to move a box but cannot because it is too heavy, he might tell the box to move, thus using words

15. *Ibid.*, p. 35.

to bring about what his activities cannot accomplish. The child's language, therefore, is in part a kind of fantasy, a word magic. A second explanation of monologue is that words and actions, for the child, are not yet fully differentiated. When he begins to learn language, the 2 or 3-year-old child often calls an immediately present object by its name or uses a word to describe ongoing actions. Consequently, in his initial experience with language, the thing (or action) and the word for it are simultaneously present, and the two are seen as a whole. The word is in a sense part of the thing, and vice versa. It takes a long time for the child to fully disassociate the word from its referent; he must learn that the word bears a totally arbitrary relation to that which it refers to and is not a part of it. Even in the period under discussion (4 to 7 years), the child has not fully grasped the relation between word and thing. Consequently, when he acts—plays with toys, draws, and so on—he tends to say the words associated with his behavior. Thus, the monologue is in a sense a part of the child's action and is not designed for the purpose of communication.

In the case of the collective monologue, much the same explanations can be employed. Sometimes the child in a group merely repeats what another says because of functional assimilation; sometimes his remarks are magically intended to produce results which he otherwise cannot achieve; and finally, his utterances often merely accompany activities in which he is engaged.

All three types of speech—repetition, monologue, and collective monologue—may be characterized as *egocentric*. Piaget does not use the term in the sense of selfish or self-serving. The young child is characterized as egocentric not because he is conceited or tries to satisfy his desires at the expense of other people, but because he is centered about himself (or his own ego in the general sense) and fails to take into account the other's point of view. When he delivers a monologue in a group, the desires of the egocentric child do not necessarily clash with those of other children; rather he is insensitive to what the others need to hear. In order to communicate, one must consider what information the listener does and does not have and what he is and is not interested in, and this the young child does not do.

One may criticize the naturalistic study of the child's language in several ways. Perhaps Piaget found the use of non-communicative language to be extensive only because of the liberal atmosphere of the school where the emphasis was on individual rather than group activity. If you will recall, the children were allowed to do what they liked, and the situation was so devised that the children learned from individual play. Under these circumstances it might be the case that the children felt no real need for communication, and consequently they did not display these abilities.

We may, however, cite as evidence against this argument an experiment by Piaget on verbal communication. Briefly, the task involved an experimenter's giving some information to one child (the speaker) who was then supposed to transmit it to another child (the listener). Piaget made clear to the speaker that his task was to communicate. These instructions presumably oriented the child toward the goal of communication rather than that of play. Therefore, the experiment might give insight into the child's ability to transmit information when he felt the need to do so. The experiment was also used to obtain information on the listener's ability to understand the speaker. Even if the speaker were communicative, did the listener comprehend what was said? However, since the methods used to assess the listener's understanding were rather poor, we will not concentrate on this aspect of the study.

Let us now describe the experiment in greater detail. In one portion, pairs of children were used as subjects. There were 30 children at ages 7 to 8 years, and 20 at ages 6 to 7 years. The experimenter sent one of the pair out of the room and told the other a story. This child, to be referred to as the speaker, was instructed to listen carefully since he would have to tell the same story to the other child whom we will call the listener. Then the experimenter read a story, repeated the difficult parts, and tried to make the speaker attend carefully. Several different stories, varying from six to nine sentences in length were used, although at any one time the speaker was required to tell only one story to the listener. Next, the listener was brought into the room, and the speaker told him the story. The experimenter took down everything that was said, and, in addition, questioned both the speaker and the listener to determine the degree to which they understood. After the experiment with stories, the same pairs of children were used to investigate communication concerning mechanical objects. This time, the examiner explained to the listener how a faucet or a syringe works. Diagrams were used to make the matter clear, and the speaker was permitted to make use of the diagram in explaining the mechanical process to the listener. Again, the experimenter recorded everything that the speaker said.

While the experiment yielded many results, we shall focus on the verbalizations of the speaker. Did children in the experiment succeed in producing communicative speech, and if not, what was their language like? In general, the experiment on communication replicated the results of Piaget's earlier naturalistic observations; that is, in both cases a substantial proportion of speech was non-communicative or egocentric. For example, the experiment on communication showed that young children often use pronouns and demonstrative adjectives—like *he, she, it, that, this*—without indicating clearly to what they are referring. In the midst of an explanation of the faucet the speaker might say "If you move it with that other thing, then it will go." This child fails to consider that the listener might not know what "it" and "that other thing" designate. This tendency is carried so far that often the speaker completely fails to name the objects involved in a mechanical explanation. The child is also poor at expressing the order of events. One child explaining how a faucet works began by telling how the water falls into the basin, and only later did he bother to say how the water goes through the pipe. Or, in telling a story the child might begin with the end and end with the beginning.

A child may also express causal relations poorly, and seldom connect the cause with its effect. For example, in telling a story in which a fairy turned certain children into swans, one child said *"There was a fairy, a wicked fairy. They turned themselves into swans."* [16] Note how the child did not express the central causal relation; it was the fairy who caused the children to become swans. He merely mentioned the two events without indicating their connection. The second sentence also illustrates the tendency to use pronouns without describing their referents. Whom does "they" refer to?

The child also often may omit large parts of the explanation or story. Even though he understands and remembers these portions (as shown by Piaget's later questioning), the child may fail to mention them. In effect he assumes that the listener already knows parts of the story or explanation. Omissions of this kind clearly reveal a lack of sensitivity to the needs of the listener.

Another aspect of egocentric speech is manifested in the observation that the child's story or explanation does not form a coherent and integrated whole. His account is fragmentary; it is merely composed of a large number of specific and unrelated items which are juxtaposed one upon the other. For example, here is one child's account of how a faucet works:

The handle is turned on and then the water runs, the little pipe is open and the water runs. There, there is no water running, there the handle is turned off, and then there is no water running, and here the water is running. There, there is no water running, and here there is water running.[17]

Clearly this explanation involves a mere collection of individual statements which are not integrated into a reasonable whole. One aspect of such juxtaposition is a tendency already described: the inability to state causal relations.

In summary, the preceding five properties of the young child's speech —the faulty use of pronouns and demonstrative adjectives, the incorrect ordering of events, the poor expression of causality, the tendency to omit important features, and finally, juxtaposition—all are concrete manifesta-

16. *Ibid.*, pp. 126–27.
17. *Ibid.*, p. 130.

tions of the child's egocentrism; that is, his inability to take the other person's point of view. With development these egocentric manifestations decrease and speech becomes more communicative. The speaker becomes aware of the views of others and adapts his speech accordingly.

Piaget's experiment on verbal communication also studies the understanding of the listener. Although the methodology was questionable, several of Piaget's impressions are of interest. The results showed that, in general, the listener does not understand the speaker very well. Part of the listener's inability to understand is clearly due to the speaker's faulty presentation. Few people could comprehend the explanation of the faucet described above. But Piaget feels that part of the listener's difficulty is due to his own patterns of thought and not to the speaker's egocentric speech. Even when the speaker is relatively clear, the listener distorts his utterances in several ways. One, the listener almost always thinks that he understands what the speaker says, even when it is very obscure. The listener very seldom asks questions to clarify a point or to obtain additional information. The listener feels confident that he has understood when in fact he has not. Two, the speaker's remarks evoke in the listener a kind of free association. In Piaget's terms, the listener assimilates the remarks into his own schemes which often bear little relation to what the speaker is attempting to communicate. For example, after listening to the story in which the bad fairy turned several children into swans, one 6-year-old child distorted the account in important ways. Instead of saying that the children were turned into swans, he maintained that they were dressed in white clothes. Then he elaborated on this propostion until the end of the story was no longer recognizable. He transformed one part of the story and, giving free rein to his imagination, went on from there to construct a new tale of his own. In brief, while the speaker fails to take account of the needs of the listener, the listener also distorts what he hears, elaborates on it, and is satisfied that he has understood, whereas, in actual fact he has not.

It is easy to see that Piaget's experiment on communication is deficient in several ways. Piaget does not make clear the methods used to assess either the speaker's or the listener's understanding of the story or explanation. The measurement of comprehension is a difficult and delicate matter that requires more attention than Piaget has given to it. Piaget also may not have fully eliminated the possibility that faulty memory, and not egocentrism may sometimes underlie the speaker's lack of ability to communicate. Perhaps the young child is not able to tell a lengthy story simply because he fails to remember large parts of it. Despite Piaget's attempts to control for the memory factor by questioning, it is not altogether clear to the reader to what extent he was successful.

Another factor to be considered is that Piaget's subjects were members of the lower class. Is it not possible that lower-class children have different verbal abilities from middle-class children? If so, Piaget is too quick to generalize his findings to children in general. While these and other criticisms may be raised and seem to have validity, one must remember that Piaget's first studies were intended as exploratory. Their aim was to uncover interesting issues for investigation, to propose preliminary hypotheses, and not to reach firm conclusions. Piaget's studies on communication seem to have fulfilled his original goals. His research raises interesting questions. For example, is it true that the young child cannot express cause and effect relations, or that the listener so extensively distorts what the speaker says? Despite its deficiencies, Piaget's research is especially valuable since it is one of the few attempts in child psychology to deal with the crucial issue of the functions of human language.

Thus far we have seen that the young child from about 4 to 7 years displays a significant amount of egocentric speech, and that the older child after about 7 years is increasingly proficient at verbal communication. Why does egocentric speech decrease as the child gets older? Piaget proposes an interesting hypothesis to explain the waning of egocentrism. When the child is young, particularly in infancy, adults take great pains to understand his thoughts and desires. The mother must know which toy the infant wants or what bothers him and is not able to rely exclusively on words to understand him. Consequently, the young child does not need to communicate clearly; even if his speech is unclear, adults will make every effort to understand him. As the child grows older, however, he is more and more thrown into the company of older children who are not as solicitous as adults. Other children do not try so hard to penetrate the obscurities of his language. Moreover, they argue with him; they challenge what he says and force him to defend himself. It is under social pressures of these kinds that the child is gradually forced to adopt better modes of communication. In the attempt to express himself and to justify his arguments, the child eventually learns to take into account the other's point of view. Not to do so is to be misunderstood and to lose the argument. In this way, then, does egocentrism diminish.

Clinical Method

Piaget's early work was in part concerned with the contents of the child's thought. He attempted to discover the spontaneous ideas of the child at different stages of his development. What is the child's conception of the nature of dreams, or what is his explanation of the fact that boats float on water? The study of content is particularly difficult, because, as we have seen in the previous section, young children have great difficulty in communicating thoughts. It is therefore crucial for the investigator of content to employ sensitive and accurate methods. Piaget has devoted careful consideration to the choice of a proper method. He has rejected the testing approach, assigned a limited role to naturalistic investigation, and adopted the clinical procedure. Let us consider each of these decisions in turn.

The essential feature of the testing method is a series of questions which are posed in the same way to all who take the test. If we are investigating the origin of the sun, for instance, we might ask all children, "Where did the sun come from?" It is important that the question be put in precisely the same way to all children. In fact, the reading of the question (the intonation, stress and so on) should be as constant as possible. If a child does not seem to understand, the examiner may repeat the question. But this is usually the maximum of flexibility permitted: the examiner may not rephrase the question or otherwise alter it. The purpose of a standardized administration is to guarantee that all subjects are faced with the same problems. Then if 4-year-olds generally give one type of answer and 8-year-olds another, the examiner may reasonably conclude that there is a real difference between the age groups. If, on the other hand, the form of the questioning varied across age groups, the examiner would not know whether the difference in answers is genuine or is due simply to the difference in questions. While the testing method has important psychological uses, Piaget feels that it is not suitable for his task—the discovery of content (or the discovery of structure, a problem to which Piaget also applied the clinical method).

The testing method has the disadvantage of inflexibility. If a child gives an interesting response, the examiner cannot pursue it. If a child misunderstands the question, the examiner cannot clarify it. If the child's answer suggests an additional topic for investigation, the examiner must leave the matter unexplored. In addition, the test procedure may be suggestive. If the child is asked, "Where did the sun come from?" the question implies that the sun did have an origin, and this idea may not have occurred to the child before. Consequently, his answer may not reveal the spontaneous contents of his thought, but may be merely a hastily considered response to a question encountered for the first time. And finally, the test method does not usually allow the examiner to establish the stability of the child's response. If a child is asked what the sum of 2 and 2 is, and says "4," his answer may be tentative or firm. If he is unsure, further questioning may induce him to change his mind. If his belief is firm, nothing will sway him. In the testing procedure the child gives an answer and that is the end of it: a tentative "4" is as good as a sure one. For these reasons, then, Piaget rejects the testing approach.

Another method for the investigation of spontaneous content is the naturalistic procedure as used in Piaget's study of infancy or language. In a sense, this is an ideal method. Suppose we observe that a child spontaneously asks the question: "Who made the sun?" The statement gives a clear insight into the content of his thought. It is immediately obvious that he believes that some agent, perhaps a person or perhaps God, intervened to create the sun, and that it did not evolve naturally. Surely this spontaneous question is far more valuable than a response to a standardized question.

The naturalistic method, however, is subject to a number of drawbacks. One may observe a child for a very long time before he will say anything of interest. Suppose we are interested in the child's conception of the origin of the sun; it is extremely unlikely that he will ask the relevant question while we are observing him. Consequently, the naturalistic method, despite its clear utility, cannot be used as the chief instrument of research. At best, naturalistic observation can serve only a subsidiary role in two ways. It can suggest questions for intensive clinical examination. If, for example, we hear a child ask, "Who made the sun?" then we can interview a large number of children to test the generality of the assumption underlying his question. Second, the naturalistic observation can serve as a check on the results of clinical questioning. If interviewing suggests that children believe that clouds are alive, then patient, naturalistic observation may furnish data to support or refute this hypothesis.

Piaget feels that the clinical method avoids the deficiencies of the testing and naturalistic procedures, and offers a number of attractive features besides. The clinical method is hard to describe since it is so flexible and provides a general framework for questioning the child rather than a set or standardized form. This account is therefore intended only as an outline of the clinical method. The basic aims of the method are to follow the child's thought without deforming it by suggestions, or by imposing the adult's views on the child. One important feature is that the experimenter tries to adopt the language of the child and keep the level of questions accessible to the child. Terms which are beyond his reach are avoided and replaced as much as possible by those which the child has spontaneously emitted. The examiner usually begins by asking a nondirective question. Instead of saying, "Who made the sun?" or "How did the sun evolve?" the examiner might ask, "How did the sun come about?" If the child does not understand, the examiner is free to rephrase the question by asking, for example, "How did the sun get there?" After the child answers, the experimenter forms an hypothesis concerning the nature of the child's beliefs. For example, if the child first answered, "It was put there," the examiner might guess that the child believes that a person created the sun. Subsequent questions are used to test this hypothesis. The examiner might then ask: "Can you tell me how it was put there?" If the child says, "God put it there," then the examiner might follow up aspects of this response. Does the child really believe in divine intervention, or is this just a superficial mimicry of what he has been taught in Sunday School? In order to answer this question the examiner may challenge the child's belief to see how firmly he holds to it. Or the examiner may wonder whether the child means to say that the sun already existed before God "put it there," or that God created it too. Further questions must be asked to decide between the two alternatives. Of course, if the examiner's hypothesis is not confirmed, he must allow the child's answers to lead him to the correct interpretation. It is easy to see that no two clinical examiners, even if they are testing the same child, will pursue the same line of questioning. It is also clear that clinical questioning is very delicate and subject to several kinds of errors. The examiner may talk too much and thereby suggest answers to the child. Or, the examiner may not talk enough and fail to pose the questions necessary for determining the child's meaning. Piaget feels that at least a year of daily practice is necessary before the examiner can achieve any proficiency at clinical questioning.

We may raise a number of criticisms of the clinical method. How do we know that Piaget is a good clinical examiner? His books give only portions of selected clinical interviews. It is possible that the published interviews are exceptional—from the point of view of method and supporting Piaget's theory—and that the unpublished protocols are poorly done. Perhaps in the latter case the examiner suggested answers to the child, asked the wrong questions, and so on. Also, we may wonder whether Piaget's diagnoses—the judgments derived from the interview— are reliable. That is, would other persons agree with the interpretations, or are Piaget's diagnoses quite idiosyncratic? It is also true that since the clinical interviews are unstandardized, it is very difficult for independent investigators to test Piaget's work. If another psychologist attempted to repeat Piaget's research and obtained different results, the Piagetian criticism could always be that he failed to use the clinical method properly. Another criticism that is raised is that Piaget usually commits a large number of methodological sins unrelated to the clinical method. For example, he does not usually report the number of subjects seen in an investigation, or their exact age, or their social background. In describing the results he presents only fragments of interviews and fails to give a statistical summary of the children's reactions. To summarize, the clinical method is deficient. Perhaps the chief objection is that it requires us to take a lot on faith: that Piaget conducts the interview without suggestion, that he interprets the results properly, and so on. As we well know, scientists prefer to take as little on faith as possible.

The deficiencies in Piaget's research are real. Yet we must be careful not to exaggerate them; we must evaluate the clinical method in the overall context of Piaget's work. Piaget felt that the early portion of his research was essentially exploratory. His goal was to open up new areas for investigation, and to propose preliminary hypotheses for further examination. The early work was not intended to prove a theory or to present definitive views on intelligence, and Piaget felt that methods should be as flexible as possible at the preliminary stages of research. It seemed premature to him to introduce rigorous procedures when almost nothing was known about the subject matter, and when it was by no means clear what the proper methods should be. If Piaget had attempted to establish every point with the maximum of certainty, then he probably would not have advanced beyond the study of children's verbal communication (one of his first research topics). Once the pioneering research has been done, then it is always possible to check the results by more standardized methods and revise the tentative hypotheses.

The Content of Thought

Piaget's early investigations of content are extensive. His two books on the subject [18] cover a large number of topics which include the child's beliefs concerning dreams, meteorology, the origin of trees, the nature of shadows, the explanation of the steam-engine, and so on. In order to illustrate this work we shall describe only one topic—the origins of the sun and moon.

According to Piaget's findings there are three stages in the child's concept of the sun and moon. The stages occur in sequence somewhere between about 3 and 12 years. Piaget does not attempt to specify precise age norms because there are large variations in responses. Here is an example of a stage 1 protocol—a 6-year-old's beliefs:

How did the sun begin?—It was when life began.—*Has there always been a sun?*—No.—*How did it begin?*—Because it knew that life had begun.—*What is it made of?*—Of fire.—*But how?*—Because there was fire up there.—*Where did the fire come from?*—From the sky.—*How was the fire made in the sky?*—It was lighted with a match.—*Where did it come from, this match?*—God threw it away. . . . *How did the moon begin?*—Because we began to be alive.—*What did that do?*—It made the moon get bigger.—*Is the moon alive?*—No . . . Yes.—*Why?*—Because we are alive. . . .[19]

The protocol illustrates three kinds of beliefs common to children in the first stage of development. The first belief is *animism*. The child

18. *The Child's Conception of the World* and *The Child's Conception of Physical Causality.*
19. *The Child's Conception of the World,* pp. 258–59.

believes that the sun and moon are alive in the same sense that people are alive; that is, the sun is credited with *knowing* that life had begun. The second belief is *artificialism*. The child asserts that the sun resulted from the actions of an outside agent. It was not a natural process that formed the sun, but an act of intervention on the part of God. The third belief illustrated by the protocol contains the idea of *participation*. The child perceives some continuing connection, or some participation, between human activities and those of things. His belief is that the moon began because people began to be alive. Note that this explanation is not artificialism, since the child does not assert that people created the moon. His conception is vague, and he merely assumes a dim relation between people and the planets; he believes that there is some sort of influence or participation between them.

The second stage of the child's concept of the sun and moon is transitionary. The child continues to believe in artificialism and animism, but less blatantly than before. The following excerpt involves an 8-year-old child:

. . . *How did the sun begin?*—It was a big cloud that made it.—*Where did the cloud come from?*—From the smoke.—*And where did the smoke come from?*—From houses. . . . *How did the clouds make the sun shine?*—It's a light which makes it shine.—*What light?*—A big light, it is someone in Heaven who has set fire to it. . . .[20]

Note that at the beginning of the protocol the child invoked only natural phenomena to explain the sun's origin. The sun was formed by clouds which in turn derived from the smoke. However, when asked where the smoke came from, the child proposed an artificialist explanation. The smoke came from houses and, by implication, from fires which people created. Artificialism is even more apparent in the second part of the protocol where the child maintains that someone in Heaven has created a light that makes the sun shine.

In the third stage, the child gives up notions of artificialism, animism, and participation. While his explanations are crude and incorrect, he attributes the sun's formation to natural processes in which human or divine agents have no role. Sometimes, of course, the child's accounts are based on what he has been told in school, and sometimes they are not; even then the child proposes explanations invoking physical processes of the planets' origins.

Moral Judgment and Behavior

Piaget's early work covered a wide range of topics including verbal communication, concepts of physical causality, and moral judgment and

20. *Ibid.,* p. 274.

behavior. This last topic will be considered now. Piaget begins his study
of moral behavior and judgment with a detailed consideration of children's
games of marbles. He describes how children conceive of the game and
follow its rules. At first glance it may seem quite unusual to study morality
by means of the apparently trivial game of marbles. Our intuitive definition
of morality probably relates to such matters as lying and stealing, and not
to mere games. But according to Piaget the essential aspect of morality is
the tendency to accept and follow a system of rules which usually regulate
interpersonal behavior. Our society has gradually developed norms which
control how an individual treats others, behaves toward property, and so
on, and these regulations, supplemented by the individual's own conceptions, constitute the moral system. On closer inspection it would seem as
if the rules governing the game of marbles fulfill all the defining conditions
of a moral system. The rules control how individuals behave toward one
another in terms of the actions which comprise the game; they determine
individual and property rights; and they are a cultural product which has
been passed down from generation to generation. The game of marbles
also has a unique advantage from the point of view of child psychology.
The rules have been developed largely by children, and the game is played
almost exclusively by children. Therefore, the child's conception of the
game and his playing of it reflect the workings of his own mind and is
subject to little adult influence. Unlike rules dealing with lying or stealing,
marbles is the child's game, not the adult's. If we question the child about
the game, his answers do not simply parrot the teachings of adults, but
give a genuine indication of his own thought. But is not the game just play,
something that is not at all taken seriously, and that therefore bears no
relation to morality which is a grave matter? We may answer this criticism
by pointing out that the child does take the game seriously. While a game
has its "fun" aspects, if one observes children playing, one realizes that they
are deeply engrossed in their activities, consider the other players' actions
of some importance, and are not entirely disinterested in the outcomes. Is
the adult who "plays" the stock market very different?

To study children's behavior in the game of marbles, Piaget first
acquired a thorough knowledge of the rules of the game. Then he asked
about 20 boys, ranging from 4 to 12 or 13 years of age, to show him how
to play. (In Switzerland the game of marbles is played exclusively by
boys.) In the course of his game with the child, Piaget tried to appear as
ignorant as possible about the rules so that the child would feel that he
had to explain them. In this way Piaget was able to determine both
whether the child understood the rules, and, if so, whether he followed
them. Sometimes Piaget observed pairs of children, particularly younger
ones, play the game without him. Piaget also questioned the child about
the nature of the rules. He was interested, for example, in whether the

child believed that the rules might be changed and in the child's conception of the origin of rules.

Let us consider the practice of rules, or moral behavior. From about ages 4 to 7 years, an *egocentric* stage occurs where children do not know or follow the rules, but they insist that they do. As an example of this stage, let us examine the following:

Piaget separately examined two boys who were in the same class at school, who lived in the same house and often played marbles with one another. The first boy described and played by a set of rules which was highly unusual and idiosyncratic. The second boy did not understand the first boy's rules and moreover proposed an unusual system of his own. Thus, each of the boys, who often played "together," in fact followed his own system of rules which bore little relation to the other child's. There was little notion of "winning," in the adult sense, and little genuine competition between the two players. For the young child "winning" means "having a good time" and it was, therefore, quite possible for all players to win in this particular game. Each child was merely playing an individual game and did not really need the other. At the same time, the children believed that they were playing like other children and that they knew and followed the rules quite well.

The behavior at marbles is similar to the speech of children of the same age and is, therefore, called egocentric. In both cases the child is centered about himself and fails to take into account another person's point of view. In the game of marbles the young child plays for himself and not with someone else. He has his own set of rules and is relatively uninfluenced by what the other does. In the case of speech, the child talks by himself and not with someone else. He speaks for his own purposes, and his monologue is relatively unaffected by the other's comments. Egocentrism is therefore a tendency common to both speech and moral behavior.

The next stage, that of *incipient cooperation*, lasts from about 7 to 10 or 11 years. The game begins to acquire a genuinely social character, and the child has a much firmer grasp of the rules. While his knowledge of the game is not perfect, he has mastered the basic rules and attempts to learn the rest. The child of this stage both cooperates and competes with his partner. There is cooperation in the sense that the child agrees with his partner on a common set of rules which are then followed. (Cooperation does not mean here that the two or more children assist each other to attain a common goal.) There is competition in the sense that each child tries to win for himself, while at the same time he adheres to the mutually agreed upon framework. Nevertheless, play is not yet fully mature. Since the child has not yet mastered all of the rules, the game does not proceed smoothly, and there are difficulties and conflicts. Again, there is a parallel between play and speech. In both instances, the child of about 7 years of age begins to take into account an external point of view. In marbles he allows a set of rules to govern his behavior, and he interacts with the partner. In speech he tries to anticipate what the listener needs to know, and he accepts linguistic conventions which facilitate real interaction.

The final stage of moral behavior is that of *genuine cooperation* which begins at about 11 or 12 years of age, and is the stage in which the child acquires a thorough mastery of the rules. As before, he agrees with the others on the way to play the game, and it is within this common framework that he tries to win. In addition, however, the older child shows a kind of legalistic fascination with the rules. He enjoys settling differences of opinion concerning the rules, inventing new rules, and elaborating on them. He even tries to anticipate all of the possible contingencies that may arise. Piaget tells a delightful anecdote about the legalistic tendencies of this stage. He observed a group of boys aged 10 and 11 who were preparing to have a snowball fight. Before getting on with it, they devoted a considerable amount of time to dividing themselves into teams, electing officers, devising an elaborate set of rules to regulate the throwing of snowballs, and deciding on a system of punishments for transgressors. Before they had actually settled on all these legalistic aspects of the game, it was time to return home, and no snowball game had been played. Yet, all the players seemed content with their afternoon.

We may summarize by stating, then, that there are three major stages of the practice of rules: *egocentrism*, where each child does not know the rules or how to apply them but thinks he does; *incipient cooperation*, where mastery of the rules has improved and children begin to share them in order to compete; and finally, the stage of *genuine cooperation*, where children know the rules well and enjoy elaborating upon them.

After establishing the child's knowledge and practice of rules, Piaget went on to question the child about their inviolability. He asked the child whether the rules might be changed, whether they always existed in their present form, and how they originated. In determining the child's conception of the rules, Piaget of course used the clinical method (as he always did in establishing knowledge of the rules). He found that there are two major stages in notions concerning the inviolability of rules. The first stage which is in turn divided into two parts lasts from about 4 or 5 years to about 9 or 10 years. Thus it overlaps the first two stages of the practice of rules (egocentrism and incipient cooperation). In the first part of the first stage, which we shall call the *absolutistic* stage, the child believes that some authority originated the rules of marbles, and that no one ever played the game before that authority played it. Moreover, the authority conveys on the rules a sacred, unchangeable character: they are absolute and cannot be altered. Here is part of a protocol of a 5-year-old illustrating some of these beliefs:

> . . . *How did you get to know the rules?*—When I was quite little my brother showed me. My Daddy showed my brother.—*And how did your daddy know?*—My Daddy just knew. No one told him. . . . *Tell me who was born first, your daddy or your granddad?*—My Daddy was born before my granddad.—*Who invented the game of marbles?*—My Daddy did. . . .[21]

We see that the child believes that the rules emerged, fully formed, from his father who is so prestigious that he was born before his own father.

While believing in the sanctity of rules, the young child from about 4 to 6 years in the first part of stage 1 is also willing to accept changes in the rules. He agrees to place the marbles in a circle, whereas a square is the usual convention. This seems paradoxical: the child thinks that the rules are sacred but easily consents to their modification. Piaget feels that the child's acceptance of changes is only apparent. He has such a poor grasp of what the rules are that he believes the changes to be merely alternative and quite legitimate versions of the rules. In other words, the child consents to alterations only because he does not know that they really are alterations.

In the latter part of the first stage (from about 6 to 10 years), the child's knowledge of the rules increases, and he is consequently able to recognize a real change in the rules when it is proposed. Now he refuses to accept these alterations and asserts that the rules are immutable. For example, Piaget asked one boy of 6 years to invent a new game, and he refused, saying "I've never invented games." Then, after Piaget suggested a new game of marbles to him, the boy played it for a time. But when asked, "Could this game ever become a fair game?" the boy responded, "No, because it's not the same [as the usual game of marbles]." [22]

If you will recall, many of the children who are in stage 1 of the conception of rules are simultaneously in stage 1 of the practice of rules (egocentrism). This means that at the same time that the child believes the rules to be sacred and immutable, he also does not know them too well and does not follow them. Again we seem to be faced with a paradox: how can he place so much faith in the same rules that he consistently breaks? To understand this apparent contradiction, we must consider the child's acquisition of rules. Usually he learns them from an older child whom he considers similar to adults, and whom he therefore imbues with the same respect and authority that he gives to adults. In Piaget's terms,

21. *Moral Judgment*, p. 55.
22. *Ibid.*, p. 60.

there is a relationship of *constraint* or *unilateral respect* between older and younger children; the former's authority is unconditionally accepted so that the younger child assigns to the rules the same authority that he considers the older child to have. Since the adult and the older child are infallible, so are the rules which they propagate. In addition, the young child is egocentric. As we saw in the case of language, he cannot take the point of view of others. Since he is wrapped up in his own concerns, he cannot understand the value of rules which protect the interests of others. It is not so much that he is selfish; rather he does not perceive the legitimate needs that other persons have. Since this is so, he does not understand the purpose of rules. For him they are merely external things which cannot be changed.

We can say, then, that the young child imbues rules with absolute respect since they derive from a prestigious person, and that he sees the rules as external objects which cannot be changed because his egocentrism prevents him from understanding the purpose of rules.

Piaget then notes that all of the factors mentioned above—the relation of unilateral respect, egocentrism, the conception of the rules as authoritative and external—prevent the young child from participation in the formation of rules. Since the young child cannot assume the older child's point of view, how can he cooperate in developing fair rules? Because the young child does not participate in making the rules, they remain quite external to him. The rules are not really his; they are a kind of foreign body imposed on him. It should come as no surprise that they do not effectively transform his behavior. In other words, because the child has not cooperated in devising the rules, he does not understand them, and, therefore, is not able to follow them.

In the second stage of the conception of rules, beginning at about 10 or 11 years, the child believes that the rules can be changed, that they originated through human invention, and that they are maintained only by mutual consent among equals. Consequently, the child will agree to a modification of the game so long as all of the other players agree, and so long as the change is a fair one. Since he himself participates as an equal in the invention of new rules, he feels obligated to follow the rules and does so.

To explain the shift from the absolutistic morality of the younger child to the flexibility of the older child, Piaget proposes a social learning theory. He begins by noting that as the child in Western society grows older, he becomes progressively free of parental and other adult supervision. During the first five years or so of life the child is very closely tied to his parents. After that point he goes to school, spends an increasing amount of time with peers, and generally assumes greater responsibility for his own life. As these events take place, the child gradually learns to make decisions for himself and does not necessarily accept as authoritative the views of other persons who are now considered his equals. In other words, the child escapes from the attitude of unilateral respect toward elders and begins to adopt a position of mutual respect. As a result of this development he does not unquestioningly accept rules as binding and immutable. Because he now sees himself as the equal of others, he desires to assist in the formation and modification of the moral code.

Another and related factor influencing the decline of the absolutistic concept of rules is the child's increasing contact with divergent points of view. As the child widens his sphere of contacts beyond the immediate family, he discovers that there are diverse and conflicting opinions and customs. He finds that not everyone accepts the views promulgated by his parents. This conflict between what he has been taught and what other people believe forces the child to reassess his own position and to resolve the differences in opinion. In attempting to do so, the child reasons about rules and comes to the conclusion that they must, to some extent, be arbitrary and, therefore, changeable.

To summarize, as he grows older the child evolves from a position of submission to adults to one of equality. He is confronted also with beliefs contradictory to those he has been taught. Both of these experiences influence the child so that he sees rules as having a human, and hence fallible, origin, and to agree to participate in their formation and alteration. Since the child now has a hand in the formation of rules, they no longer exist as a foreign entity imposed on his conscience; they no longer exist as a code which may be unequestioningly respected, occasionally obeyed, and seldom understood. The child now chooses to follow rules which are his own or at least freely agreed upon.

Piaget goes on to examine the development of judgments concerning explicitly moral situations. In order to study this he told children stories which posed a moral dilemma and asked them to resolve it. For example, if a child stole some apples, what would his punishment be? In this way Piaget attempted to discover the child's conception of justice, punishment, lying, and similar matters. To illustrate these investigations, we will focus on the conception of goodness and naughtiness.

Piaget presented his subjects with a series of stories of two types. In one story, the central character performed an act which unintentionally resulted in considerable damage; in the other, he caused a negligible amount of damage as a result of a deliberately improper act. The subject's task was to decide who was good and who was naughty.

Here is an example of the first type:

A little boy who was called Augustus once noticed that his father's ink-pot was empty. One day that his father was away he thought of filling the ink-pot so as to help his father, and so that he should find it full when he came home. But while he was opening the ink-bottle he made a big blot on the table cloth.[23]

The corresponding story involving negligible damage is as follows:

There was a little boy called Julian. His father had gone out and Julian thought it would be fun to play with his father's ink-pot. First he played with the pen, and then he made a little blot on the table cloth.[24]

After telling each pair of stories, Piaget asked whether the two children were equally guilty, and which of the two was the naughtiest and why. He used the clinical method to probe the child's responses. The results were that until the age of 10, children give two kinds of answers. One of the answers maintains that the character's guilt is determined by the nature of his motives. The boy who wanted to help his father but caused a great deal of damage is less guilty than the boy who engaged in an improper act which resulted in negligible damage. Piaget calls this a "subjective" conception of responsibility since the child takes into account the motives (the subjective state) of the character in the story. The second type of judgment found in this stage (and found, moreover, in many of the same children who sometimes give a subjective answer) is less mature. This answer maintains that the character's guilt is determined not by his motives, but by the sheer amount of damage he has caused. The boy who wanted to help his father is nevertheless guilty because he made a large stain; whereas the boy playing with the pen is not guilty since his stain was so small. Consider this protocol, from a girl of 7 years:

. . . *Which is the most naughty?*—The one who made the big blot. —*Why?*— Because it was big.—*Why did he make a big blot?*—To be helpful.—*And why did the other one make a little blot?*—Because he was always touching things. He made a little blot.—*Then which of them is the naughtiest?*—The one who made a big blot. [25]

It is evident from the protocol that the child was perfectly aware of each character's intentions, and yet ignored them. What determines guilt is not intention but quantity of damage. Piaget characterizes such a response as a case of *moral realism.* The judgment is "realistic" in the sense that the criterion of guilt is not subjective (the intention) but material or "real" (the amount of damage). The child considers only the facts of damage, not the subjective state of motive. Also, the child's judgment observes the letter and not the spirit of the law. The rule (in this case, "Thou shalt not spill ink") is an absolute, so that any action which conforms to it is good, and any which does not is bad.

23. *Ibid.,* p. 122.
24. *Ibid.,* p. 122.
25. *Ibid.,* p. 126.

Piaget finds that the young child's moral realism is pervasive. Consider the definition of a lie. One 6-year-old gave a typical response in saying: "It's when you say naughty words." [26] He went on to agree that "fool" is a lie because it is a word you should not say. We see then that the child's definition is "realistic": a lie is a bad thing and does not at all refer to the intention to deceive. A second example concerns young children's comparison of the magnitude of lies. In order to study this sort of judgment Piaget read the children two stories. In one story a boy was frightened by a dog and told his mother that the dog was "as big as a cow." In a second story a boy deliberately deceived his mother about his school grades. Young children often maintained that the story about the dog was a greater lie than the story about the grades. The reason was that seeing a dog the size of a cow was a less probable event than getting good grades. In the case of the dog there is a much greater discrepancy between actual facts (the real size of the dog) and the lie (the dog being as large as a cow) than in the case of grades, where the lie (a good grade) seems almost as likely as the fact (a bad grade). In other words, seeing a dog as large as a cow is far less likely to occur than having good grades and, therefore, appears to be a bigger lie. Intention to deceive is irrelevant, and the important criterion has to do with the probability of occurrence of the facts. Thus the young child's judgment of lies is as "realistic" as his decision concerning goodness and naughtiness. It focusses on the external or material aspect of the question and fails to take into account the intentional or subjective aspect.

Why does a significant proportion of the young child's responses involve moral realism? Part of the reason is probably that parents are sometimes "realistic" themselves. Some adults punish the child more for breaking 15 cups unintentionally than for purposely destroying one cup. But this is not the whole story. Parents punish a statement intended to deceive (a real lie) more than a mere exaggeration (for example, the dog as big as a cow). The child, however, thinks that the exaggeration is naughtier than the intention to deceive, so it seems that the child's judgment does not simply reflect the punishments which he has actually received from adults. It is apparent, then, that two additional factors are involved. One factor is the relation of unilateral respect. Since the parent is respected, so are his rules. If the parent forbids the breaking of cups, then the act of doing so is bad regardless of intention. Another factor is the child's egocentric patterns of thought. Since he cannot assume points of view different from his own, he cannot see the other's need for truth, and consequently, he is not aware of the fact that his "lies," which he himself often appears to believe in, are deceiving the listener. Unilateral

26. *Ibid.*, p. 141.

respect and egocentrism, then, contribute to moral realism just as they do to the concept of rules as inviolable and sacred.

The child gradually abandons moral realism in favor of a more "subjective" approach. In judgments of goodness and naughtiness he focusses on motivation, not extent of damage. In judgments of lying he considers the intention to deceive, not just the likelihood that the event could have occurred. As was the case in the conception of rules, the child's progress is due largely to his new independence from the family, to his increased interaction with others, to his contact with divergent views, and to similar factors.

We may make several comments concerning moral behavior and judgment. First, Piaget emphasizes that the various stages overlap, that the same child may be in both stages simultaneously depending upon the content of a particular situation, and that primitive forms of moral judgment are often characteristic of adults as well as children. Neither the stages nor the course of their development are clearcut, and Piaget does not wish to give an impression of orderliness where little is to be found. Second, Piaget's social learning theory—that primitive moral judgment derives in fact from unilateral respect, and mature conceptions from cooperation and similar factors—is speculative because there is no direct evidence linking adult constraint with moral realism. Nevertheless, the theory points in interesting directions. The effect of the social environment on intellectual processes has hardly been considered. Undoubtedly the theory will require clarification and elaboration, particularly with regard to the reciprocal effect which seems to exist between cooperation and the diminution of egocentrism. Does the child take the other's point of view mainly because the two persons interact, or do they interact mainly because they can each take the other's point of view? Or, as seems more plausible, could it be that there is a complex relationship between cooperation and the passing of egocentrism?

A third comment is that Piaget's theory, like Freud's, is somewhat pessimistic. According to Freud it is inevitable for both social and biological reasons that the child will experience an Oedipal conflict, the result of which will be the adoption of a harsh and authoritarian superego or conscience. For Piaget, too, it seems inevitable that the young child will display egocentric thought, and that he will stand in a relation of unilateral respect to the adult. Egocentrism defines certain properties of thought observed in young children which appear to be unavoidable and which must be overcome before the child can reach a more mature level of cognitive functioning. Unilateral respect is inevitable too; even if the parent tries, he cannot create a total atmosphere of mutual respect. The parent must arbitrarily impose upon the child some regulations because the child cannot understand their complex rationale. Since egocentrism and unilateral respect are inevitable, so is their product, moral realism.

A fourth comment is that Piaget has not yet fully demonstrated that the moral judgments elicited by his questioning on stories correspond to moral judgments in "real life." Piaget's arguments may be convincing— for example that children take the game of marbles seriously—but no amount of argument can resolve the issue. What is required is naturalistic study. We need to see whether moral realism, for example, is indeed found in children's moral judgments in the natural situation. A fifth comment concerning moral behavior and judgment is that Piaget's work has certainly fulfilled its original purpose: to stimulate further experimentation and theorizing. Moral judgment has been a popular topic for research, and in the main, independent investigators' findings have been consonant with Piaget's.[27]

Reasoning

Piaget's early work touched upon the child's reasoning too. The research again was preliminary, and as we shall see in Chapter Four, he later intensively elaborated upon the same topics. At this point we will consider several types of reasoning: syncretism, juxtaposition, and ordinal and part-whole relations.

In one of his studies Piaget presented 35 9-year-old boys and girls with a series of proverbs and a collection of explanatory sentences. The child's task was to connect each proverb with the proper explanatory sentence. For example, one proverb is, "Drunken once will get drunk again." The sentence which expressed the same idea is, "It is difficult to break old habits," and not, "Some people are continually drunk." Piaget also questioned each child concerning the reasons for his choice.

One 8-year-old child said that the sentence corresponding to "When the cat's away the mice can play" is "Some people get very excited but never do anything." When Piaget asked his justification, he responded:

Because the words are about the same. . . . It means that some people get very excited, but afterwards they do nothing, they are too tired. There are some people who get excited. It's like when cats run after hens or chicks. They come and rest in the shade and go to sleep. There are lots

---

27. For a review of this literature see L. Kohlberg, "The Development of Moral Character and Moral Ideology," in M. L. Hoffman and L. W. Hoffman, *Review of Child Development Research*, Vol. I. (New York: Russell Sage Foundation) 1964, 383–432.

*of people who run about a great deal, who get too excited. Then afterwards
they are worn out and go to bed.*[28]

The child's process of reasoning is certainly very confused. One way
we may characterize it is in terms of *syncretism*, a tendency to connect a
series of separate ideas into one confused whole. In the present case the
child tries to tie together an absent cat with excited people. The child
assigns to disparate things a similarity which is almost unfathomable to
the adult. How does the tendency toward syncretism work? According to
Piaget, when the child reads the proverb he constructs an interpretation
of it. This interpretation may be only loosely related to the real meaning of
the proverb because the child, in effect, free associates when he hears the
words.

In the case of the subject whose protocol was described above, subsequent questioning revealed that he interpreted the proverb as meaning
"The cat runs after the mice." The child then searched among the alternative sentences to find the one corresponding to the proverb. His interpretation or understanding guided this process, so that he viewed the
sentences in terms of his interpretation of the original proverb. In Piaget's
terminology, the child assimilates the sentences into the scheme which
originally contributed toward his understanding. The subject cited thus
perceived a similarity between his understanding of, "The cat runs after
the mice," and the sentence, "People get excited. . . ." Then, after the
child has interpreted a proverb and seen a relation between the interpretation and a sentence, he says that the sentence and the proverb have the
same meaning. By means of an intermediary—the scheme which enabled
him to understand in the first place—he has conglomerated two apparently
disparate items. In a sense, syncretism is a case of assimilation gone wild.
The child does not accommodate to the real meaning of the proverb;
rather, he assimilates it into his own scheme, and then he goes on in the
same way to assimilate the sentence into this scheme too.

Now we will consider the phenomenon of *juxtaposition*. If you will
recall, in his study of verbal communication Piaget found that young
children seldom express causal relations. In describing some mechanical
device, the child merely says that *a* and *b* occurred; he does not say that
a caused *b*. Instead of being related one to the other, the two events are
merely juxtaposed; that is, placed one after the other. In order to investigate this matter more directly, Piaget performed an experiment on 40
children from about 6 to 10 years of age. He gave each child an incomplete sentence ending with the word "because," and asked him to complete it. For example, he might ask, "Water gets hot because . . ." If the
child answered, "the fire was turned on," then Piaget might continue by

28. *Language and Thought*, p. 149.

asking, "And the fire was turned on because . . ." In this way, he attempted to determine if children could use the notion of causality when they are almost directly asked to do so. The responses to the sentences and to clinical questioning revealed a frequent inability to express causal relations. Here are some examples: [29]

. . . *the man fell from his bicycle, because* he broke his arm. . . . *I had a bath, because* afterwards I was clean. . . . *I've lost my pen because* I'm not writing. . . . *He fell off his bike, because* he fell and then he hurt himself. . . .[30]

At least two explanations of the child's responses are possible. According to one explanation the child's answers express sophisticated relationships. The sentence "I had a bath, because *afterwards I was clean*" means "We can tell that I had a bath because afterwards I was clean" or "My cleanliness implies that I had taken a bath." A second interpretation of the same sentence is that the child has a poor understanding of causality: he reverses cause and effect and merely juxtaposes one event after the other. Which explanation is correct? A number of factors seem to support the second interpretation which is juxtaposition. In his natural speech the child seldom uses the word "because" or other similar words to express relations, causal or otherwise, between events. Also, some of the answers to Piaget's test do not reveal sophisticated relationships of the type proposed by the first hypothesis. An example is: "He fell off his bike, because *he fell and then he hurt himself.*" This statement does not directly connect falling with injury; the two events are merely juxtaposed. The more accurate interpretation of the child's responses seems to be that they reveal a failure to perceive causality (let alone more sophisticated relations) and indicate a tendency merely to place events one after the other without specifying the relations among them.

Juxtaposition can also be seen in another and different context; namely, the child's drawing. In depicting a bicycle, for instance, the child draws many of the parts but does not synthesize them into a proper whole. He may draw the chain but not connect it to the wheel; he may draw the seat but not attach it to the frame. We see that the child considers only isolated events and ignores the relations between them.

Since syncretism and juxtaposition seem to be opposites, their simultaneous existence in the young child poses a paradox. How can the same child both ignore the parts in favor of the whole (syncretism) and ignore the whole in favor of the parts (juxtaposition)? Piaget attempts to resolve the paradox by arguing that both juxtaposition and syncretism are expressions of a common mode of thought—the inability to think about several

29. The sentence to be completed is in italic type, and the child's answer is in roman.
30. *Judgment and Reasoning,* pp. 17–18.

aspects of a situation simultaneously. Juxtaposition involves failing to see any relation among the parts of a whole, and the result is that they are seen as discrete and unrelated to each other. The child is thus unable to think simultaneously about the parts as separate things *and* about the relations which unite them. Similarly, in the use of syncretism the child perceives a whole or the common relationships, but fails to recognize the differences within the whole. He also has focussed on one aspect of the situation at the expense of the other. In other words, since the child cannot focus simultaneously both on the differences among things and on their common relationships, he is apt to see either a succession of unrelated events (juxtaposition) or a conglomerated whole (syncretism). Both types of distortions result from the same deficiency in thought.

In yet another investigation Piaget studied relational thinking. He presented a number of children with this problem: "Edith is fairer (or has fairer hair) than Suzanne; Edith is darker than Lili. Which is the darkest, Edith, Suzanne, or Lili?" [31] The problem in effect involves what Piaget was later to call *ordinal relationships*. Suppose we know that b is a smaller number than c, and that b is a larger number than a. Which is the largest number? The answer of course, is c. If we substitute Lili for a, Edith for b, Suzanne for c, and "has lighter hair than" for "is a smaller number than," then we have the same problem in the two cases: both deal with the understanding of relations of ordering, whether these be in terms of lightness of color, size of number, etc. Both problems present the child with partial information concerning the ordering (e.g. that $b < c$, and $b > a$) and ask him to deduce the entire ordering (that $a < b < c$). Piaget found that children even as old as 13 years found the problem to be very difficult. For example, a 9-year-old said: "You can't tell, because it says that Edith is the fairest and the darkest." [32] Piaget again explains their difficulty in terms of an inability to consider several aspects of a situation simultaneously. It is because the child cannot at the same time focus on $b < c$ and $b > a$ that he fails to deduce $a < b < c$, or that Suzanne is the darkest of the lot.

Another investigation yielded remarkably similar results. The study dealt explicitly with the relations of the part to the whole. The aim was to discover whether the child believed that the part was *included in* the whole. The questions were phrased in terms of the relations between cities (the parts) and countries (the whole). Here is an example:

Stu (7;8) says that "Geneva is in Switzerland" *and that* "Switzerland is bigger [than Geneva]." *But Genevans are not Swiss.* "Then where must you come from to be Swiss?"*—*"From Switzerland." *We draw a circle*

31. *Ibid.*, p. 87.
32. *Ibid.*, p. 88.

representing Switzerland, and ask Stu to put the cantons in their places. . . . Stu inscribes within the circle three or four smaller ones—Geneva, Vaud, etc., but he still maintains that Genevans are not Swiss people. The Swiss are the inhabitants of the big circle.[33]

Note that at the outset the child seems to maintain that the city is part of a larger whole (*"Geneva is in Switzerland"*). But when he is questioned about the matter, he denies that Genevans are Swiss or that the part is in fact included in the whole. The child again sees part and whole separately: they are unrelated entities.

We see in summarizing that: Piaget's studies of reasoning find that the child has a tendency to group together various different events into a loose and confused whole (syncretism); that he sometimes fails to see the relations among separate events (juxtaposition); that he fails to understand ordinal relations; and that he cannot deal with the relations between a part and the whole of which it is a member. All of these types of reasoning reveal a common deficiency: an inability to think simultaneously about several aspects of a situation.

Piaget makes an extremely interesting general comment about his investigations. He postulates that his findings, since they are the results of questioning children, hold true on the "plane of verbal thought" but not on the "plane of action." That is to say, while children may fail a problem when its solution requires verbal expression, they may be quite able to deal with the same dilemma on a practical, behavioral level. However, when the child first solves problems on the plane of action, he then must relearn his solutions on the plane of verbal thought. In a sense, action is more advanced than verbal thought (for the child from 7 to 11 years); the latter lags behind the former. Piaget terms the lag a *"vertical décalage."* The verticality refers to an ascending age scale: what the child learns at age 7 on the plane of action, he must restructure at age 11 on the plane of verbal thought. "Décalage" refers to the gap or lag.

GENERAL SUMMARY AND CONCLUSIONS

Piaget's early work is greatly varied. The first studies deal with the child's use of language. Naturalistic observation reveals that children below the age of 7 years often fail to use speech as a vehicle for transmitting information to one another, and instead, frequently repeat another's remarks or engage in individual or collective monologues. An experiment confirms these findings: when young children are given the explicit task of conveying information to another child, they fail to communicate. They

33. *Ibid.*, p. 123.

do not consider the informational needs of the listener. Moreover, the listener distorts what the speaker says by giving it idiosyncratic interpretations.

In other investigations Piaget uses the clinical method. He rejects the testing approach because of its rigidity, and the naturalistic approach because of its failure to yield a sufficient amount of relevant information. The clinical approach, he feels, is more flexible and, therefore, especially well suited to the exploratory aims of initial stages of research. He uses the clinical method to investigate the child's conception of the world, and finds that the child exhibits several primitive thought patterns. *Animism* is the tendency to consider natural events to be alive in the same sense as human beings are. *Artificialism* is the tendency to believe that some agent —human or divine—created natural events. *Participation* is the vague idea that human actions and natural processes interact and are related.

A further study, again using the clinical method in part, deals with moral judgment and behavior. Children below the age of 7 years fail to follow the rules of a game while at the same time believe that the rules are sacred and inviolable. Older children display both a greater tendency to follow the rules and to believe that they can be changed. In explicitly moral situations young children believe that guilt and moral responsibility are determined not by intention but by the amount of damage produced. These "realistic" moral tendencies are seen in the case of lying as well, and decline with age.

In studies of reasoning, Piaget finds that the young child's thought is characterized by *syncretism*: the tendency to group together into a confused whole several apparently unrelated things or events; and by *juxtaposition*, the failure to see the real connections among several things or events; and the failure to understand either part-whole or ordinal relations. All of these tendencies reflect a common pattern of thought: the inability to consider several aspects of a situation simultaneously.

Piaget employs a social learning theory to explain the child's development particularly in the areas of language and moral judgment. He postulates, for example, that the child's primitive moral judgment is the result of egocentric thought tendencies and the relation of unilateral respect toward the adult. The child's moral judgment becomes more mature when he adopts a position of mutual respect toward adults and comes into contact with new social institutions and points of view.

There are several comments we may make concerning Piaget's early research. First, what is the relation between the various findings? The young child is egocentric in communication, has an absolutistic concept of rules, is realistic in his moral judgment, and in his reasoning displays syncretism and juxtaposition. These varied terms at first may seem to refer to different and unrelated phenomena. One might think that moral realism and syncretism, for instance, refer to different patterns of thought, and that there is no commonality between them. But Piaget feels that such a view is mistaken: there is indeed a strong similarity among many of the young child's reactions to the problems posed by the various investigations.

The common pattern underlying these apparently diverse reactions is the inability to deal with several aspects of a situation simultaneously. This is due to the egocentric nature of the child's thought or the incapacity to shift attention from one to another aspect of a situation. In the case of speech, the young child cannot consider *both* the other's point of view and his own at once, and therefore centers solely on his own point of view. In the case of rules, the young child fails to consider both his own interests and the needs of others. Consequently, he often breaks the rules. He sees the origin of rules from a limited perspective too. Emanating from a person whom he regards as prestigious, they must be prestigious too. The child fails to consider both the parent's prestige and his reasons for devising the rules. In the case of moral judgment the child cannot consider both degree of damage and intention, and he bases his judgment entirely on the former. As far as reasoning is concerned, we have already seen how both syncretism and juxtaposition are expressions of a single tendency; namely, that of focussing on a limited aspect of the problem. The same may be said of the understanding of ordinal and part-whole relations. In the former the child considers only certain pairs of relations but not others; in the latter, he focusses on the part but not the whole, or vice versa.

As the child grows older and comes into contact with opposing points of view and varied social institutions, his thought goes through a process of decentration. In speech, he considers both what he wants to express and the listener's needs. In games, he considers the other's interests as well as his own, and is therefore willing to follow and modify the rules. In moral judgment, he considers both the outcomes of a person's behavior and its intent. And in reasoning, he tries to consider the complexities of problems; that is, both the differences and similarities among the same set of events. Thus, the child decenters his thought just as in the sensorimotor period the infant decentered his behavior. The newborn *acts* as if the world is centered about himself and must learn to behave in more adaptive ways. Similarly, the young child *thinks* from a limited perspective and must widen it. Both infant and young child must decenter; the former, his action and the latter, his thought.

In addition to characterizing the young child's thought in terms of centration, Piaget occasionally described it in Freudian terms. Freud described several primitive mental operations usually found in certain kinds of mental illness and in the deepest layers of the normal person's unconscious. Freud felt that this type of thinking, called "autistic thought," displayed certain regularities. For instance, it shows a tendency to fuse disparate things into one image. Thus, in a dream we may perceive a character who is a "condensation" of two distinct persons. In his early work Piaget proposes that the thought of the child is intermediate between autistic and adult thinking. For example, the child's syncretism is similar to, but more mature than, the tendency toward condensation. While at the beginning of his career Piaget borrowed a few ideas from psycho-analysis, he was never a disciple of Freud but always an independent investigator. As time went on his limited dependence on Freud diminished further with the result that Piaget's later work is totally devoid of Freudian concepts.

Piaget not only abandoned Freudian ideas, but became dissatisfied with the clinical method as administered at that time. He came to feel that it relied too heavily on language. The child thinks in non-verbal ways too, and the exclusively verbal clinical method was not always effective in tapping these thought processes. Consequently, he turned to somewhat different methods which we will describe in the next chapter.

Despite their methodological deficiencies, Piaget's early investigations may be considered among the most interesting of his achievements. The major part of the early studies dealt with *socially and practically relevant* phenomena: the child's ability to communicate information, to follow rules, and to make moral judgments. All these matters are obviously important for the child's practical success in the world and for his interactions with others.

By contrast Piaget's later work deals, as we shall see, with more abstract phenomena: the child's understanding of number or classification. These have less obvious relevance to the child's ordinary activities. Probably, his ability to understand the cardinality of number makes less of a difference to his daily life than his ability to communicate to other children. Also, in his early books, Piaget showed a strong interest in the role of social factors in development. Later research, as we shall see, convinced Piaget that other factors of equal importance were involved. With time his interests have tended to focus on these factors rather than on the social environment.

Finally, we may note that the explanatory concepts which evolved from Piaget's early work are vague. They are stated in ordinary language and are often not entirely clear. Much confusion, for example, has arisen over the concept of egocentrism. But as we have stated repeatedly, Piaget fully recognized that his early concepts were only preliminary and tentative, not final and conclusive. He hoped that his early work would stimulate research by others, and that he himself could clarify his concepts at a later time. The first of his expectations has been fulfilled: there has been much research on moral judgment, for example. We will see in the next chapter how Piaget has elaborated and even formalized some of his early and tentative notions, like ordinal and part-whole relations.

4

the years 2 through 11:
piaget's later work

This chapter deals with aspects of Piaget's later work (approximately from 1940 onward) on the child from about 2 to 11 years. As was shown in Chapter One, this portion of Piaget's research and theory is voluminous and covers such matters as the child's conception of chance, space, geometry, movement, number, and other topics. Since we cannot review all of the later work here, we shall focus on what we consider to be basic issues and concepts which reappear in and apply to almost all of Piaget's recent writings. We will consider (a) the revised clinical method; (b) the child's classification of objects or events; (c) his ability to place them in ordinal relations; (d) his concept of number (particularly its conservation over transformations); (e) the nature of his mental imagery; (f) some general characteristics of thought; and (g) Piaget's explanation of development in terms of the equilibration theory.

THE REVISED CLINICAL METHOD

We saw in Chapter Three that Piaget's original clinical method was highly dependent on verbalizations. The examiner posed the questions in words, and the child was required to give the answers in the same way. The examiner's questions usually did not refer to things or events which were immediately present, and the problems did not always involve concrete objects which the child could manipulate or even see. For example, the examiner might depict a child who had unwittingly broken some cups and might then ask the subject being questioned for a judgment concerning the child's naughtiness and the punishment to be meted out. In such a situation as this the subject is required to do several things. He must interpret the examiner's description so as to picture the scene to himself; he must make a special effort to comprehend certain crucial aspects of the question, like the word "naughty"; and he must express his judgment in words.

After some experience with this method, Piaget came to feel that it was faulty because it relied too heavily on language. The child might not understand everything said to him, particularly if the words did not always refer to concrete objects, and even if the child did understand, perhaps he could not adequately express in words the full extent of his knowledge. Consequently, Piaget modified his procedures, and the result is what we shall call "the revised clinical method." The new method involves several features. First, the examiner's questions refer to concrete objects or events which the child has before him. No longer must the child imagine these things merely on the basis of a verbal description. Second, an effort is made to let the child express his answer by manipulating the objects, and not solely express himself through language. For example, let us suppose that the examiner wishes to know whether the child can form two distinct classes. To investigate the matter he might present the child with an array of circles and squares all mixed together in no order, ask him to put together the ones that belong together, or sort out two distinct piles. What the child *does* with the objects—what sort of piles he makes—and not what he says about them, constitutes the primary data of the study. If after encouragement a child still cannot form a pile of circles separate from a pile of squares, then the examiner might conclude that he does not have the classification skills under investigation.

While completely non-verbal tests are desirable, it is often hard to invent them. This is especially true for Piaget since he usually investigates the child's understanding of abstract concepts that are not easily manifested in the simple manipulation of concrete materials. The revised clinical method, therefore, must often depend for its data on the child's verbal responses. But even when this is necessary, the child's answers refer to a problem stated in terms of concrete materials which are present. A third feature of the revised clinical method is not new: the examiner's questioning is flexible. Rather than employ a standardized list of questions, he modifies them or adds new ones as the situation demands. As before, Piaget still feels that there is no point either in asking a child a question that he does not understand or in failing to clarify an answer. To summarize, the revised clinical method involves posing questions concerning concrete materials; allowing the child to "answer" by manipulating the materials, if this is at all possible; and, as in the earlier clinical method, stating questions and pursuing answers in a flexible and unstandardized way. Whether or not the revised clinical procedure gives an accurate assessment of the child's abilities is a matter for lively debate. Some critics feel that the method is still too verbal and therefore inadequate,[1] whereas other investigators have performed studies which indicate otherwise.[2] The issue is not settled yet. Nevertheless, the revised clinical method is less exclusively verbal than Piaget's earlier procedure and attempts to give an accurate assessment of the child's thought processes which may be in a large measure nonverbal.

CLASSIFICATION

Piaget has used the revised clinical method to study classification in the child. The preceding chapters have already touched on this and related matters, and it may be useful to review some of the material here. We saw that there is a primitive sort of motor classification in the sensorimotor period (0 to about 2 years) when the infant applies to objects in the environment abbreviations of familiar schemes. For example, Lucienne saw a toy parrot hanging above her crib and kicked her feet very slightly. This was an abbreviation of a scheme which she could quite easily have applied to the present situation. It seemed as if her action classified the parrot as a "thing to be swung." Moreover, the abbreviation shows that the behavior was becoming internalized. Eventually it could be replaced by the thought: "That's the parrot; that's something I can swing." But the abbreviated schemes are not yet instances of legitimate classification. One reason is that the schemes apply to individual objects over a period of time and not to a collection of objects. For example, Lucienne kicked from time to time whenever she saw parrots and thus indicated recognition. But this recognition does not imply that she considered the parrots to belong to a class. Mature classification, on the other hand, involves the conception of a collection of things, whether they are immediately present or imagined. A second reason why it is not possible to credit Lucienne with classification has to do with *inclusion relations* which will be ex-

1. M. D. S. Braine, "Piaget on Reasoning; a Methodological Critique and Alternative Proposals." In W. Kessen and C. Kuhlmann, Eds., "Thought in the Young Child," *Monographs of the Society for Research in Child Development,* 1962, 27, No. 2.
2. B. Fleischmann, S. Gilmore, and H. Ginsburg, "The Strength of Nonconservation." *Journal of Experimental Child Psychology,* 1966, 4, pp. 353–68.

panded on below. Briefly, this refers to the ability to construct a hierarchical classification, such that toy parrots are a sub-class of a larger
more inclusive class like toys-in-general.

From about 2 to 4 years the child begins to classify collections of
objects in a way that is quite primitive. He uses the pre-concept. Sometimes
he fails to see that one individual member of a class remains the same
individual despite slight perceptual changes; and sometimes he thinks that
two different members of the same class are the same individual. Between
5 and 10 years, the child's classification is still faulty in several ways. There
is the phenomenon of juxtaposition, the inability to see that several objects
are indeed members of the same class. There is also syncretism, the tendency to group together a number of disparate events into an ill-defined
and illogical whole.

As was pointed out, Piaget's investigations of the pre-concept, syncretism, and juxtaposition were preliminary and tentative. First, there
existed methodological defects: the data were almost exclusively verbal
so that Piaget's interpretation was based largely on what the child said.
Secondly, Piaget's concepts—syncretism, juxtaposition, the pre-concept—
were somewhat vague and needed elaboration. Consequently, Piaget has
recently (in the 1950's) returned to the study of classification in the
child from about 2 to 12 years. These recent investigations make use of
the revised clinical method; also they modify the notions of pre-concept,
syncretism, and juxtaposition, and suggest new ways of conceptualizing
the child's classificatory activities.

Some Properties of a Class

Before examining Piaget's research into classification, we must be clear
about what he means by a class. Suppose we have before us a number
of objects all mixed together. The array contains a large red triangle, a
small blue circle, a large pink circle, and a small black triangle. All of the
objects are discriminably different one from the other. That is, there is
no difficulty in perceiving that any one object is different from any of
the others. For example, the large red triangle is very obviously larger and
redder than the small black triangle. Suppose too that we wish to place
these objects into two different classes. One way of doing this is to put
in one separate pile the large red triangle and the small black triangle. In
the second pile would go the small blue circle and the large pink circle.
If the original array contained additional triangular objects, regardless of
their size or color, they would of course go in the first pile. Similarly all
other circular objects would go in the second pile. The two piles each
represent a class. Of course, we might classify the objects in another way.
We could put in one pile the two small objects (regardless of their color

or shape) and in the second pile the two large objects. There are usually many different classes that one may form from a given array of objects.

Piaget makes a number of points about the classes formed from the original array (for purposes of illustration consider just our first example, the class of triangles and the class of circles): (a) No object is a member of both classes simultaneously. For example, the large red triangle is in the class of triangles and not also in the class of circles. Thus, the classes are mutually exclusive or disjoint. This holds even if there are more than two classes formed. (For example, we might divide some animal pictures into the classes of lions, tigers, and elephants, all of which are disjoint.)

(b) All members of a class share some similarity. For example, the small blue circle and the large pink circle both share the property of circularity. Circularity is the defining property of the class; that is, we include in the class of circles any object which is circular. Another way of putting it is to say that circularity is the *intension* of the class. The defining property or intension of the other class is triangularity.

(c) Each class may be described in terms of a list of its members. Instead of describing a class in terms of its defining property or intension (for example, the class of triangular objects), we may simply list the objects in the class (for example, large red triangle and small black triangle). Such a list is the *extension* of the class.

(d) The defining property of a class determines what objects are placed in it. Another way of stating this is that intension defines extension. For example, if we know that one class is to be formed on the basis of triangularity and another on the basis of circularity, we can predict the content of the list of objects in each class.

These are some fundamental properties of classes. (There are other crucial attributes too, like inclusion relations which we will discuss later.) Piaget then asks whether the child classifies objects in accordance with these properties. When asked to group objects, does the child form mutually exclusive classes? Do his classes have defining properties which determine the list of objects in each class?

Piaget discovers three stages of development. The first two—both of which we may call *preoperational*—occur roughly during the years 2 to 7. The third stage—that of *concrete operations*—occurs roughly from the years 7 to 11.

Stage 1

To investigate these issues, Piaget performed a number of experiments which used the revised clinical method. In one study, he tested a number of children from about 2 to 5 years of age. They were presented with flat geometric shapes of wood and of plastic. The shapes included squares, triangles, rings, and half-rings all of which were in several colors. The shapes were mixed together and the child was told: "Put together things that are alike." Sometimes additional instructions were given: "Put them so that they're all the same" or "Put them here if they're the same, and then over there if they're different from this one but the same as each other." [3]

The children displayed several methods of grouping the objects. One method is called the *small partial alignment*. With this method the child uses only *some* of the objects in the original array and puts them together in several ways apparently without any over-all guiding plan. For example, one child began by putting six half-rings (semi-circles) of various colors in a straight line; then she put a yellow triangle on top of a blue square; later she put a red square in between two blue triangles; then put squares and triangles in no particular order, in a straight line. There are several points to note about this performance. Sometimes similarities among objects determine the collection. For example, the subject whose performance was described above began with a line of half-rings. At other times the same child grouped things on the basis of no detectable similarity; that is, she put a yellow triangle on a blue square, or a red square between two blue triangles. In both of these cases, there is no similiarity of either color or form.

It is clear that small partial alignments are not true classes for several reasons. One of them is that intension does not define extension; that is, no defining property determined which geometric forms were put in various collections. The child does not operate under an over-all guiding plan like a system of rules (defining properties) which organize the way in which he arranges the objects.

Other children of this age use the geometric figures to construct an interesting form or picture. One child arranged a number of circles and squares to represent a long vertical object and then proclaimed it to be the Eiffel Tower; another child placed a number of half-rings in between several squares, all in a horizontal line, and described the result as a bridge. Piaget calls these productions *complex objects*. It is obvious that like the small partial alignments, and like some other types of collections not described here, the complex object is not a class. Figures are not placed in the complex object because they share some defining property; rather, extension is determined solely by the requirements of the picture under construction.

In another investigation, Piaget presented children of the same age with non-geometric figures for classification—little toys which included people, houses, animals, and so on. Once again, the results showed an

3. *Early Growth of Logic*, p. 21.

inability to form classes. One child put two dolls in a cradle, then two wheelbarrows together, then a horse. When the examiner asked the child for all the objects like a horse, she gave him all the animals and then a baby and two trees. This example illustrates the fact that although the young child perceives similarities among the objects, these do not fully determine what objects go into the collection. That is, the child saw that all animals were in some respect similar and gave them to the examiner when he asked for objects like the horse. If the child had stopped there, she might have formed a class which was based on the defining property of "animalness." However, she went on to throw in the baby and two trees. The similarity (intension) that she first perceived did not fully determine which objects were to be grouped together (extension). It is as if the child forgot about the initial defining property (animalness) and then switched to some other.

We may make several comments on these investigations. First, they make clear the nature of the revised clinical method. The examiner gives the child concrete objects to work with. The task instructions and questions are still, of course, verbal, but they refer to real things that the child can manipulate. The child is required to say very little. Most of his responses are not verbal but behavioral. He does not have to say that all of the animals do or do not go together; rather, he can put them together or fail to do so.

Second, although the revised clinical method is an improvement over what was used before, we wonder whether the task was entirely clear to the child. The instructions (e.g., "Put together things that are alike") seem rather vague and susceptible to many interpretations. We suspect that different methods of presenting the task to the child might produce entirely different results. Piaget considered this objection and tried an essentially non-verbal method. He began to classify the objects himself and asked the child to do the same thing. The result again was not true classification, but "complex objects," etc. While this method was not successful, it does not exhaust the possibilities. Other procedures might work and should be explored.

Stage 2

Children from about 5 to 7 years produce collections which seem to be real classes. When presented with the situation described earlier, one child produced two large collections, one which contained all the polygons and the other the curvilinear forms. Moreover, each of these collections was subdivided further. The polygons, for instance, contained separate piles of squares, triangles, etc., and the curvilinear forms involved separate collections of circles, half-rings, and so on. Thus, the child not only seems

FIGURE 1

CLASSIFICATION OF
GEOMETRIC OBJECTS

to form classes, but arranges them hierarchically, as in Figure 1. There are two general collections (polygons and curvilinear forms) at the top of the hierarchy and these both branch out into several sub-collections below (squares, triangles, etc.). The child's activities may be characterized in several additional ways. (a) He places in the appropriate collection *all* of the objects which were in the initial array given him. The younger child did not do this; he left some objects unclassified. (b) Intension fully defines extension. That is to say, if the child defines a collection on the basis of the defining property of circularity, *all* circles go into that pile, and *none* is placed in any other pile. (c) At a given level of the hierarchy, similar defining properties are used to determine collections. For example, at the lower level of the hierarchy in Figure 1, all of the collections are defined in terms of geometric form—squares, triangles, etc. It is not the case that some collections are defined by form and some by color. To summarize, it would seem that the child from about 5 to 7 years produces rather elaborate hierarchical collections which deserve to be called true classes.

Piaget feels, however, that the child of this stage fails to comprehend one crucial aspect of the hierarchy he has constructed. He does not understand the relations among the different levels of the hierarchy. This is the problem of *class inclusion* which we will now illustrate. Suppose we are given a randomly organized array of blue and red squares and black and white circles. We construct an arrangement (see Figure 2) such that there are two major collections (squares vs. circles) and within each of these there are two further sub-divisions (blue vs. red squares and black vs. white circles). Thus, there is a hierarchy whose higher level is defined by shape and whose lower level is defined by color. Consider for the moment only one half of the hierarchy; namely, the squares which are divided into blue and red. If we understand inclusion relations, then we can make statements of this sort: (a) *All* of the squares are either blue or red. (b) There are more squares than there are blue squares. (c) There are more squares than there are red squares. (d) If the red squares are taken away from the squares, then the blue ones are left. (e) If the blue squares are taken away from the squares, then the red ones are left. These, then, are some of the possible statements about inclusion relations—the relations of the parts to the whole, of the whole to the parts, and the parts to the parts. They may seem very obvious, but so do many principles which children fail to understand.

Piaget investigated the understanding of inclusion relations in children of various ages. Let us consider now the child from about 5 to 7 years. Piaget presented each of his subjects with a number of pictures of flowers and other things. The child was first required to group the pictures in any way he wished, and then he was asked a number of questions bearing on inclusion relations. The results concerning spontaneous classification replicated what was found earlier: the child from 5 to 7 years constructs collections which seem to involve a hierarchy. One child formed two large collections: flowers vs. other things; then he further subdivided the flowers into primulas vs. other kinds of flowers. In terms of Figure 3, he seemed to have constructed the top two levels of the hierarchy. (He did not make a further sub-division in terms of yellow vs. other primulas.) It would seem that the construction of such a hierarchy implies the understanding of inclusion relations. If the subject divided the flowers into primulas vs. other kinds, must he not understand that there are more flowers than there are primulas? The results of Piaget's questioning, however, point to different conclusions. Consider this protocol of a child aged 6 years 2 months:

. . . *A little girl takes all the yellow primulas and makes a bunch of them, or else she makes a bunch of all the primulas. Which way does she have the bigger bunch?*—The one with the yellow primulas will be bigger. [*He then counted the yellow primulas and the other primulas and found*

FIGURE 2

CLASSIFICATION OF
SQUARES AND CIRCLES

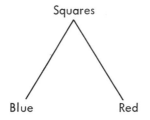

Squares

Blue   Red

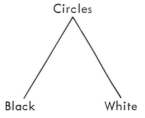

Circles

Black   White

FIGURE 3

CLASSIFICATION OF
FLOWERS AND OTHER THINGS

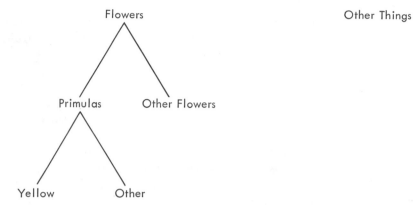

that there were four of each kind] Oh no, it's the same thing . . .—*And
which will be bigger: a bunch made up of the primulas or one of all the
flowers?*—They're both the same. . . .[4]

Although this child had earlier constructed a hierarchical arrangement of the materials, he maintained that the yellow primulas did not
form a smaller collection than the primulas as a whole; and that the primulas did not form a smaller collection than the flowers as a whole. Both
of these answers, of course, are quite wrong. In both cases, the part is
smaller than the whole from which it derives.

What is the explanation of the child's inability to comprehend inclusion relations? Piaget postulates that once the child has divided a whole
into two sub-groupings, he cannot then think simultaneously in terms of
the larger collection and the sub-divisions which he has constructed from
it. For example, suppose a child divides a collection of flowers (the whole)
into primulas vs. other flowers (sub-divisions of the whole). When he is
asked "Are there more primulas or more flowers," he must consider both
the original collection (flowers) and one of his sub-divisions (primulas)
at the same time. He must compare the "size" of one against that of the
other. Under these conditions, he focusses or *centers* on the collection he
can see (the primulas) and ignores the original collection (all of the
flowers), which is no longer present in its initial state (a collection of the
primulas and other flowers all mixed together). And since he centers on
the part, ignoring the whole, his answers to inclusion questions are often
wrong.

4. *Ibid.*, p. 102.

Stage 3

Children from about 7 to 11 years of age are both capable of constructing hierarchical classifications and comprehending inclusion. For example, after constructing a hierarchy one child of 9 years and 2 months was asked:

Which would make a bigger bunch: one of all the primulas or one of all the yellow primulas?—All the primulas, of course. You'd be taking the yellow ones as well.—*And all the primulas or all the flowers?*—If you take all the flowers, you take the primulas too.[5]

This protocol makes quite clear the child's ability to think simultaneously in terms of the whole and its parts (e.g., "If you take all the flowers, you take the primulas too"). While he physically separates the flowers into primulas and other kinds, he is able to reason both about the original whole and its part at the same time. His thought has *decentered* from exclusive preoccupation with the part *or* the whole.

Piaget also found that when the child of this age was asked the same questions about objects that were not present, he often failed to give correct answers. Apparently, the child's classification is *concrete*: he understands the inclusion relations of a group of objects he can see, but fails to comprehend the same relations when imaginary classes are involved. The gap between verbal and concrete reasoning is another example of *vertical décalage*. We may summarize by stating that the child from 7 to 11 has reached the most advanced stage as far as the classification of concrete objects is concerned: he can construct a hierarchical arrangement and understand the relations among the levels of the hierarchy. Piaget then proposes that this accomplishment can be described in terms of a logico-mathematical model. Let us explore this idea.

Rationale for the Use of a
Logico-Mathematical Model

We have seen that Piaget attempts to describe the basic processes underlying the classification of objects or events. He proposes that the stage 1 child (2 to 4 or 5 years) fails to construct hierarchical arrangements partly because after a short while he forgets the defining property (intension) which he has used to form a collection. The stage 2 child (5 to 7 years) can construct a hierarchy because he can use a defining property to determine which objects go in a collection; but at the same

5. *Ibid.*, p. 109.

time he cannot understand inclusion relations because of the inability to simultaneously consider several immediately present collections and the larger one from which they were derived. The stage 3 child (7 to 11 years) can correctly answer questions concerning inclusion because of his ability to think of original classes and their derivatives at the same time.

Thus far, we have described these basic processes (the ability to think simultaneously of subclasses and larger classes) in terms of the ordinary language. Many psychologists believe that this is the proper procedure; but others, including Piaget, feel that descriptions of structure should be phrased, as much as possible, in a formal language like mathematics.

Let us consider first, however, some aspects of the use of the common language. Most psychological theories have been stated in this way. Freud, for example, wrote exclusively in German and not in logic nor mathematics, and no doubt there is not a single formula in the entire corpus of psychoanalytic doctrine. Another example from another point on the psychological spectrum is Tolman, an experimental psychologist, who produced his theories of learning in ordinary English and made use of only a few (and non-essential) symbols. Tolman and Freud are hardly isolated examples. Today, too, the major part of psychological theorizing is done in English, or Russian, and so forth. Several advantages are usually claimed for this procedure. The ordinary language may be richer and subtler than formal languages and also it is generally easier to read than mathematics or logic.

However, another approach to this problem is possible. Piaget feels that for scientific purposes the ordinary language is fundamentally ambiguous and must be supplemented by formal approaches. Anyone even slightly familiar with the history of psychology knows that most, if not all, psychological theories stated in the common language have been vague and easily susceptible to misinterpretation. Even today there are many fruitless arguments over the meaning of words like "concept" or "ego" or "learning." As an example, let us consider the word "thought," which we have used without definition quite frequently. No doubt "thought" means quite different things to different readers. To some it may mean "ideas," and to some "consciousness"; to others it may mean "mental effort," "meditation," "concentration," "opinion," and so forth. Is it any wonder that a given psychological theory which uses words like this will elicit a variety of interpretations and, hence, considerable argument and misunderstanding? Perhaps a prime example of the difficulty is Piaget's own use of verbal theories in his early work. Considerable confusion still surrounds the terms "egocentrism," "moral realism," and so forth.

Piaget feels, then, that the ordinary language produces obscure and ambiguous psychological theorizing, and must, therefore, be supplemented, if not replaced by other modes of description. The physical sciences have convincingly shown that mathematics is an extremely powerful tool for communicating certain precise ideas. Piaget feels that it would be fruitful for psychologists to adopt a similar approach, and has himself attempted to do so in the case of classification and other matters. Let us now explore his formal description of the structure of classification.

Grouping I

The formal description called a Grouping [6] begins with this situation: we have a classification hierarchy of the sort constructed by the 7 to 11 year old children in Piaget's experiments (see Figure 4). This is

FIGURE 4

CLASSIFICATION HIERARCHY

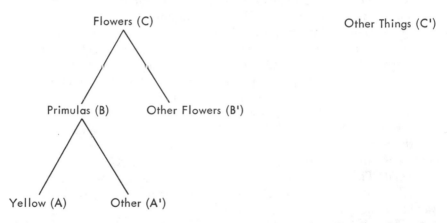

what we start with (that is, it is a given) and the Grouping describes what the child can do with the hierarchy. At the top of the hierarchy that the child has constructed are the two classes, flowers which we shall symbolize as (C) and other things (C'). On the middle level of the hierarchy we find primulas (B) and other flowers (B'). On the lowest level there are yellow primulas (A) and primulas of other colors (A'). Each of the classes (A, A', B, B', C, C') is an *element* of the system. There is one *binary*

6. Our exposition of Grouping I is simplified and incomplete; for example, we have defined only one binary operator. We have kept the mathematical development at a very informal level. The reader interested in pursuing the matter should see Jean Piaget, *Traité de Logique* (Paris: Colin, 1949), and also J. B. Grize's recent formalization of Piaget's system as described in E. W. Beth and Jean Piaget, *Mathematical Epistemology and Psychology* (Dordrecht–Holland: D. Reidel Publishing Company, 1966).

operator that may be applied to the elements; namely, *combining*. We will symbolize combining by +, although the reader should be aware that combining classes is not precisely equivalent to adding numbers. The operator + is binary since it can be applied to only two elements at a time. Just as we can add only two numbers at any one time, so we can only combine two classes at a time.

Given the elements and the binary operator, the five *properties* describe the ways in which the operator may be applied to the elements.

The first property is *composition* (usually referred to in mathematics as *closure*) which states that when we combine any two elements of the system the result will be another element of the system. For example, if we combine the yellow primulas with the primulas of other colors, we get the general class of primulas. This may be written as $A + A' = B$. Or if we combine the yellow primulas with all the primulas, we get all the primulas. We may write this as $A + B = B$. This property describes aspects of the child's ability to understand a hierarchy. For example, he can mentally construct a larger class by combining its subclasses.

The second property is *associativity*, which may best be illustrated in a concrete manner. Suppose we want to combine three classes such as yellow primulas, primulas, and flowers (A, B, and C, respectively). Remember that we cannot just add all three of them together simultaneously since the operator (combining) is binary; that is, it can be applied to only two elements at a time. Given this limitation, there are at least two ways of adding A, B, and C. We might first combine the yellow primulas and the primulas and get primulas. That is, we do $A + B = B$. Then we might combine this result (B) with flowers-in-general (C) and get flowers-in-general. Thus, we do $B + C = C$. To summarize, we first perform $A + B = B$ and then $B + C = C$ so that our final result is C. Another way of stating this is $(A + B) + C = C$.

There is yet a second way of doing the combining of classes. We could start by combining the yellow primulas (A) with the *combination* of primulas and flowers in general (B + C), and finish with the same result: flowers-in-general, (C). Thus we can write $A + (B + C) = C$. Note that the final result of performing the operation by either method is C, so that the two methods may be considered equivalent. We may write this equivalence as $(A + B) + C = A + (B + C)$. This equation expresses the fact that the child can combine classes in different orders and can realize that the results are equivalent.

The third property is *identity* which states that there is a special element in the system (the "nothing" element), which when combined with any of the other elements produces no change. If we combine the nothing element with the yellow primulas the result will be the yellow primulas. If we symbolize nothing by 0, then we have $A + 0 = A$. More concretely, if we do not combine the yellow primulas with any of the other classes, then, of course, we still have the yellow primulas.

The fourth property is *negation* or *inverse* which states that for any element (class) in the system, there is another element (the inverse) which when combined with the first produces the nothing element. That is, if we add to the class of yellow primulas its inverse, then we are left with nothing. The inverse is equivalent to the operation of taking away the same class. If we start with yellow primulas and combine with this class its inverse, we are in effect taking away the yellow primulas with the result that we are left with nothing. We can write this as $A + (-A) = 0$ or $A - A = 0$. The inverse rule might apply to a train of thought like this: "Suppose I combine the yellow primulas with all of the other primulas. Then I have all of the primulas. But if I take away [inverse or negation] all of the other primulas, then I am left again just with the yellow primulas." Note how this train of thought is *reversible*. First the other primulas are added, but later they are taken away, so that the thinker is once again at the point where he started. Negation then is one kind of reversibility.

The inverse also may be used to express aspects of class inclusion. Suppose we start with the class of primulas (B) and take away (or add the inverse of) the primulas which are not yellow (A'). This operation leaves us with the yellow primulas (A). We may write this as $A = B + (-A')$ or $A = B - A'$. This type of reasoning underlies the child's ability to say that there are *more* primulas than yellow ones; that the yellow primulas are *included* in the class of primulas; or that the yellow primulas are only some of the primulas.

The fifth property actually has several aspects. One of them has to do with special identity elements. Suppose we combine the class of yellow primulas with itself. The result is yellow primulas. We may write this as $A + A = A$. In this equation A functions as an identity element like 0. Adding A to A is liking adding 0 to A: the result, A, is unchanged. Piaget calls this *tautology*. Another aspect is *resorption*. If we combine the class of yellow primulas with the class of primulas, the result is primulas. We may write this as $A + B = B$. Here too, A functions as an identity element. Adding A to B is like adding 0 to B; the result, B, is unchanged. In a sense, this is another way of looking at inclusion relations. The yellow primulas must be included in the class of primulas (or must be some of the primulas) since adding the former to the latter does not change the latter.

These, then, are some of the aspects of Grouping I and are intended as a formal description of the processes underlying the child's classification. The model involves elements (classes), the binary operator of combining, and five properties governing the application of the operator to the elements.

Discussion of Grouping I

A few general remarks should be made concerning Grouping I. First, Piaget's use of mathematics is not at all meant to imply that the child understands the logico-mathematical model in any explicit sense. It is obvious that most children have never heard of the special identity element, let alone Grouping I. Clearly the child is not a mathematician at this level. In fact, he often cannot describe in *any* clear way, mathematical or otherwise, how he went about solving a particular problem. His report is often incoherent. Piaget uses the logico-mathematical model, therefore, not to characterize the child's consciousness, but to describe the processes underlying his classification.

Second, Grouping I is not metrically quantitative in the sense that it does not involve numbers. The operations involve classes which may be of any size. It does not matter whether there are five yellow primulas and six white ones, or 5000 yellow primulas and 300 white ones. In both cases there are more primulas than there are white primulas, and so forth.

Third, we may expand on our earlier point that the Grouping is intended to describe the structure of the child's classification. Piaget is not interested in the minor details of the child's performance; that is, whether he is classifying flowers or fish, or whether he first put the flowers in an arrangement and then the animals. Piaget instead attempts to capture the essence of the child's activities and to identify the processes underlying them. The Grouping is Piaget's way of describing these processes in a clear way. Therefore, the Grouping is not simply a protocol listing everything that the child does. It is instead an abstraction which describes basic processes like the ability to mentally combine two smaller classes into a larger one, or to take away one class from another.

The Grouping also is a comprehensive and integrated structure. It is comprehensive since it describes the processes underlying everything that the child can do in classification. The Grouping describes the potentialities of the child, and not necessarily what he does in any one task at any one time. Let us suppose that a child constructs a hierarchy of classes. In doing so he may not make use of inclusion relations. In this case, the Grouping does not so much describe what the child actually does, but what he is capable of doing under the proper conditions.

Also, the Grouping is an integrated system in the sense that each of the properties does not stand alone but is related to all of the others. On the mathematical level this is easy to see. The property of associativity describes the order in which elements may be combined, but the property of composition or closure is needed to interpret the result of the associative combination. In other words, associativity shows that two different orders of combining elements are equivalent, and composition reveals that both of these orders of combination result in another element which must be in the system. Thus, the property of associativity would be meaningless without the property of composition. We cannot have one property without the other. This feature of the Grouping is, of course, intended to reflect an important aspect of the child's activities: the child's successful classification (including the understanding of inclusion) presupposes a complex, an *interrelated whole*, of mental operations. For example, suppose the child recognizes that there are more primulas than yellow primulas. This achievement implies a number of interrelated mental acts. The child must be aware that the primulas (which are no longer before him in a single collection) are the combination of yellow primulas and primulas of other colors $(A + A' = B)$. He must also be aware that when yellow primulas are taken away from the primulas, there remain primulas of other colors $(B - A = A')$. These, then, are some of the operations underlying the child's answer to a question concerning inclusion. When the child correctly answers the question, he may not first actually perform all these operations. However, they are implicit in his answer; he could not answer correctly if it were not possible for him to perform all the operations involved in the classification system. To summarize, any particular response that the child makes to a classification problem cannot be considered in isolation. His response presupposes a complex structure, and it is this which Piaget describes as the Grouping. The Grouping, in other words, describes the mental operations which make it possible for the child to "really" understand classification.

Fourth, the Grouping explains and predicts behavior. Insofar as the Grouping describes the processes underlying the child's classification, it may be said to explain his performance. The Grouping states that the child can combine two classes to get a larger one. This operation, among others, underlies the child's ability to understand inclusion relations and in this sense explains it. Insofar as the Grouping is general it may be said to predict behavior. The Grouping is not limited to the objects Piaget used to study classification. Because the Grouping provides a description of structure, it goes beyond the details of any particular problem and allows us to predict what the child's performance is like on other similar tasks.

Fifth, Piaget has described several other Groupings all of which refer to the child's ability (from 7 to 11) to deal with concrete objects. Therefore, stage 3 is termed *concrete operational*.

SUMMARY AND CONCLUSIONS

Piaget's early work (in the 1920's and 1930's) dealt with classification in a preliminary way. In the 1950's he returned to the problem, using the revised clinical method. He presented 2 to 11-year-old children with an array of objects to be classified. The findings were that in *stage 1* (2 to 5 years) the child fails to use consistently a clear rule or defining property to sort the objects into different classes. He instead constructs graphic collections which are small partial alignments or interesting forms. In *stage 2* (5 to 7 years), the child sorts the objects by a reasonable defining property and even constructs a hierarchical classification, but he fails to comprehend inclusion relations. Stages 1 and 2 are termed *preoperational*. In stage 3, which is *concrete operational* (7 to 11 years), the child has a mature notion of class, particularly when concrete objects are involved. He sorts them by defining properties, understands the relations between class and subclass, and so forth. In order to describe in a clear way the processes underlying the child's activities, Piaget proposes a logico-mathematical model which he calls Grouping I. This Grouping involves some elements, a binary operator, and five properties relating the operator to the elements. Also, the Grouping is not metrically quantitative in the sense that it does not matter how big or small (in numerical terms) are the various classes involved. The child, of course is not conscious of the Grouping; rather the Grouping is intended to describe the basic structures of his activities. It seems to be the case, however, that Piaget has not specified as precisely as is desirable, how all aspects of the Grouping are related to the child's activities.

Piaget stresses that the age norms describing classification are only approximate. A particular child may pass from stage 1 to stage 2 at 6 years, and not necessarily at 4 or 5 years. One child may spend three years in stage 1 while another child may spend four years in the same stage. Piaget does maintain, however, that the *sequence* of development is invariant. The child must first be characterized by stage 1 before he can advance to stage 2 and then to stage 3. Piaget also points out that a child may not necessarily be in the same stage of development with respect to different areas of cognition. That is to say, a child may be in stage 1 with respect to classification, and in stage 2 of number development. Thus, a child may be slightly more advanced in some categories of thought than in others.

Yet another major issue concerning classification remains to be covered. Why does the child pass from one stage of development to the next? How does he acquire the ability to deal with inclusion relations, for example? We will consider Piaget's theory of development—equilibration theory—at the end of this chapter.

RELATIONS

In Chapters Two and Three we have already reviewed several aspects of relations, a problem (like classification) with which Piaget has been concerned since his earliest work in psychology. We saw that in the sensori-motor period the infant displays precursors of relations. He can broadly discriminate within the dimensions of numerosity, intensity of muscular effort, and loudness of sounds (among other dimensions). In the case of numerosity, you will recall that Laurent said "papa" when Piaget said "papa"; that Laurent said "bababa" when Piaget said "papa-papa"; and that Laurent said "papapapa" in response to "papapapapapapa." Laurent's imitation, although not exact, nevertheless implies an ability to discrim-inate or hear the difference among several sounds which differed in number of repetitions of one syllable. Similarly, in the case of muscular effort, Laurent appeared able to detect the difference among the variations in vigor with which he swung a chain, and also he was able to discriminate among sounds of different degrees of loudness. Thus, the infant can dif-ferentiate gradations within different kinds of stimuli: some things are louder than others, or more numerous, or bigger, and so forth. He can perceive differences in various aspects of his world. The ability to make such discriminations is a prerequisite for reasoning about differences.

Piaget's early research on the child from about 5 to 10 years investi-gated reasoning about differences, but not the perception of differences. He presented children with this verbal problem (among others): "Edith is fairer (or has fairer hair) than Suzanne; Edith is darker than Lili. Which is the darkest, Edith, Suzanne or Lili?" [7] The results showed that children from 5 to 10 years are unable to deal with problems of this sort, called transitivity, at a verbal level.

As in the case of classification, Piaget returned to the problem of rela-tions in his later work. Using the revised clinical method, he performed several interesting studies on *ordinal relations*, which we will now charac-terize briefly.

Some Properties of Ordinal Relations

Piaget's definition of ordinal relations involves several features. Sup-pose we have several numbers, such as, 17, 65, 25, 3, and 1,001. It is possible to arrange them in order of increasing size. We may use the symbol $<$ to stand for "is a smaller number than" and write $3 < 17 < 25 < 65 < 1,001$. The sequence is an ordering of the numbers with the smallest being first, the next smallest second, and so forth. Note that the absolute size of the numbers makes no difference. The second number does not have to be exactly one more than the first or exactly twice as big as the first. The last number, so long as it is larger than 65, may be of any size whatsoever. Also, we do not need to have zero as the beginning of the series. The only re-quirements for ordering the numbers are that they are different from one

7. *Judgment and Reasoning*, p. 87.

another; that one number is smaller than all the rest; that another is larger than all the rest; and that any number in between the smallest and the largest is both larger than the one immediately preceding it in the series, and smaller than the one immediately following it. Of course, orderings are not limited to numbers. We may also order sounds on the dimension of loudness. Suppose sound *a* is very soft, *b* is much louder than *a*, and *c* is slightly more loud than *b*. Then we have $a < b < c$, where $<$ means "is softer than." Again the precise degree of loudness does not affect the ordering.

Piaget's work deals with such matters as the child's ability to construct orderings or ordinal relations and to manipulate them in various ways. These studies, involving children from about 4 to 8 years of age, usually detect three distinct stages of development: stage 1 lasting from about 4 to 5; stage 2 from about 5 to 6; and stage 3 from about 7 and above. The first two stages are *pre-operational* and the last is *concrete operational*. While the age norms are approximate, the sequence is crucial.

Stage 1

One study was concerned with the ability to construct an ordering of a collection of ten sticks which differed only in size. We will call the shortest of the sticks (about 9 cm. in length) A, the next larger B, and so on through J, the largest (about 16 cm. in length). A differed from B by about .8 cm., and this also was true of B and C, etc. Piaget presented the child with the sticks in a randomly organized array and asked him to select the smallest of the lot. After this was done, Piaget gave an instruction like this: "Now try to put first the smallest, then one a little bit bigger, then another a little bit bigger, and so on." [8] In another study the child was asked to make a staircase from the sticks.

When confronted with this problem children in stage 1 showed several reactions, none of which was successful. Some children produced random arrangements of the sticks, like H, E, B, J, etc. Other children managed to order a few of the sticks, but not all of them. An example of this reaction is A, B, C, D, H, F, E, etc. A more advanced reaction also appeared which may be considered a transition to the next stage. The child started with some stick, like B, apparently selected at random; then took another stick, like H, and made the top of it extend slightly above the top of B. A third stick, for example A, was made to extend slightly beyond the top of B, and so forth. The result was that the tops of the sticks form an ordering; H is slightly higher than B, and A slightly higher than H, and so forth, as in Figure 5. But the bottoms of the sticks also differed in

8. *Child's Conception of Number,* pp. 124–25.

FIGURE 5

ORDERING OF STICKS

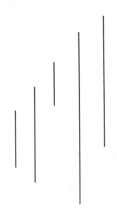

a random way, and failed to lie on a straight line as they should. Thus, the child constructs an ordering, but only by ignoring the length of each stick. This procedure frees him from the necessity of comparing each stick with the one immediately preceding it and with the one to follow. One way of characterizing the child's activities is to say that he focusses (centers) on one aspect of the problem (putting the tops in order) but ignores another, equally important aspect (arranging the bottoms in a straight line). To summarize, the child at this stage frequently cannot form a systematic ordering of any number of objects, although sometimes he can order a few of them.

Stage 2

Presented with the same problem, children in the second stage generally succeed in constructing the ordinal arrangement of sticks, so that $A < B < C < D < E < F < G < H < I < J$. But the child does not build the orderings without difficulty. Sometimes he begins by ignoring the bottoms of the sticks, as in stage 1. Sometimes he makes many errors, like $A < D < B$, etc., and takes a long time to recognize and correct them. He continually rearranges his ordering, and shifts the sticks from one position to another. Essentially the child's procedure is one of trial-and-error. He lacks an overall plan or guiding principle. For example, if he has chosen A as the smallest, he might then choose another small one, like D, and line it up next to A. Then he might choose another small one, like C, and place it next to D and see that it is smaller than D. Since this is so, he might rearrange the sticks placing C after A but before D. What the child fails to do after beginning with A, is to look for a stick that is longer than A but smaller than all the ones remaining. If this rule is followed, then each step of the ordering can be constructed without any difficulty. However, the child at this stage does not employ such a logical procedure. He fails to make systematic comparisons between a given stick and the one immediately preceding it and all those following.

This tendency was further revealed by the addition of one more problem. After constructing the ordering A through J, the children were given a new collection of ten sticks, $a, b, c, d, e, f, g, h, i, j$. Each of these new sticks could fit in between a pair of sticks of the first series. That is to say, if the new set of sticks were ordered correctly along with the first set, the arrangement would be: $A < a < B < b < C < c < D < d < E < e < F < f < G < g < H < h < I < i < J < j$. The child's task was to do precisely this; to fit the new sticks into the ordering already constructed (A through J), so as to make a new ordinal arrangement involving all 20 sticks.

Children of this stage had great difficulty with the problem. In fact, many failed to solve it. Part of one child's ordering was $C\ e\ d\ D$, and another produced $H\ g\ G\ I\ h\ j\ c$, and so forth. Other children succeeded in producing the correct ordering, but only after considerable trial-and-error.

These difficulties seem due to several factors. One factor appears to be that the child perceives the original series as a whole and finds it hard to break up the series into smaller units. Also, children of this stage do not approach the problem with a guiding principle. They fail to use a rule like, "Start with the smallest of a–j; insert it in between the pair of smallest sticks in A–J; then take the smallest of b–j and insert it between the smallest pair of sticks in B–J; and so forth." Not only did the children fail to use a rule like this, but they also had difficulty in deciding that a given element of a–j was at the same time bigger than one stick in A–J and smaller than the next larger stick in A–J. In order to place d properly, the child must see that $d < E$ and that $D < d$. He must *coordinate* these two relations, but he fails to do so consistently. That is, some children would take e and seeing that it was larger than B would place it right after B. They failed to consider whether e was at the same time smaller than C, and therefore made an error.

After investigating the child's ability to construct an ordering and place new elements in it, Piaget went on to study the child's ability to construct equivalences between two separate orderings (which involve equal numbers of elements). Let us take a class with 15 boys and 15 girls and order each of these groups in terms of height. We find the shortest boy, the next to shortest boy, etc., and we do the same for girls. We can see that the two orderings are equivalent in some ways and different in others. Some differences are that the height of the shortest boy may be 48 inches, whereas the height of the shortest girl is 44 inches. Also, the second shortest boy may be four inches taller than the shortest one, whereas the second shortest girl is only one inch taller than the shortest girl. Despite these real differences, there are important similarities between the two orderings. The boy who is 48 inches tall and the girl who is 44 inches tall, despite their difference in height, are equivalent in terms of their position in the ordering. They are both the shortest. The same holds true, of course, for the tallest boy and girl, the next to tallest, and so forth.

Piaget then raises the issue of whether the young child can recognize the equivalences between two distinct orderings. Does he understand that two objects, while differing in height, for example, can at the same time be equivalent in terms of their relative position in an ordering? To study the matter he first presented children with ten dolls, A–J, which were presented in a random display, and which could be arranged in order of height; and with ten sticks, A'–J', also randomly arranged, which could be ordered in size. The sticks were smaller than the dolls, and the differences between adjacent pairs of sticks were smaller than between pairs of dolls. The child was told that the dolls are going for a walk, and that each of them must have the proper stick. The intention of the instructions, of course, was to get the child to produce an ordering of the dolls and of the sticks, and to make each member of one ordering correspond to the appropriate member of the other ordering. Thus, doll A should have stick A', doll B should have stick B', and so on. Piaget calls this process the placing of orderings into one-to-one correspondence.

The results showed that children of this stage can produce a one-to-one correspondence of dolls and sticks, but only in a trial-and-error fashion. The most common procedure is to order the dolls (by trial-and-error) and then to order the sticks (by trial-and-error). Only after two separate orderings have been constructed are the elements of each put into one-to-one correspondence. That is, the child first identifies the largest doll, the next to largest doll, and completes the ordering of dolls; then he goes on to order the sticks. It is only after this is done that the child places the largest stick with the largest doll, the next to largest stick with the next to largest doll, and so forth. While this procedure works, it is somewhat cumbersome. An easier method is to begin by identifying the largest (or smallest) doll and the largest (or smallest) stick and immediately placing the two together. The second step is to choose the largest doll and stick of all those remaining and to place them together, and so forth. In any event, the child in this stage does succeed in setting the two orders into one-to-one correspondence. He seems to have established that the orderings are equivalent.

The next problem concerns the stability of the equivalence estab-

FIGURE 6

THE EQUIVALENCE OF
RELATIVE POSITION
(DOLLS AND STICKS)

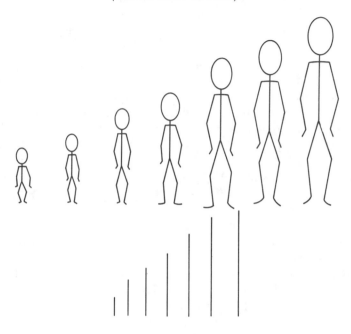

lished by one-to-one correspondence. Let us suppose that the sticks are placed very close together with their order preserved (as in Figure 6). The shortest stick is closest to the third tallest doll; the second stick is closest to the fourth tallest doll, and so forth. Does the child recognize that the second tallest stick is *still* equivalent to the second tallest doll, even though the former is now closest to the fourth tallest doll? That is does the child *conserve* the equivalence of relative position when the overt one-to-one correspondence is destroyed?

Piaget presented this and similar problems to a number of children. He placed the sticks close together and asked which stick "goes with" which doll. Piaget discovered several methods of attacking the problem. The most primitive reaction is to assert that a doll is equivalent to the stick closest to it. Thus, the second largest stick and fourth largest doll are considered to belong together simply because one is below the other.

The child's judgment is dominated by *spatial* relations. Other children try to solve the problem by counting, but they fail to do so properly. For example, one child said that the fourth largest stick was equivalent to the third largest doll. The reason for his mistake was that he noticed that there were three sticks preceding the fourth largest stick; he then counted out three dolls, stopped there, and identified the third doll with the fourth stick. This method is quite frequent among children of this stage; that is, they find a doll corresponding to the nth stick, count the preceding $n - 1$ sticks, then count the dolls, stopping at the $n - 1$th element. The child confuses the position to be found (say stick 4) with the number of preceding elements (3).

Stage 3

After about the age of 6–7 years, the child is successful in all of the tasks we have described. If he is asked to construct a single ordering of sticks differing in size, he does so quite easily. His ordering is guided by an overall plan. He usually begins with the smallest (or sometimes, with the largest), then the next to smallest, and so forth, in sequence until the ordering is complete. His strategy may be characterized as starting with the smallest and continuing to take the smallest of everything that is left, until the sticks have been exhausted. When asked to place additional sticks $(a-j)$ in their proper positions within the ordering $(A-J)$ already constructed, the child does so with almost no errors. The process underlying his achievement is the comparison of one of the new sticks (say d) with two in the original ordering simultaneously. That is, in order to ascertain d's proper position, he determines that it is at the same time bigger than D but smaller than E. To phrase the matter differently, he coordinates two inverse relations—bigger and smaller than.

In a similar way the concrete operational child easily places two separate orderings into one-to-one correspondence. One child immediately put the biggest doll with the biggest ball (balls were sometimes used in place of sticks), the next to biggest doll with the next to biggest ball, and so forth. His strategy was to identify the biggest doll and ball of all those remaining and to place the two together at once. This procedure is more economical than that of the younger child who first orders the dolls, then the balls, and finally begins to put them together. When this one-to-one correspondence is destroyed, the child conserves the equivalence of relative position. He realizes that the smallest doll is still equivalent to the smallest ball and not to the ball to which it happens to be closest in space. In summarizing the material on the concrete operational child, then, we can state that he is adept at understanding and manipulating ordinal relations. However, as in the case of classification, one limitation applies: he can deal with relations on a concrete level only; that is, when objects are present. Nevertheless, his thought is far more advanced than that of the child in stages 1 and 2. He can construct orderings, put two such orderings into one-to-one correspondence, and conserve the resulting equivalences. As in the case of classification, the processes underlying the child's ability to manipulate relations form integrated and comprehensive structures. Each of his mental operations cannot be understood without reference to the others of which he is capable. These processes must be interpreted in terms of complex *systems* of operations. To describe these systems, Piaget has developed several logico-mathematical models, similar to Grouping I (although they of course deal with relations, not classes). Also, he has investigated several other aspects of ordinal relations, such as *transitivity* (if $a > b$ and $b > c$, then $a > c$), which we will not cover here.

NUMBER

The ability to understand classes and relations, according to Piaget, is basic to mature concepts in many areas. The several Groupings which describe the processes underlying the older child's performance in problems of classes and relations, may also be used to characterize his concepts of space, chance, geometry, and so forth. Since we cannot review all of these concepts, we will concentrate on one that is particularly interesting and that has received considerable attention in the American and English research literature; namely, the concept of (whole) number.

First, we must be clear on what Piaget does and does not mean by the concept of number. He does *not* mean and is *not* interested in computational abilities as taught in the first few grades of school. Whether the child can add 2 and 2, or subtract 3 from 5 is not the issue. The reason for Piaget's lack of interest in these matters is that simple addition and subtraction of whole numbers, as well as other manipulations of them, can be carried out entirely by rote and without understanding. The child can simply memorize the addition and subtraction tables and fail to comprehend the basic concepts underlying them. Piaget does not deny that it is necessary to memorize the facts of addition and subtraction; for purposes of computation, we all must do so. He asserts, however, that for mature understanding of number, such rote memorization is not sufficient and must be accompanied by the mastery of certain basic ideas.

Among these ideas are one-to-one correspondence and conservation. Let us first consider one-to-one correspondence. Suppose we are presented with a collection or set of discrete objects as in Figure 7. The size of the objects, their color, and so forth, are completely irrelevant. All that is required is that the set contain a finite number of discrete objects. We

FIGURE 7

COLLECTION OF OBJECTS

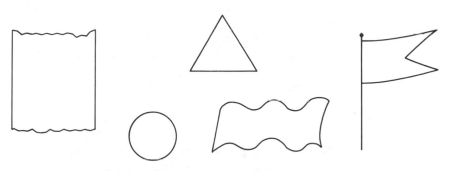

are then given a box of objects and are required to construct from it another set which has the same number property as the first set. It does not matter whether the objects in the second set (which we will call set B) are the same color, size, and so on as those in the first set (set A). Whether set A contains elephants and set B contains geraniums is irrelevant. The only requirement is that they have the same number. One way of constructing a set B so that it will have the same number property as A is by counting the objects in A (say there are seven) and then take out of the box the same number of objects. This procedure, which of course is quite adequate, probably occurs first to adults. But suppose we cannot count. Suppose we do not know the number of objects in set A. Even with these limitations there is a simple way of constructing a new set, B, which will have the same number property as A. This method merely involves putting next to each member of set A one, and only one, new object. These new objects, after the one-to-one correspondence has been established, form a set, B, with the same number as A. Of course we do not really have to physically place each new object next to one in A; we can note the one-to-one correspondence mentally. That is, we can "say to ourselves": "This new object corresponds to the first in the line of set A; etc." The important idea is not the physical placing together of the sets, but the pairing of one member in set A with one in set B, however this is done.

Although very simple, the idea of one-to-one correspondence is basic and powerful, and may be used in a variety of situations. If we want to determine whether there are the same number of seats as people in an auditorium, all we have to do is ask everyone to sit down. If all the people are in seats (in one-to-one correspondence with the seats) and if none of the seats is empty, then the numbers (whatever they may be) of people and seats are equal. If there are people standing, then this defines the relation of more people than seats. If there are empty seats, then this defines the relation of more seats than people. In brief, one-to-one correspondence establishes that any two sets—regardless of the nature of the objects comprising them—are equivalent in number. Counting or other procedures are not needed. Lack of one-to-one correspondence establishes that one set is larger than the other (and one smaller than the other).

The second basic idea which Piaget investigates is *conservation*. Suppose that we have established that sets A and B are equal in number, as in Figure 8A. That is, we have put set A in a line, and below each member of set A we have put a new object. The line of the new objects is set B. Suppose that we then compress the members of set B, as in Figure 8B, so that the perceptual one-to-one correspondence is destroyed. Now each member of set B is not directly below a different member of set A. The problem is whether the two sets which now differ in physical arrangement still are equal in number. In other words, is the equivalence established in Figure 8A conserved when the rearrangement shown in Figure 8B is performed? To adults, this may seem like a foolish question. Of course, the equality of numbers has not changed! But the problem is whether children accept this simple and basic idea too. If they do not, then their world of number must be very chaotic indeed. If number is seen to change whenever mere physical arrangement is altered, then the child fails to appreciate certain basic constancies or invariances in his environment.

Piaget has conducted a number of investigations on the child's understanding of these two basic ideas; that is, one-to-one correspondence, and conservation of the equivalence of two numbers. He finds that young

FIGURE 8

CONSERVATION OF NUMBER

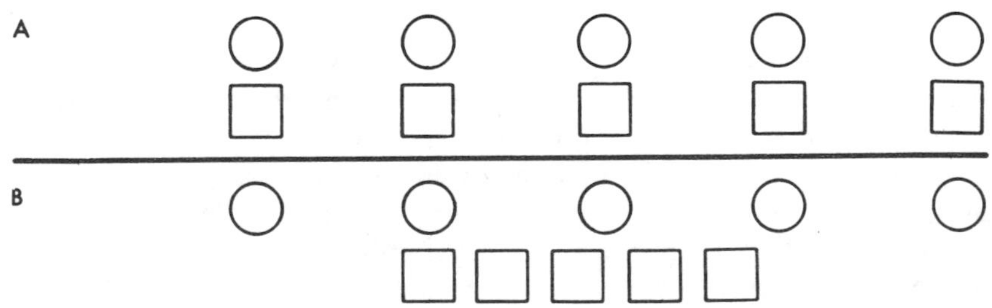

children fail to understand these two notions, and that a period of development is required before the child achieves the mental operations necessary for thorough comprehension of number. Let us now review the experiments.

Stage 1

In order to study the ability to construct sets of equivalent number, Piaget presented children with a variety of problems. The simplest of these involved placing before the child a row of six or seven pennies or buttons or sweets, etc. The examiner then asked the child to pick out the "same number" or "as many" from a large collection of similar objects. Thus the child was given set A and was required to construct a second set, B, which was equivalent in number. The children were, of course, not told how to construct set B. Here is a protocol describing how a stage 1 child, 4 years and 7 months of age, dealt with the problem. Piaget had placed six sweets in a row and told the child that they belonged to his friend Roger:

"Put as many sweets here as there are there. Those . . . are for Roger. You are to take as many as he has." (He made a compact row of about ten, which was shorter than the model.)—*"Are they the same?"*— "Not yet" (adding some).—*"And now?"*—"Yes."—*"Why?"*—"Because they're like that" (indicating the length).[9]

The example makes clear the predominant tendency of this stage. The child does not use the method of one-to-one correspondence. Instead, he thinks that the two sets are equivalent in number if they have the same lengths. In Piaget's terms, the child *centers* on one dimension—the length —of set A (Roger's sweets or the model) and bases his construction of set B solely in terms of that one dimension. The result is pictured in Figure 9. The lengths of the two rows are equal, but their numbers are not. The new row is denser, that is, there are smaller spaces between the sweets, than Roger's row, but the child ignores this fact and concentrates only on the lengths. Since he fails to *coordinate* the two dimensions of length and density at the same time, he cannot construct sets equivalent in number except when very small numbers are involved, or except by accident.

In another investigation, Piaget tried to make the child understand the principle of one-to-one correspondence, and then performed the conservation experiment. In this study, set A was a row of ten vases and set B consisted of flowers. One child, 4 years and 4 months of age,

9. *Ibid.*, p. 75.

FIGURE 9

FAILURE TO
CONSTRUCT EQUAL SETS

put 13 flowers close together in a row opposite 10 vases rather more spaced out, although he had counted the vases from 1 to 10. Since the rows were the same length, he thought that the flowers and vases were "the same." "Then you can put the flowers into the vases?"—"Yes." He did so, and found he had 3 flowers [left] over.[10]

The child, then, initially constructed set B so as to make it the same length as set A and thought that the two sets were therefore equal in number. The examiner then made the child construct a one-to-one correspondence between the flowers and vases; that is, the child put each flower in a vase. The result was ten flowers in ten vases (or two sets equivalent in number), and the three extra flowers were discarded. The question now is whether the child realizes that the two sets are really equivalent in number. Does the child *conserve* the equivalence despite a mere physical rearrangement of the objects? To find out, Piaget continued the experiment with the same child.

The flowers were taken out and bunched together in front of the vases. [That is, they formed a shorter row than did the vases.] "Is there the same number of vases and flowers?"—"No."—"Where are there more?"—"There are more vases"—"If we put the flowers back into the vases, will there be one flower in each vase?"—"Yes."—"Why?"—"Because there are enough." (The vases were closed up and the flowers spaced out.)—"And now?"—"There are more flowers."[11]

Note that after the child had himself established a one-to-one correspondence between the flowers and vases, he failed to conserve the numerical equivalence of the two sets. When the flowers were put into a shorter row than the vases, the child believed that the numbers were no longer equal and that now there were more vases. He maintained this even though he realized that the one-to-one correspondence could be reestablished; that is, that the flowers could be returned to the vases.

10. *Ibid.*, p. 50.
11. *Ibid.*, p. 50.

Then when the row of vases was made shorter than that of the flowers, he changed his mind once again. He asserted that now there were more flowers. Clearly, this child centered on the lengths of the rows and used only this information to make judgments of equivalence or lack of equivalence of number. When the rows were the same length (as when the flowers were in the vases), he said that they were equal in number. When the rows differed in length, he believed that the longer line had the greater number.

Piaget also investigated the role of counting. The question is how counting the two sets affects the child's judgment. One child, 5 years and 3 months of age, failed the conservation problem. He said that set A (six glasses) was greater than set B (six bottles) because one was longer than the other. Then the examiner said:

*"Can you count?"—"Yes."—"How many glasses are there?"—"Six."
—"And how many bottles?"—"Six."—"So there's the same number of glasses and bottles?"—"There are more where it's bigger [that is, longer]."* [12]

This examination shows that while the child can count, the act is meaningless. Although he can recite a string of numbers, he does not comprehend what they signify. The fact that he counted six bottles and also six glasses does not imply to him that the sets are equal in number. For him, equality of number is determined solely by equality of lengths, and counting is an extraneous and irrelevant act, which does not assure either the equivalence of sets or its conservation.

Stage 2

The child of this stage easily constructs two sets equivalent in number, but fails to conserve the equivalence when the sets are rearranged. Per, a child of 5 years, 7 months

*had no difficulty in making a row of 6 sweets corresponding to the model. [Piaget uses "model" to refer to set A, the row to be copied, and "copy" to refer to set B.] The model was then closed up: "I've got more."
—"Why?"—"Because it's a longer line. (The process was reversed)—Now there are more there, because it's a big line." But a moment later, Per said the opposite: "Are there more here [referring to the longer row]?"—"No."
—"Why not?"—"Because it's long."—"And there [the shorter row]?"—
"There are more there, because there's a little bundle [The child meant that the shorter row was denser].—"Then are there more in a little bundle than in a big line?"—"Yes." After this Per went back to using length as*

12. *Ibid.*, p. 45.

the criterion, made the two rows the same length again and said: "Now they're both the same." [13]

The protocol shows that the child of this stage easily constructs a set equal in number to another. He also establishes the equivalence by the method of one-to-one correspondence. That is, in order to construct set B he places a new sweet just below each in set A. But the one-to-one correspondence is not fully understood; it is just "perceptual." When set B is made shorter than set A, the child fails to conserve the equivalence which he so easily constructed. The protocol also shows that the child is ambivalent about the criteria used to establish equality or inequality of number. Sometimes he maintains that the longer row has more because it is longer; at other times he believes that the shorter row has more because it is denser. In Piaget's terms the child sometimes *centers* on the lengths (ignoring densities) and sometimes centers on the densities (ignoring lengths). This tendency is an improvement over what occurs in the previous stage, since the younger child (in stage 1) consistently centers on only one of the two dimensions, usually length, and does not consider the other, usually density, at all. By contrast, the child in stage 2 has widened the sphere of his centrations. He notices, albeit at different times, that both dimensions may be relevant. He uses the information from either of these dimensions separately to make his judgment. This use of partial information is called *regulations*. We will see next how the child in the period of concrete operations *coordinates* the two dimensions.

Stage 3

The results of this stage are easy to describe. The child can now construct a set numerically equivalent to another set, and can conserve their equivalence despite changes in physical arrangement. Here is a protocol illustrating this stage:

"Take the same number of pennies as there are there [there were 6 in set A]." He made a row of 6 under the model, but put his much closer together so that there was no spatial correspondence between the rows. Both ends of the model extended beyond those of the copy. "Have you got the same number?"—"Yes."—"Are you and that boy [referring to the hypothetical owner of set A] just as rich as one another?"—"Yes."— (The pennies of the model were then closed up and his own were spaced out.)—"And now?"—"The same."—"Exactly?"—"Yes."—"Why are they the same?"—"Because you've put them closer together." [14]

This protocol contains several interesting features. One feature is that in making set B equal to set A, the concrete operational child does

13. *Ibid.*, p. 79.
14. *Ibid.*, p. 82.

not bother to place each element in B directly under each element in A. He does not need to rely on the perception of spatial proximity between the elements of each set. How then does he construct numerically equivalent sets? One method, of course, is simply to count the number of objects in set A, and then merely count out the same number for set B. Probably some children used this method, but Piaget concluded from his clinical examinations that other children did not use counting. They seemed to use the method of one-to-one correspondence, but in a more sophisticated way than the younger child. The concrete operational child's technique may be described as follows: to construct set B equal to set A, he puts out one penny for the first penny in set A, and so forth. It does not matter *where* he puts the members of set B. The only crucial requirement is that he match each member in set A with one and only one member in set B (a non-spatial one-to-one correspondence). He must not forget to put out a penny for each member of set A (that is, he cannot skip any member of set A), and must not put out more than one penny for each member of set A (that is, he must not count any member of set A twice).

The process of establishing sets equal in number may be described in terms of classes and relations. As far as relations are concerned, the child uses the method of *vicariant ordering*. Suppose set A (the model) is a line of pennies, and the child must construct a set B (the copy) from a large supply of candies. He begins by pointing at the penny on the extreme left and puts out a sweet. Then he points to the second penny from the left, puts out a sweet for it, and continues until he has exhausted the line of pennies. This process of pointing to one penny at a time, being careful to count each penny once and only once, is an ordering. It is equivalent to saying: "This penny comes first, this one second, this one third. . . ." and so forth. In a way, the ordering of pennies is like arranging a series of sticks or dolls in order of height. There is a first stick, a second stick, and so forth, just as there is a first penny and a second one.

Therefore, something like the ability to construct ordinal relations underlies the child's construction of sets equivalent in number. Despite the evident similarity, the two processes—constructing ordinal relations (as in ordering the sticks) and vicariant ordering (the pennies)—are not identical. In the case of the sticks, there is one and only one shortest stick which must come first in the series, one and only one second shortest stick which must come second in the series, and so forth. In the case of the pennies, it does not matter which penny is considered first in the series, which comes second, etc. One could start counting at the extreme left, at the extreme right, in the middle or wherever one pleased, just so long as one is careful not to omit pointing to each of the pennies and not to point to any of them more than once. The ordering of pennies is called "vicariant" for this very reason: the order in which the pennies are counted does not matter.

Other aspects of relations are involved too. When the child puts out one and only one sweet for each penny, he is *coordinating* two orderings. This is similar to the problem of dolls and sticks. Just as the child can give to the shortest doll the shortest stick, to the second shortest doll the second shortest stick, and so forth, so can he place the first sweet with the first penny, the second sweet with the second penny, and so forth. Of course, the one-to-one correspondence of pennies and sweets is vicariant, whereas the one-to-one correspondence of dolls and sticks is not. In the latter instance, there is one and only one stick (the shortest) which goes with the shortest doll, and so forth. In the case of pennies and sweets, it does not matter which sweet is placed into correspondence with any penny, so long as one and only one sweet is used for each penny.

The construction of equivalent sets also involves *classification*. To the child, the pennies in set A, for instance, are in some ways all the same and in some ways different from one another. They are different in that a certain penny is counted first, another one second, and so forth. They are the same in that it does not matter which is counted first, which second, and so forth. In other words, it is only the child's act of pointing to each in turn that differentiates the pennies; otherwise, they are all equivalent. Insofar as each of the pennies is an element equivalent to all the rest, they are all members of the same class. The same is true, of course, of the sweets in set B.

Thus far we have seen how the child's ability to construct sets equivalent in number may be analyzed into a number of component skills. Underlying the child's overt performance (e.g., placing on a table seven sweets corresponding to seven pennies) are a number of *concrete operations*: vicariant ordering, one-to-one correspondence of two vicariant orderings, and classification. Some of the operations involve classes and others relations. Thus, number is a union of classes and relations. The operations are *concrete* since the child can apply them only to objects which are immediately present. They are *operations* since they are actions which the child performs mentally and which have the added property of being reversible. This means that for each particular mental action, for instance addition, the child can perform its opposite action, in this case subtraction, which leaves him where he started. As operations, they may also be described in terms of overall structures or systems, that is, in terms of the Groupings, an example of which we have given in the case of classification.[15]

15. Strictly speaking, in the case of number Piaget uses a somewhat different logico-mathematical model, called the *Group*. The essential difference between the Groupings and the Group is that the fifth Grouping operation, tautology (e.g., $A + A = A$), is not used in the Group. Tautology does not apply to number since there $A + A = 2A$, not A. Therefore, the Group must be used for number.

In the stage of concrete operations, the child can also conserve number. After he has constructed two sets equivalent in number, the child recognizes that the sets remain equivalent despite mere physical rearrangement of the sets. If the seven sweets are compressed to make a short line while the line of seven pennies remains the same the two sets are nevertheless still equal in number. The equivalence has been conserved.

What enables the concrete operational child to conserve while the preoperational (stages 1 and 2) child fails to do so? Recall the mechanism underlying the preoperational child's failure: centration. The younger child centers on only a limited amount of the information available. When the row of sweets is compressed, he notices only that the line of pennies is now longer than the line of sweets. He ignores the fact that the line of sweets is denser (has smaller spaces between adjacent elements), and bases his judgment only on the lengths. The preoperational child knows that *empirical reversibility* is possible: he realizes that if the sweets were returned to their original positions, there would be one sweet for each penny. This knowledge does not help, however; despite it, he feels that the number of a set changes when its appearance is altered. Perceptual factors have too strong a hold on him at this stage. They are not yet sufficiently controlled by mental actions which can compensate for apparent discrepancies in visually perceived information.

By contrast, the concrete operational child decenters his attention. He attends to both of the relevant dimensions and uses this information in several ways. (a) He notices that the line of pennies has become longer than the line of sweets *and* that the line of sweets has become denser than the line of pennies. Moreover, he coordinates the two dimensions. He mentally manipulates the visual data available to him. This mental activity leads him to realize that while the length of the line of pennies increases (relative to the sweets) by a certain amount, the density of the line of sweets increases by an equivalent amount. In other words, the child conceives that the pennies' increase in length is balanced by, or compensated for, by the sweets' increase in density: there is a relation of *reciprocity* or *compensation* between length and density. In effect, one increase cancels out the other with the result that the sets remain equivalent in number. This reciprocity is one form of *reversibility*. Since the increase in length counteracts the increase in density, the result is a return, or a reversal, to the original situation, which is equal number.

(b) The concrete operational child also comes to use the operation of *negation*. We have already seen that when the row of sweets is compressed, the concrete operational child realizes that the sweets' increase in density is reciprocated by the pennies' increase in length, and that, as a result of these reciprocal transformations, the number of the two sets remains equivalent. The concrete operational child is also able to imagine that these changes can be annulled or *negated*. He reasons that the action of contracting the sweets can be negated by the inverse action of spreading them out. The one action is annulled by the other. Such annullment or negation is another form of reversibility; that is, the child mentally reverses the action of contracting the row of sweets. As a result he attributes equal numbers to the two sets. Note that the stage 3 child both reverses the act of contracting and recognizes that the final result is the original arrangement of sweets and pennies. The stage 2 child, who is capable of *empirical reversibility*, recognizes that the sweets can be returned to their original position but does not focus on or reverse the act of rearrangement. He attends to states, not transformations.

(c) The concrete operational child sometimes uses an *identity* argument. He reasons that the numbers must be the same since the same objects are involved: nothing has been added or taken away.

To summarize, the stage 3 child, having entered the period of concrete operations, can construct two sets equivalent in number, and can conserve this equivalence despite changes in appearance. Underlying these achievements are a number of thought processes. The ability to construct equivalent sets requires *vicariant ordering* and *classification*. The ability to conserve, which is acquired as a result of the decentration of the child's attention, is supported by three types of operation which are sometimes explicitly expressed in the child's justification of his response: *reciprocity*, *negation*, and *identity*. These are aspects of *concrete* operations, which may be described by the *Groupings*. The child does not perform all of the thought processes each time he is presented with a problem of constructing equal sets, nor does he refer to all three arguments when asked for a justification of conservation. He might only refer to one or perhaps two of them. He is, however, *capable* of performing all the concrete operations, although he may not always do so. In fact, after a period of time the concrete operational child takes conservation for granted. He immediately recognizes that number is conserved and does not need to prove conservation to himself by means of negation or reciprocity. When asked why number is conserved, he thinks that the question is silly and that the fact of conservation is self-evident. Conservation has become a matter of logical necessity for him, which is evidence that he has acquired an underlying structure of mental operations with each one interdependent upon the other and none of which is performed in isolation.

MENTAL IMAGERY

Piaget conceptualizes cognition in terms of two major aspects: the *operative* and the *figurative*. The more dynamic aspect, the operative, refers to *actions* whose result is some transformation or change of reality. These actions may be either overt or internal. Examples of overt actions abound in the sensorimotor period. The infant kicks to shake a rattle, or uses a stick to draw an object close. The present chapter has covered two major subdivisions of internalized actions: the isolated and unrelated actions of preoperational thought, and the structured and coordinated ones of concrete operational thought.

By contrast, the figurative aspect refers to actions by which the child produces a "copy" of reality, and in this instance cognition concentrates on the states of reality rather than its transformations. Piaget makes three subdivisions among the figurative aspects of cognition. One is perception, which is a system which functions by means of the senses and requires an immediately present object. It is through perception that the child achieves a copy of the things that are around him. This copy is often inexact, as in the case of the visual illusions. A second subdivision is imitation, by which the child reproduces the actions of persons or things. It is true that imitation involves action on the part of the child; but these actions nevertheless fall under the figurative aspect since they produce a copy of reality. A third portion of the figurative aspect, and the one on which we will concentrate here, is mental imagery. As we saw in Chapter Three, mental imagery refers to personal and idiosyncratic internal events which stand for or represent absent objects or events. When we "picture" to ourselves our first bicycle, or the stroll we took last week, then we are using mental imagery.

History

Mental imagery was one of the first topics studied by experimental psychologists. At the end of the 19th century the school of Wundt used the introspective method to analyze the nature of mental imagery. The Wundtians believed that images were composed of a bundle of sensations tied together by means of association. At the beginning of the 20th century the study of imagery fell into disrepute for two reasons. One, the Wurzburg psychologists found that much of thought did not seem to involve imagery at all, and two, the behaviorist revolution which occurred in the United States maintained that the introspective method was a poor one. The behaviorists felt that the data of introspection—one's impressions of one's own consciousness—were not public enough. How could another psychologist determine if an introspection were reliable and accurate? As a result of the behaviorist attack on the method of introspection, the study of imagery was considered "unscientific" and was largely abandoned. Recently, however, psychologists have shown a renewed interest in the ancient problem of imagery. A number of investigators have used physiological techniques, for example, to study images occurring during sleep; that is, the dream.

Piaget, however, in contrast to modern investigators, has been studying imagery since at least the 1930's. In Chapter Three we discussed Piaget's work on imagery in the young child up to the age of 4 years. If you will recall, this theory proposed that mental images do not occur until about the middle of the second year. Before this time the child did not possess mental representations of his environment, and, as a result, reacted mainly to events occurring in the present. After imagery makes its appearance the child can represent to himself both events that occurred in the past and objects that are no longer perceptually present. If you will recall too, we discovered that, according to Piaget's theory, imagery results from imitation. At first the child overtly imitates the actions of things or people; later, his imitation becomes internalized and abbreviated. It is through this internal activity that images arise. Clearly, Piaget's views contrast strongly with Wundt's. Images are not merely bundles of sensations which are connected by association; rather, the construction of images involves the activity of internalized imitation.

In the 1950's Piaget returned to the study of imagery. His later work deals with children above the age of 4, and poses a number of interesting questions. For example, are there different types of images at different stages of intellectual development? Are the images of the pre-operational stages different from those occurring at the concrete operational stage? If so, what is the relation between the images and the mental operations of a given stage?

Method

While these questions are interesting, the study of mental images is very difficult, especially in the case of children. Images are personal, idiosyncratic events which cannot be viewed directly. One cannot "see" another person's imagery; the investigator must, therefore, infer their existence and nature from other phenomena, such as a verbal report. Piaget has used a variety of methods to study imagery. One of these methods is to ask a person to describe his own images. But language is not fully adequate for this task, or even for describing something as concrete as the immediate perception of an object. We are never able to convey by words the precise nature of what we see. In our attempt to describe percepts, we inevitably emphasize certain features and neglect others. We have difficulty in describing shades of colors, or gradations of textures. We cannot give an impression of the entire percept at once, but must describe its details in sequence, and thereby often lose the essence of the whole. If language so poorly conveys perceptual events which continue to remain before our eyes for further inspection, how much more difficult is it to describe mental images which are fleeting and unstable?

Another method of studying mental images is by drawing. Here the person is asked to draw an object previously presented. Since the object is no longer present, he must produce an image of it to yield the drawing. The drawing, therefore, gives some insight into the nature of the image, which is the internal "picture" of the object. The method of drawing, however, presents several shortcomings. Drawing is not a simple and direct reflection of images, and also it involves other processes. Some persons have poor memory. If they have forgotten their image of an object, they cannot very well draw it. Other persons simply cannot draw well. It is not their image that is at fault, but their artistic skill.

A third method attempts to bypass the shortcomings of original drawings. The subject is given a collection of drawings made by the experimenter, and must select from them the one most closely corresponding to his image of what he had previously observed. This method, of course, is not affected by variations in subjects' artistic abilities and reduces the difficulties created by a poor evocative memory. But even the method of selection from a collection of drawings is not altogether satisfactory. One problem is that the drawings presented are not likely to be exact copies of the person's mental image. The drawings may omit details of the original image or add some. In either event, the subject's choice does not give a fully accurate indication of his image.

To study imagery, Piaget has used all of these methods—verbal report, drawing, and selection of drawings—either alone or in combination. As is customary with the explorations carried out by the Geneva school, the methods were supplemented by verbal questioning carried out in the clinical manner.

Major Findings

One experiment was concerned with *kinetic images*, or the imagery of an object's movement. Children from about 4 to 8 years of age were presented with two identical blocks, one on top of the other (see Figure 10a). Each subject was asked to draw the situation, and generally did this quite well. Then the top block was moved so that it slightly overlapped the bottom one, as in Figure 10b. After the child had had a chance to look at this for a while, the top block was returned to its original position (Figure 10a). The child was then asked to draw the block in its displaced position (Figure 10b), which was, of course, no longer visible. After this, a collection of drawings was presented. This

FIGURE 10

MOVEMENT OF BLOCKS

contained a correct rendering of Figure 10b as well as an assortment of incorrect drawings which represented errors typically made by children of this age. The child was asked to select the drawing which he felt corresponded most closely to what he had seen. In the final step another control was added. The top block was once again displaced, and the child was asked to draw the situation while it was present. If he could accurately draw the blocks when present, then any of his previous errors of drawing (when the blocks were absent) must be due to faulty imagery or memory and not to faulty drawing ability.

To summarize, the child first drew the displaced blocks after they were no longer visible; then he selected from a group of drawings one resembling the displaced blocks; and finally, when the displaced blocks were once again before him, he drew them.

The findings show that before the age of 7 years, children can draw the displaced blocks quite correctly when they are present, but not when they are absent; nor can the children choose a drawing which corresponds to the situation. In general, children of about 4 and 5 years produced and selected drawings of the types A through D (see Figure 11), whereas children of 6 years made errors like those of types F and G. It was only at 7 years that over 75 per cent of the subjects both drew and chose the correct drawings.

FIGURE 11

DRAWING OF BLOCKS

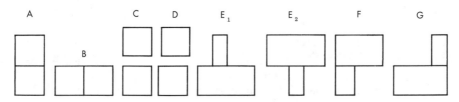

The responses of the younger child would seem to indicate that he forms only a very general picture of the situation; that is, that one block has been moved. When asked to draw the exact details, he is unable to do so. He therefore reproduces this general impression of movement by detaching the top block from the bottom (cf. C and D), by a symetrical movement of shrinking or enlargement of one of the two blocks (cf. E_1 and E_2) or, finally, by the retention of one common boundary or identical line for the two blocks, in addition to making certain changes of the other side of the blocks (cf. F and G). His image does not appear to correspond to the actual situation. The child seems to center on one dimension, that is, on one particular aspect of the situation; for example, the overlapping of the top block in Figures E_2 and F, or the overlapping of the bottom block in Figures E_1 and G, but he does not coordinate the movement of one block with the final state of the two blocks. Apparently the child does not analyze the situation in sufficient detail; he merely forms a global impression of what has happened. He is aware that the block has moved, but the intimate details of the movement and the ensuing displacement seem to have escaped his attention. As a result, his mental image is inadequate.

Another study concerned *transformational* imagery. In this case, the child views an object which actually changes shape or form rather than position, as in kinetic imagery. The experimenter first presented subjects with a piece of wire in the form of a semi-circle and then transformed the wire into a straight line. The child was asked to draw this sequence: the initial state, the intervening forms, and the final result. Other methods of testing—selection of drawings, verbal description, and so forth—were also used. Figure 12 illustrates some typical drawings of the younger children. One major finding was that the child below 8 or 9 years strongly underestimates the length of the straight wire. That is, the child judges the final state of the transformation to be shorter than the initial state. Piaget interprets this result in terms of *boundaries*. The child has established his

FIGURE 12

DRAWING OF WIRES

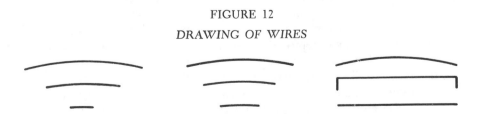

imaginary vertical boundaries, or vertical lines, from both ends of the wire and feels that the straight line should not cross those boundaries. He therefore draws the straight lines so as to remain within the boundary, and this results in incorrect drawings since a semi-circle straightened out covers a longer horizontal distance. The findings show that although the child frequently draws the straight line shorter, only on very rare occasions does he draw it longer than the semi-circle. Another major finding was that the young child has great difficulty in imagining the intermediary stages of the transformations; that is, what happens in between the initial and final states. Thus, the preoperational child's imagery is deficient in two ways: he not only fails to imagine the final state accurately, but, at the same time, he is unable to give a correct rendering of the transformations which have occurred during the change of wire from semi-circle to straight line.

Piaget gives two reasons for these errors. In the first place, the young child is unable to *conserve* the length of the wire. We have discussed earlier the preoperational child's inability to conserve number. In this instance it is length that he fails to conserve. This means that for him a change in shape automatically entails an ensuing change in length. Second, the young child does not consider the transformations from the one state to the other as being a continuous sequence of changes. He seems instead to consider each intermediary step as a discrete one which bears little or no relationship to the one prior to it or to the one following it. Therefore, we can conclude that the preoperational child does not have an adequate representation of the sequence of events. Only when he becomes capable of conserving length and is able to decenter from the states to the transformations will he be able to visualize the whole process of transformation from semi-circle to straight wire in its entirety and, consequently, produce a correct image of the situation.

A third type of imagery is *static* imagery. In this instance the image reproduces a collection of objects, a scene, or a picture; in brief, any event or object where the elements remain unchanged in either shape or position. Piaget finds that the child is able to produce adequate static imagery earlier than the kinetic or transformational varieties.

Piaget makes a further distinction concerning imagery. Some images are *reproductory*. They reproduce something that the person has already seen; that is, they attempt to copy a model which has already been presented perceptually. *Anticipatory* images, on the other hand, involve the anticipation of future events, or of changes in form or location. In this situation the child sees an object and is asked to predict what it would look like after some change in form or position. Kinetic and transformational images may be reproductory or anticipatory. That is, we can either reproduce or anticipate a movement or a transformation. But static images can be only reproductory. It is not useful to talk of anticipating the future condition of an event which never changes.

We have seen only a small sampling of Piaget's experiments on imagery. Their results, together with those of a great many more studies, have led Piaget to draw the following general conclusions concerning imagery and its relation to intelligence as a whole. First, imagery develops over time. The 2-year-old does not possess the same type of images as the 10-year-old. The evolution of imagery, however, is not as dramatic as that of the cognitive operations which display a clearcut sequence of stages. There appears to be only one major turning point in the development of images. This seems to occur at around the age of 7 or 8 years and corresponds to the onset of the period of concrete operations. Before the break, that is, from the age of 1½ to about 7 years, the child seems capable of producing only static images with any degree of accuracy, and even these are far from perfect. He cannot represent correctly the movements of an object or even simple physical transformations; the images he produces for such situations are grossly deformed.

Piaget believes that the reason for this deficiency is a tendency to concentrate on the initial and final states of a given situation and to neglect the intervening events which are responsible for the changes. We have already seen this tendency, which is called *centration*, operating in the case of conservation. If you will, recall the situation where the child was presented with a line of vases, each of which contained a flower. The flowers were removed from the vases and spread apart. When this occurs, the young child usually believes that there are more flowers than vases, since the line of flowers is now longer than the line of vases. He has *centered* on the lengths and ignored a number of other factors. He has failed to decenter and to consider the density of the lines, as well as their length; and he has ignored the intermediary transformation (the removal and spacing of the flowers). Thus, the child focusses mainly on the initial and final states (the flowers in the vases and the flowers spaced out); and fails to integrate these impressions with all else that has occurred.

It is also true that before the age of 7 or 8 imagery is extremely static. In fact, it seems to dominate the child's thought processes. As a result, he produces a distorted picture of reality characterized by an emphasis on superficial features which are each isolated from others and not coordinated into a coherent whole.

From about the age of 7 years onward, however, the child becomes capable of producing images which can both reproduce and anticipate kinetic and transformational situations. This improvement is due to the fact that he can now imagine not only the initial and final states, but also the intermediary transformations. His imagery has become less static. It is never possible to reproduce *all* these intervening events, since in some cases (like the pouring of liquid) they occur rapidly. But the child recognizes that a sequence is involved, and that there has been a series of intervening steps between the initial and final states.

One might ask why reproductory and anticipatory images seem to appear simultaneously in the concrete operational child. It would seem easier, for example, to reproduce movements than to anticipate them. Therefore, one might well expect reproductory images to appear sooner. Piaget feels that the reason for their simultaneous appearance is that reproductory images also require an element of anticipation, or rather of re-anticipation. For example, suppose we have seen a wire transformed from a semi-circle into a straight line. When asked to reproduce the transformation, we are influenced by our knowledge of the final state; that is, that the wire has become a straight line. In other words, we do not start from the beginning with no inkling of what is to follow; we re-anticipate the final state and use this knowledge to reconstruct the transformation. Therefore, even reproductory images involve anticipation, and this fact explains why they do not appear before anticipatory images.

A final question concerns the relation between dynamic images—kinetic and transformational—and the concrete operations. That is, kinetic and transformational images occur at approximately the same time as the child becomes capable of the concrete operations; what then is the relation between the operative and figurative aspects of thought at this stage? The answer seems to be that although images and operations are different sorts of entities, the presence of one assists the functioning of the other. For example, consider the number conservation task involving flowers and vases. The concrete operational child can form accurate transformational images of the displacement of the flowers. After the transformation has been done, he correctly pictures the way in which the flowers have been removed from the vases. His ability to form images of this sort does not *guarantee* that he can conserve number: as we have already seen, the processes underlying conservation are not solely perceptual or imaginal. Nevertheless, the child who has a correct image of the transformation is certainly ahead of the child who does not. In other words, images are a useful and necessary auxiliary to thought during the concrete operational stage. By providing relatively accurate representations of the world, images assist the process of reasoning although they do not cause it.

Summary and Conclusions

Images represent absent objects or events. They are "symbols," in the sense of bearing some resemblance to the object represented, and are personal and idiosyncratic. Images do not give as complete and detailed a reproduction of the object as is provided by direct perception. Images first make their appearance around the middle of the second year of life, and they arise from a process of imitation which gradually becomes internalized. Until the age of approximately 7 years, the child is only able to produce correct mental images of static situations. He concentrates on states, rather than transformations. After the age of about 7 years, the child becomes capable of correct kinetic and transformational imagery. This new ability helps the child's understanding of reality: he now has available a more accurate and detailed rendering of the events on which he will focus his reasoning. Images, therefore, form a very necessary complement to the thought processes during the stage of concrete operations. Previous to that time, the static images of the preoperational period were in a sense detrimental to thought: they directed the child toward consideration of isolated states, rather than transformations of objects.

GENERAL CHARACTERISTICS OF PREOPERATIONAL AND CONCRETE OPERATIONAL THOUGHT

We have reviewed cognitive development in a number of separate and specific areas: the child's notions of classes, relations, number, and imagery. It would seem useful at this time to take a broader look at the child's mental development. We will therefore describe some common threads running through the child's approach to particular problems, and we will consider some general points which Piaget raises concerning cognitive growth.

Regularities and Irregularities

Piaget's theory describes a sequence of stages of cognitive development. For example, in the case of conservation of number we have seen how the child of about 4 years tends to center on either the length of the rows or on their density; how the child of about 5 or 6 begins to decenter and, instead of concentrating on only one dimension, centers alternately on both length and density; and how the child of about 7 and above coordinates both of the dimensions simultaneously and relates them to the transformations performed.

Piaget has gone to great lengths to dispel some misinterpretations concerning his stage theory. He points out, first, that the ages at which the stages occur vary considerably both within and among cultures. Not all Genevan children attain stage 2 of number development at 6 years; and children in Martinique lag behind Genevans by approximately 4 years.

Second, the course of an individual's development is continuous. The child is not one day characterized by stage 1 and the next by stage 2. Rather the transition is gradual, and occurs over a long period of time, and the child exhibits many forms of behavior intermediary between the two stages. Third, the child is not always in the same stage of development in regard to different substantive areas. He may be characterized by stage 2 in the case of classes, and stage 1 in the case of relations. It is unlikely, however, that he will be in stage 1 for classes and stage 3 for relations. Fourth, the child may even display different levels of achievement in regard to problems involving similar mental operations. This phenomenon, called *horizontal décalage*, has been extensively studied in the case of the several conservations.

Thus far, we have described only the conservation of number; that is, the child's ability to recognize that the number property of a set remains invariant despite irrelevant changes such as the mere physical rearrangement of the set. Piaget has also investigated several other conservations which include continuous quantity, substance, weight, and volume. The *conservation of continuous quantity* may be defined by this situation. The child is presented with two identical beakers (A and B), each filled with equal amounts of liquid (see Figure 13), and is asked whether the two glasses contain the same amount or not the same amount to drink. After he agrees to the equivalence of quantities, the liquid is poured by either the experimenter or the child from one of the two identical beakers (say B) into a third, dissimilarly shaped beaker (C). The column of the liquid in the third glass (and the glass itself) is both shorter and

FIGURE 13

CONSERVATION OF
CONTINUOUS QUANTITIES

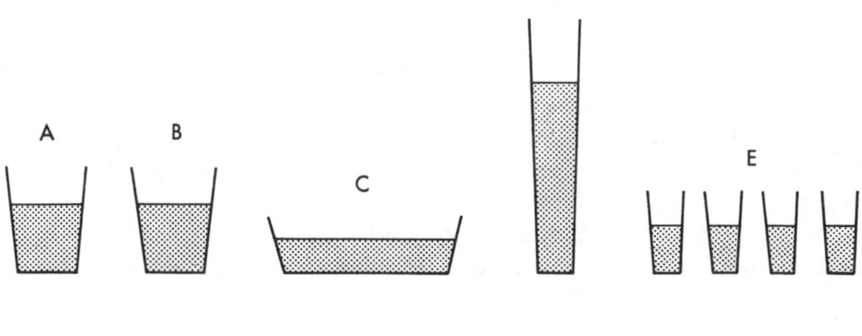

wider than that in the remaining original glass (A). The child is now asked whether the two beakers (now A and C) contain equal amounts. If he asserts that they do he is asked to explain why. The liquid in C is then returned to the original beaker B and the child is again asked if A and B contain identical amounts. The above manipulation is repeated, this time with a glass (D) which is taller and thinner than the original beakers. Finally the liquid of either A or B is poured into a set (E) of about three or four smaller glasses and the same questions are asked of the child. If the child continuously asserts in each case that the amount that has been poured from B into the different beakers is always the same as the amount remaining in the original beaker (A), then he has conserved continuous quantity. That is, he recognizes that merely pouring the liquid from B to C or D or E, does not increase or decrease the quantity; the "amount" of liquid remains the same (or is conserved) whether it is in B or in C. Since the quantities A and B were equal, and since pouring the liquid of B into C does not change its quantity, then the quantities in A and C must also be equal. If the child does not consistently assert this equality, then he has failed to conserve.

In the case of *conservation of substance*, the child is presented with two identical balls of plasticene (or clay, etc.). He is first asked whether there is the same amount of plasticene in both balls. If he does not think so he is asked to take away or add some clay to make them identical. Then, the experimenter changes one of the balls to a sausage shape, while the child watches. The child must now decide whether or not the ball and the sausage have equal amounts of substance. As in the liquid situation, the ball is changed into a variety of different shapes. If the child consistently asserts that the ball and the new shapes do have equal amounts of substance, then he has conserved substance. He has recognized that merely changing the shape does not alter the amount of matter involved.

To test the *conservation of weight*, the experimenter again presents the child with two identical balls of plasticene and places them on a balance. The child sees that the two balls weigh the same. Then they are removed from the balance and one ball is transformed into the shape of a sausage. The child is asked to anticipate the results of placing the ball and the sausage on the two sides of the balance. Will they still remain balanced or will one side be heavier than the other? The question is whether the child recognizes that weight is conserved despite changes in shape. Here again a series of changes are made to one of the balls and the question as to the identity of weight is repeated.

In the case of *conservation of volume*, two balls of plasticene are placed in two identical beakers, each filled with equal quantities of liquid. The child sees that the balls displace an equal volume of liquid in both beakers. Or, in the child's terms, the liquid goes up an equal distance in both cases. Then the balls are removed from the beakers, and one ball is changed into the shape of a sausage. The question now is whether the child recognizes that both ball and sausage continue to displace equal volumes, or whether the water goes up an equal amount in both cases.

All of these conservations are similar. They involve a first phase in which the child must recognize that two amounts—liquid quantity, substance, weight or volume—are equal. Most children above the age of 4 years are quite successful in this task. All of the conservations also involve a visible transformation which may be done by either the child or the experimenter. While the child watches, or as a result of his own actions, the liquid is poured from one beaker to another, or the ball is changed into a sausage. It is quite apparent that no liquid or plasticene is added or taken away. It is also apparent that things now *look* different. The column of liquid is shorter and wider, and the ball is now a sausage. And finally, all of the conservations involve a second phase in which the child must once again judge whether the amount in question is still the same. Of course, it is, and the issue is whether the child will recognize this or be misled by the changes in appearance he has observed.

Piaget's general findings are that there is a sequence of development with regard to each of the conservations. Children begin by failing to conserve, and require a period of development before they are able to succeed at the task. For example, in the case of continuous quantities, children are not able to conserve until about the age of 6 or 7 years. In the first phase of the problem (two identical beakers, each filled with equal amounts of liquid), the youngest children, around 4 or 5 years of age, correctly conclude that the amounts of liquid are equal. Since the child has either poured out the liquid into the second beaker, or has told the experimenter when to stop pouring, this is not surprising. If asked to justify the identity, the child will say that the water comes up to the same place in each glass so that the amounts are equal. When the liquid in one beaker is poured into a third glass which is different in shape from the first two, the child now maintains that the amounts are no longer equal. One glass has more to drink than the other. Asked to explain his answer, he says that the glass with the taller column of liquid has the greater amount. His judgment of amount is tied exclusively to the heights of the columns of liquid: when the heights are the same (as in phase 1), he thinks that the amounts are the same; when they are different (as in phase 2), then the amounts must be different too.

In stage 2, the child of 5 or 6 years vacillates in his responses to the conservation problem. While he usually fails to conserve, his approach to the problem varies from time to time. In the second phase of the experiment (when one beaker is shorter and wider than the other), he sometimes says that the taller beaker has more to drink, and sometimes maintains that the wider one has the greater amount. Unlike the stage 1 child, he does not concentrate exclusively on the heights of the columns of liquid, but sometimes bases his judgments on the widths as well.

In stage 3, the child is capable of conservation. When asked why the amounts do not change after the pouring, he gives at least one of several reasons. One is that if the liquid in C were returned to its original container, B, then the two initial beakers, A and B, would contain identical columns of liquid. This is the *negation* argument. A second reason is the *identity* argument: it's the same water. You haven't added any or taken any away. A third argument, involving *compensation* or *reciprocity*, is that the third glass, C, is shorter than the original beaker, A, but what C lost in height was compensated by C's gain in width; therefore, the amount in C must be equal to the amount in A.

In the case of conservation of substance, weight, and volume, a similar progression to that of quantity appears. In the first stage, the child fails to conserve apparently because he concentrates on only one of the stimulus dimensions involved. That is, in the case of weight he may say that the sausage is heavier than the ball because the former is longer. In the second stage, he again fails to conserve, although now he vacillates between the two dimensions involved. For instance, he may sometimes believe that the ball is heavier because it is wider, and at other times assert that the sausage is heavier because it is longer. In the third stage, the child conserves, for reasons similar to those cited for continuous quantities.

While all the conservations follow a similar course of development, there is a striking irregularity as well—the phenomenon of horizontal décalage, already alluded to. This refers to the fact, which has been well substantiated, that the child masters the conservation of discontinuous quantity and substance at about age 6 or 7; does not achieve stage 3 of the conservation of weight until age 9 or 10; does not understand the conservation of volume until approximately 11 or 12. In each case the arguments used are the same, sometimes even involving the same words. But having mastered conservation in one substantive area, like substance, he is not able to generalize immediately to another area like that of weight. First he acquires conservation of discontinuous quantity and substance, and then weight, and then volume. This décalage, or lack of immediate transfer, illustrates how concrete is the thought of the child during the ages of about 7 to 11 years. His reasoning is tied to particular situations and objects; his mental operations in one area may not be applied to another, no matter how useful this might be.

To summarize, we have described a number of irregularities in the course of development. First, the ages at which children attain various stages of development vary both within and among cultures. Second, an individual child's behavior takes many forms other than those Piaget describes as being typical of the various stages. Piaget's stages are idealized abstractions; they describe only selected and salient points on an irregular continuum of development. Third, the child may be in different stages of development with regard to different areas of functioning. And fourth, the child may be in different stages of development with regard to problems involving similar mental operations; this is called horizontal décalage.

We have emphasized the irregularities of development. But there are striking regularities too. One of these is that within Western cultures; that is, Switzerland, England, the United States, Canada, children progress through the various stages in the order described by Piaget. In the case of conservation of continuous quantities, for example, research shows [16] that Swiss, English, American, and Canadian children first fail to conserve, then vacillate in their response, and later conserve. While children in these cultures do not necessarily achieve the various stages at the same average ages, the sequence of development—the order of the stages—seems identical in all cases. Even in other very different cultures,[17] like the Chinese, the same sequence of stages appears. Thus, there is great cross-cultural generality to Piaget's findings.

Another regularity in development is that in each of the two major periods of development which we have discussed in this chapter (the preoperational and concrete operational periods) the child approaches different substantive problems in similar ways. There appear to be some general "traits" which characterize the thought of the preoperational child, and some different traits manifested in the concrete operational child's cognition. Consider first the child from about 4 to 7 years in the preoperational period. (Remember that this age designation is only approximate, since a child as old as 9 or 10 years typically shows a preoperational approach to the conservation of volume.) One general characteristic of his cognitive activity is centration. He tends to focus on a limited amount of the information available. In the conservation of number, he judges two sets equal when they are the same length, and he ignores another relevant variable, the density. In the conservation of continuous quantity, he judges two amounts equal when the heights of the columns of liquid are the same and ignores the width, or he may focus on the width alone and ignore the height. In the construction of ordinal relations (the problem of ordering ten sticks in terms of height), he suc-

16. The following book reports a number of relevant replications. K. Lovell, *The Growth of Basic Mathematical and Scientific Concepts in Children* (London: University of London Press, 1961).
17. J. J. Goodnow and G. Bethon, "Piaget's Tasks: the Effects of Schooling and Intelligence." *Child Development*, 1966, 37, pp. 573–82.

ceeds only by considering the tops of the sticks and ignoring the bottoms, or vice versa. In all these problems, the preoperational child deploys his attention in overly limited ways. He focusses on one dimension of a situation, fails to make use of another, equally relevant dimension, and therefore cannot appreciate the relations between the two.

The notion of centration is somewhat similar to Piaget's earlier concept of juxtaposition which is the tendency to think in terms of the parts of a situation and not integrate them into a whole. By contrast, the concrete operational child is characterized by *decentration*. He tends to focus on several dimensions of a problem simultaneously and to relate these dimensions. In the conservation of number, he coordinates length *and* density: two sets have the same number when the first is longer than the second but the second is denser than the first. In the conservation of continuous quantity, he recognizes that amounts are equal when one column of liquid is at the same time taller but narrower than a second. In the construction of ordinal relations, he determines whether a given object is simultaneously bigger than some objects and smaller than others. In all these problems, the concrete operational child attends to several aspects of the situation at once.

The thought of the preoperational child is *static* in the sense that it centers on states. In the conservation of substance he focusses on the shape of plasticene (sometimes a ball and sometimes a sausage) and ignores the transformation, that is, the change from one state to the other. In the conservation of continuous quantity he focusses on the heights of the columns of liquid and not on the act of pouring. In the area of imagery he lacks adequate representations of an object's shift from one position to another. In general, he concentrates on the static states of a situation and not on its dynamic transformations. The concrete operational child, on the other hand, is attuned to changes. In the conservations he concentrates on the transformation: the act of pouring the liquid, or spreading apart a set of objects, or deforming a ball into a sausage. He forms more or less accurate images of the changes which have taken place, and, therefore, can reason, for example, that as a set expands in length it simultaneously decreases in density.

The preoperational child's thought lacks *reversibility*. He may be able to predict an empirical reversibility as, for instance, in the case of the liquids where he would agree that if the water were poured back into B, there would be the same quantity as before. But this empirical reversibility does not change the fact that now he believes there is more (or less) water in the new glass C. It is as if pouring from B to C, and from C to B were totally unrelated actions. The older child, on the other hand, realizes that pouring from C to B reverses or negates the action of pouring from B to C. He is aware that it is the same action performed in another direction. By carrying out the action mentally, that is, by reversing the pouring in his mind, he is able to ascertain that the quantity of water in C (the lower wider glass) is the same as in B. He can perform a mental operation which leads him to a certain conclusion, and then do the reverse of this operation which enables him to return to his original starting point.

The concrete operational child can also perform another type of reversibility when operating on relations. This is reciprocity. For instance, in the example of liquid quantity, when the child says that one glass is longer and thinner, whereas the other is shorter and wider, he is cancelling out the differences between the two glasses by an action of reciprocity. One difference balances out the other, with the result that they have a reciprocal relationship.

To summarize, the preoperational child's thought is irreversible and attentive to limited amounts of information, which are particularly the static states of reality. The concrete operational child focusses on several aspects of a situation simultaneously, is sensitive to transformations, and can reverse the direction of his thinking. Piaget conceives of these three aspects of thought—centration-decentration, static-dynamic, irreversibility-reversibility—as interdependent. If the child centers on the static aspects of a situation, he is unlikely to appreciate transformations. If he does not represent transformations, he is unlikely to reverse his thought. By decentering he comes to be aware of the transformations, which thus lead to reversibility in his thought. In conclusion, we can see that one aspect of thought is not isolated from the rest. Even though the nature of the system may vary with the development of the child, thought processes form an integrated system.

DEVELOPMENT AND LEARNING

We have described the major differences between the thought of the preoperational child and that of the concrete operational child in such areas as classes, relations, number, and imagery. We have postponed until now consideration of the mechanisms of transition. Why is it that the preoperational child's thought advances to a higher level? What factors produce change and improvement? Piaget feels that mental growth involves two processes: *development*, which results in genuine learning, and *learning* in the narrow sense. The first of these, development, is spontaneous and vital; the second, learning in the narrow sense, is provoked and limited to certain situations. Let us consider first the process of development which we find to be influenced by four factors.

The first factor affecting development is *maturation*. Heredity equips the child with various physical structures affecting his intellectual development. These structures, the most important of which for cognitive abilities is the central nervous system, take time to reach their highest level of development. The brain of the newborn, for example, is smaller and lighter than that of the adolescent. It is obvious that the maturation of physical structures plays some role in cognitive development. The simplest example involves motor coordination. The newborn's muscles and other structures are not sufficiently developed to permit walking. Since he cannot get around in the world, the newborn can obviously know very little about it. Other examples abound. One of the factors underlying the newborn's inability to speak is undoubtedly an underdeveloped vocal apparatus. One of the variables producing his weakness at abstract reasoning is in all probability an insufficiently mature brain. It is clear, then, that immature physical systems often contribute to deficits in cognitive functioning.

But what role does physical maturation play in intellectual growth and advance? Some persons, most notably Gesell, have felt that such maturation is the chief factor explaining development. According to this hypothesis, the process of physical maturation is the most important and direct influence on all aspects of psychological functioning. Piaget feels that this position is too extreme for several reasons. One is our lack of understanding of the maturation of the central nervous system. How can one base a theory on maturation when so little is known about it? Second, it is clear that maturation does not explain everything. For example, children in Martinique reach the concrete operational stage about 4 years later than do children in Switzerland. It would seem unlikely that Swiss children's brains are 4 years more mature than the children's in Martinique. A much more likely explanation is that cultural factors contribute heavily to the differences in development. It is apparent, then, that physiological maturation undoubtedly affects cognitive development, often in ways we do not understand, but it is not the only factor.

A second influence on development is experience or contact with objects. To acquire the notion of object permanence, the infant must obviously experience things disappearing and reappearing. In order to classify objects, the child must first see some of them. To speak a language, the infant must first hear people talking. Piaget feels that contact with objects leads to two types of mental experience. On the one hand, *physical experience* involves actions which abstract or extract the physical properties of objects. This type of experience results, for example, in knowledge that strawberries are red, or that one object is heavier than another. Hence the knowledge is drawn directly from the objects themselves. Another type of experience is *logical-mathematical* experience which results in knowledge that is acquired through an internal coordination of the individual's actions, and not through physical experience.

Take, for example, the simple numerical concept that a given set of elements has one number property regardless of its physical arrangement. Figure 14 illustrates this. Set A has 10 elements. When it is rearranged

FIGURE 14

TWO SETS

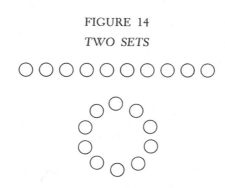

into set B, it still has 10, even though the two sets look quite different. Does physical experience alone induce the child to recognize this property of the sets? Piaget's answer is no. The accurate perception of the physical properties of set A and those of its rearrangement does not convey to the child that both have the same number. Physical experience, then, is not sufficient for a concept of number. What is required is a different kind of experience, *logical-mathematical* experience, in which knowledge is not a direct result of perceiving objects, but of actions performed on objects. To illustrate the logical-mathematical factor, Piaget cites a friend's childhood experience. At the age of about 4 or 5 years,

> *. . . he was seated on the ground in his garden and he was counting pebbles. Now to count these pebbles he put them in a row and he counted them one, two, three up to ten. Then he finished counting them and started to count them in the other direction. He began by the end and once again found he had ten. He found this marvelous. . . . So he put them in a circle and counted them that way and found ten once again.*[18]

Through repetitions of counting and recounting, of arranging and rearranging, the child learned an important property of number: it stays the same despite different orders of counting and despite physical arrangements. In this case, Piaget maintains, the child did not discover a physical property of the pebbles; rather he learned something about his own actions

18. Jean Piaget, "Development and Learning." In *Piaget Rediscovered*, R. E. Ripple and V. N. Rockcastle, eds. (Ithaca, New York: Cornell University, 1964), p. 12.

of ordering and counting. The important experience, then, derived primarily from his own actions (logical-mathematical experience) and only secondarily from the world of things (physical experience). Both these types of experience are not, however, sufficient to explain development. One reason is that they omit social factors.

A third factor influencing cognitive development is *social transmission*. This phrase is used in a very broad sense. It may refer to a parent explaining some problem to a child, or to a child's obtaining information by reading a book, or to a teacher giving instruction in a class, or to a child discussing a question with his peers, or to a child's imitation of a model. Certainly, the social transmission of knowledge promotes cognitive development. But again, social transmission is not sufficient. Unless the child is prepared to understand the information which is conveyed to him, social transmission will not be effective. Another way of saying this is that to receive the information the child must possess cognitive structures which can assimilate it. The 5-year-old cannot learn the calculus however well it is socially transmitted because he does not have the prerequisite structures.

American and Russian psychologists have proposed that one specific type of social factor, namely the child's own language, is vital for the development of behavior. In very general terms, their thesis is that around the age of 4 or 5 years the child uses internal speech to control and organize his activities. Language "mediates" between external events and the child's response. Without an internal linguistic system the child's responses are directly contingent upon external events; but with such a system the child can represent external events, delay responding to them, and can thereby control his own behavior.

Piaget's view is in strong contrast to the above. While not denying that language is an important human acquisition or that internal speech sometimes controls behavior, Piaget feels that logical thinking is primarily non-linguistic and derives from action. As we have seen, cognition may be viewed in terms of two aspects, the figurative and the operative. Piaget feels that images (part of the figurative aspect), for example, are often non-verbal. At a year and a half of age the infant has images of things or events even though he can hardly speak at all. Piaget proposes that the infant's images and other representations derive from imitating the actions of persons or things, and not from language.

To take an example from the operative aspect of thought, let us consider classification. We have seen that the preoperational child in stage 1 cannot produce a hierarchical arrangement of objects and does not understand inclusion relations. This is so despite the fact that the child can use all of the relevant words involved. He can say "blue triangles," or "red circles," or "more of these," or "some of these." Even though the language is available the preoperational child cannot classify. Also, it has been found that deaf children, for whom language is lacking or minimal, are capable of classification once they have reached a certain age. Therefore, classification and other kinds of thinking are not fully dependent on language. This is not, however, to assert that language plays no role in the development of classification or other mental operations. For example, the presence of nouns in the language may stimulate the child to think in terms of discrete classes. Also, the ability to verbalize a thought structure, like class inclusion, may help to consolidate and generalize it. Nevertheless, for Piaget, thought involves more than language. It involves representations (visual images, auditory images, mental symbols, etc.) and operations (internalized actions, like combining and taking away).

A fourth factor affecting development is *equilibration,* which in a way integrates the effects of the other three factors, none of which is sufficient in itself to explain mental development. Equilibration refers to the child's self-regulatory processes. As a result of these, he progressively attains a higher degree of equilibrium at each stage of development. The equilibration process is the backbone of mental growth.

Before considering the self-regulatory process, let us review the concept of equilibrium. Piaget has borrowed this notion from physics and has modified it to apply to human intelligence. The concept of equilibrium, which is not novel in psychology, refers to a state of balance or harmony between at least two elements which have previously been in a state of disequilibrium. Freud, for example, makes use of a similar principle when he states that a person tends toward a release of tension. For Piaget (unlike Freud) equilibrium does not have the connotation of a static state of repose between a closed system and its environment. Rather, equilibrium, when applied to intellectual processes, implies an active balance or harmony. It involves a system of exchanges between an open system and its surroundings. The child is always active. He does not merely receive information from his environment like a sponge soaking up water. Rather, he attempts to understand things, to structure his experience, and to bring coherence and stability to his world. Thus, a cognitive system which has attained a high degree of equilibrium is not at rest. It interacts with the environment. The system attempts to deal with environmental events in terms of its structures (assimilation), and it can modify itself in line with environmental demands (accommodation). When in equilibrium the cognitive system need not distort events to assimilate them; nor need it change very much to accommodate to new events. Equilibrium then, involves activity, openness, and a state of relative harmony with the environment.

Piaget describes equilibrium in terms of three major characteristics.

First there is the *field of application* of the equilibrium. This relates to the objects or properties of objects which the person acts upon. For instance, in visual perception the field of equilibrium is the visual field, that is, the objects which a person can apprehend visually at a glance. In the case of classification, the field of equilibrium is considerably wider. It involves the extension (the list of members) of the particular class under consideration. This list may, of course, contain a variety of objects. The greater the field of application, the more powerful is the equilibrium.

Another characteristic of equilibrium is *mobility*, which is defined in terms of the spatial and temporal distances that separate the person and the elements of the above mentioned field. The greater these distances, the more mobile the equilibrium, or the more flexible the mental operations necessary to cover these distances. Here again a comparison between visual perception and classification may be useful. Perceptual mobility is restricted; the spatial and temporal distances between the elements of the immediate visual field are small and call for a relatively limited number of mental activities. Mature classification, on the other hand (for example, when an adult thinks of the class of elephants), involves representation of objects which are not present. The spatial and temporal distances between the elements are unlimited. Classification, even in the case of immediately present objects, also calls for a variety of mental operations, as we have seen in Grouping I. The equilibrium involved in the operations of the classification structure is therefore more mobile than that of the perceptual system.

A third characteristic of equilibrium is *stability*, which is defined by the person's capacity to compensate [19] by actions or mental operations for changes in the elements without disturbing the whole previous structure. Once again in perception the equilibrium is partial and limited. If new elements are introduced into the visual field, perception is changed. This can be seen most clearly in the case of visual illusions. Parallel lines are not seen as parallel if they are placed close to curved lines. In classification, however, the introduction of new elements does not destroy the system. The structure easily incorporates the new elements and does not change. For example, if we classify animals into elephants and non-elephants, and if we discover that zebras exist, they can easily be classified under non-elephants. Thus the classification system can take into account additional elements without distortion, whereas the perceptual system is affected, even distorted, by the addition of new elements. The former, therefore, presents a greater degree of equilibrium than the latter.

19. Here we use compensation in a general sense, not in the narrow sense in which it was used in the case of conservation.

Throughout development the child moves from states of a lesser to those of a greater degree of equilibrium. The tendency toward equilibrium results in an increase in coherence and stability; this stability is acquired by activity on the part of the child. The child is active in the sense that he compensates for changes in the world, either by means of overt actions, as in the sensorimotor period, or by internal mental operations, as in the older child. With age the equilibrium becomes more stable because the child can anticipate changes and compensate in advance.

The equilibration process is the mechanism by which the child moves from one state of equilibrium to the next. Piaget describes this progression in terms of strategies and the probability of adoption of a particular strategy. As an illustration consider the acquisition of the conservation of continuous quantities. If you will recall, the problem involves understanding that a given quantity of liquid remains the same despite visible transformations which change the appearance. First, the child approaches the problem by focussing on a single dimension, say the heights of the columns of liquid. This is the most probable strategy since it is simple and requires the least effort. It is also a strategy which results in an inaccurate assessment of the situation since it is based on static states of the environment and not on the transformations between the states. The child uses strategy 1 for a period of time. Eventually two factors lead him to a second strategy which focusses on the other dimension of the situation, that is, on the widths of the column of liquid. One factor is the salience of the stimulus. When the liquid is poured into an extremely short and wide beaker, the width "stands out": it is salient and forces itself on the child's attention. A second factor is subjective: the child feels "a lack of satisfaction about always using the same solution when it is not accompanied by certainty." [20] For two reasons, then, the child adapts strategy 2, focussing on widths. But this strategy too is incorrect and unstable. The child feels a lack of certainty about the new solution. Also the heights again force themselves on the child's attention. The result is a third strategy, an oscillation between the two dimensions. At one time the child centers on heights, at another on widths. He still focusses, however, only on states, and the result is inconsistency in his responses. If he focusses on heights, he is led to assert that one beaker has more to drink; if he focusses on widths he concludes that the other beaker has more to drink.

But strategy 3 also has some constructive effects. When the child oscillates between heights and widths, he begins to see that one does not change without an inverse change in the other. In other words, the con-

<hr>

20. Jean Piaget, "Equilibration and the Development of Logical Structures," in *Discussions on Child Development, Vol. IV*, J. M. Tanner and B. Inhelder, eds. (London: Tavistock Publications, Ltd., 1960), p. 103.

tradictions which the child experiences in strategy 3 lead to a fourth solution. The child becomes aware of the transformations, that is the pouring from one beaker to the other. Now his strategy is to coordinate the two dimensions, to relate them to the transformation, and this leads to successful conservation. With the attainment of conservation he has acquired a high degree of equilibrium. Although strategy 4 was not the most likely at the outset, it has become so as a result of the previous strategies.

Piaget terms this process one of *sequential probability*. By moving from one stage to the next, and by experiencing conflicts along the way, the child develops a final strategy which leads to equilibrium. With strategy 4 the child focusses on both transformations and states and this coordination leads him to reversibility of thought. It is reversibility, in its two forms of reciprocity and negation, which allows the child to compensate satisfactorily for the changes in reality and which, in the final analysis, accounts for the equilibrium. Equilibration is therefore a process of intellectual development whereby states of disequilibrium are succeeded by states of greater equilibrium; whereby periods of incomplete understanding of reality are followed by periods of greater understanding.

The four factors, maturation, experience, social transmission, and equilibration describe what Piaget calls development. What relation does development bear toward learning? For Piaget, learning takes two forms. In the narrow sense, it consists of the acquisition over time of new responses restricted to a specific situation. For instance, in the case of the conservation of weight, if the young child observes that a ball of clay repeatedly weighs the same despite changes in shape, he may learn that the weight of this particular clay ball remains constant. He may even predict that for any new change in the same ball the weight will continue to be the same. In other words, as a result of repeated empirical observations or external reinforcements, he will have learned a law for a particular situation. This does not necessarily mean, however, that he has understood why the weight remains constant. Also, he may be unable to generalize the law to other situations with other objects. To summarize, he may have inferred a physical law, but has not acquired a new structure of thought enabling him to generalize the novel situations.

The acquisition of a new structure of mental operations is a second form of learning which results from the equilibration process. This type of learning, Piaget feels, is the only stable and lasting type. It is only when the child has the prerequisite mental structure to assimilate new experiences that true learning takes place, and the possibility to generalize to novel situations becomes feasible. In other words, genuine learning occurs when the child has available the necessary mental equipment to make use of new experiences. When the requisite cognitive structure is present, he can learn from the world and come to understand reality; when the structure is absent, new experience has only superficial effects. If there is too great a disparity between the type of experience presented to the child and his current level of cognitive structure, one of two things is likely to happen. Either the child transforms the experience into a form which he can readily assimilate and consequently does not learn what is intended, or else he merely learns a specific response which has no strength or stability, cannot be generalized, and will probably disappear soon. It is for this reason that the child's learning, in school or out, cannot be accelerated indefinitely. There are some things he is not ready to learn because the necessary cognitive structure is not yet present. If forced to deal with such material, the child does not achieve genuine learning.

A number of psychologists have attempted to investigate Piaget's notions concerning learning in the narrow sense (responses restricted to a specific situation) and learning in the wider sense (understanding based on appropriate cognitive structures). Smedslund [21] for instance, worked with the conservation of weight. After young children judged two plasticene balls to be equal in weight, Smedslund changed one to the shape of a sausage. Now the children judged that the weights were no longer equal. To teach conservation, Smedslund then had the children weigh the sausage and the ball, and thereby find that the two were equal. The external reinforcement of observing the identity of the weight was supposed to teach the children conservation. Smedslund had little success, however. After the external reinforcement, some children, it is true, were able to conserve when the same ball and sausage were involved. But in general, the children's ability to conserve did not generalize to slightly new and different situations. Also, it was not stable: the children could easily be convinced that non-conservation was true. By contrast, a child who has acquired conservation on his own, presumably by the process of equilibration, is not easily shaken in his belief.

Piaget feels, therefore, that development does not occur as a result of learning in the narrow sense. Instead, true learning occurs primarily as a result of development. That is, the child can appreciate the meaning of an external reinforcement or new experiences in general only when his structures have reached a certain point through the process of equilibration. The child can profit from external information—whether it be reinforcement or an adult's explanation or other sources—only when his cognitive structure is sufficiently prepared to assimilate it. In this sense development explains learning, and not vice versa.

21. J. Smedslund, "The Acquisition of Conservation of Substance and Weight in Children. II. External Reinforcement of Conservation of Weight and of the Operation of Addition and Substraction." *Scandanavian Journal of Psychology,* 1961, 2, pp. 71–84.

Summary and Conclusions

Piaget distinguishes between development, which produces genuine learning, and learning in the narrow sense. Development is influenced by four factors. Physical structures both limit certain aspects of cognitive development and make others possible, but maturation in itself is not sufficient to explain mental development, partly because there are obvious cultural effects on cognitive functioning. A second factor is experience. Physical experience involves gaining knowledge of objects by observing them directly. Logical mathematical experience involves an internal coordination of the individual's actions which at the outset are performed on the objects, but later do not require this physical support. However, these two types of experience are not sufficient to explain development because they omit, among other things, the effects of social influences. A third factor, social transmission, refers to the acquiring of knowledge by such techniques as reading or instruction. This factor too is insufficient to explain development partly because it ignores the role of the cognitive structures which make social influences efficient or inefficient.

A fourth factor is equilibration. This concept involves the child's self-regulatory processes which lead him through progressively more effective states of equilibrium. The notion of equilibrium refers to a system of exchanges between an open system and its surroundings. It implies a system that is in active balance with its environment. The degree of equilibrium is defined by a system's position on three dimensions: field of application, mobility, and stability. The greater the degree of these qualities, the more perfect the equilibrium. Piaget characterizes the progression from one state of equilibrium to the next in terms of the sequential probability of various strategies. Given that the child begins with a certain simple and inadequate strategy, it becomes probable that other, more complex strategies will evolve. Factors of subjective conflict and stimulus salience are influential. The final strategy resolves the conflicts which arose from the use of the simpler, inadequate strategies. This is the equilibration process.

Piaget distinguishes between learning in the narrow sense and learning in the wider sense. The former involves the mere acquisition of specific responses to particular situations. Such learning is superficial: it is unstable, impermanent, and unlikely to generalize. Learning in the wider sense is based on development. It occurs when the child has available the cognitive structures necessary for assimilating new information.

It is important to make several observations about Piaget's equilibration theory and his notions of learning. First, Piaget continually stresses activity on the part of the child. It is he who tries to assimilate the conservation problem into already available structures, and it is he who feels a subjective lack of certainty about his solution. The child does not simply react to external events but takes an active part in his own development. Second, perfect equilibrium is never fully achieved. Each period of development represents only a successively closer approximation to equilibrium, and even adolescent thought does not attain perfect equilibrium in all areas or at all times.

Third, the equilibration theory requires further elaboration. There seem to be two major aspects of Piaget's theory. One is a dissatisfaction with traditional theories of development. Maturation theory, as proposed by Gesell and others, is obviously inadequate. Piaget feels that traditional behaviorist learning approaches (learning in the narrow sense) are likewise deficient. It seems fairly clear, on the basis of Smedslund's experiments and those of other investigators, that external reinforcement cannot explain the development of such concepts as conservation. Also, observation of children in school and in their everyday activities suggests, at least to the present writers, that intellectual development depends on far more than learning in the narrow sense. The acquisition of cognitive structures which make possible genuine understanding seems to involve more than limited physical experience, external reinforcement, or similar factors. When genuine learning takes place, the child does seem to regulate his own activities: he decides what needs to be learned; he sets his own pace; he selects certain kinds of experiences, and so forth.

However, while Piaget may be correct in postulating that external reinforcement has little effect on real learning and that much of the child's development involves self-regulation, his own theory of equilibration is not entirely persuasive. There are several deficiencies. (a) Some of the theory is interesting, but requires further explication. For example, one reason for the child's progression from strategy 1 to 2 is said to be a subjective lack of satisfaction. The child does not feel certainty in his responses and therefore modifies his strategy. This hypothesis unfortunately raises more questions than it answers. What factors determine this lack of satisfaction? Why does the child use strategy 1 for so long (several years) before feeling a lack of satisfaction? Why does he use one dimension so long before the other becomes salient? Piaget's theory does not elaborate on these issues as thoroughly as one might like. (b) As far as we know, there is little *direct* evidence supporting Piaget's views on equilibration. Most studies in the area have attempted to rule out other views of the acquisition of conservation. But ruling out learning in the narrow sense, for example, does not automatically rule in equilibration theory. What seems needed is a direct experimental attack, preferably through longitudinal studies, on such notions as subjective lack of satisfaction or stimulus salience. (c) Piaget's probabilistic framework needs clarification. He proposes that strategy 1 is most *probable* at the outset, then strategy 2 becomes most probable, and so forth. It is not clear to what probability refers in this case. The individual child uses only strategy 1 for a long period of time and then adopts strategy 2. That is, use of each strategy is an all or nothing affair, and does not seem to involve probabilities, which in this case would seem to refer to a random distribution of at least two strategies. If equilibration theory is to be cast in probabilistic terms, it requires some amplification. To summarize, Piaget seems to offer a useful critique of traditional views of development, but has not sufficiently explicated his own view, which is the equilibration theory. While the child does seem to regulate his own learning, the details of the process are as yet by no means clear.

GENERAL CONCLUSIONS

In this chapter we have reviewed Piaget's later work on such issues as classes, relations, number, imagery, and equilibration. There are several general comments which we may make at this point. First (and at the risk of some repetition), Piaget is interested in the child's *competence*, and not necessarily in his ordinary performance. The focus is on the child's highest capabilities, on his potential; his performance may at times fall short of competence, because of such factors as fatigue, boredom, and so forth. In short, Piaget is interested in the optimum functioning of the child's mind, not in its average or ordinary achievement.

Second, a comparison of this chapter (reviewing Piaget's later work from the 1940's to the present) with the two chapters preceding (the work on infancy done in the 1930's, and the early work done in the 1920's) reveals that Piaget's interests have shifted with time. No longer does he study the problems commonly faced by the child or infant in his natural environment—moral judgment, verbal communication, or finding an object behind an obstacle. Instead, Piaget's philosophical, mathematical, and logical interests now determine the choice of substantive problems. The early Piaget was a functional psychologist, studying patterns of thought which had immediate importance for the child. The later Piaget is much more the "genetic epistomologist," investigating the child's understanding of various philosophical and mathematical concepts. Both kinds of approach are valuable but incomplete. The functional approach, which is favored by many American psychologists, focusses on the child's ability to deal with commonly encountered problems. But it may ignore the problem of the development of the highest mental abilities providing the environment does not present the child with opportunities for their use. Piaget's genetic epistemological approach, which is rare outside of Geneva, emphasizes the child's competence to use the most elaborate and efficient forms of thought. But it may not stress sufficiently the child's ordinary mental activities.

Third, a comparison of the later work with the earlier investigations reveals that the later Piaget emphasizes the detailed and formal description of thinking. Piaget now focusses on the development of logico-mathematical systems which attempt to model the structure of the child's thought. In this connection, we have reviewed aspects of Grouping I. Perhaps as a result of this new emphasis, Piaget now devotes less attention than formerly to a theory of transition; that is, an explanation of why it is that the child progresses from one stage to the next. If you will recall, in his work on infancy Piaget was very much concerned with learning and motivation; to explain these matters he developed such notions as functional assimilation, accommodation, and so forth. While not abandoning an interest in explaining development (or the concepts of assimilation and accommodation), Piaget recently has not focussed on these issues so sharply. He has devoted far less attention to the elaboration of equilibration theory than to the description of structure.

5

adolescence

Thus far we have reviewed the sensorimotor period (birth to 2 years), the pre-operational period (2 to 7 years), and the concrete-operational period (7 to 11 years). In Piaget's theory the final period of intellectual development is that of *formal operations,* which begins at about age 12, and is consolidated during adolescence.

There are several major themes which run through Piaget's account of adolescent thought. One is that the adolescent's system of mental operations has reached a high degree of equilibrium. This means, among other things, that the adolescent's thought is flexible and effective. He can deal efficiently with the complex problems of reasoning. Another major theme is that the adolescent can imagine the many possibilities inherent in a situation. Unlike the concrete-operational child, whose thought is tied to the concrete, the adolescent can transcend the immediate here and now. He can compensate mentally for transformations in reality, and as we have seen in the previous chapters, this is one of the determinants of equilibrium.

These general conclusions are based on a number of studies performed by Piaget and Inhelder,[1] on adolescent reasoning. These studies, which use the revised clinical method, describe the adolescent's perfor-

1. For purposes of brevity, we refer to the work on adolescence as Piaget's; nevertheless, Inhelder's contributions should be recognized.

mance on various problems involving scientific concepts. In a typical investigation, a number of adolescents were given several problems based on classical physics, chemistry, or other disciplines. In each case the adolescent was presented with some apparatus or materials (a pendulum, a balance, etc.) and was required to explain how they work. He was allowed to manipulate the apparatus, and to do experiments; in short, to behave as a scientist. The investigator kept a detailed record of the adolescent's activities and occasionally asked him a few questions if verbal clarification seemed necessary. Piaget's major question, of course, is not whether the adolescent can come up with the "right" answer. Rather, the issue is whether and how his thought differs from that of the younger child. Piaget's interest is in how the adolescent copes with scientific problems, how he experiments, and how he reasons about the observed data. As we shall see, Piaget's theory of adolescent thought is stated in terms of two logical models—the 16 Binary Operations [2] and the INRC group. These two models together describe the period of *formal operations*. Since the models are quite complex, we will consider only limited portions of Piaget's theory.

THE 16 BINARY OPERATIONS

The Pendulum Problem

In one investigation all subjects were presented with the following situation: A pendulum was constructed in the form of an object hanging from a string, and the subject was shown how to vary the length of the string, how to change the weight of the suspended object, how to release the pendulum from various heights, and how to push it with different degrees of force. The subject was required to solve what is essentially a problem in physics: to discover which of the four factors, that is, length, weight, height, or force, alone or in combination with others, affects the pendulum's frequency of oscillation (how fast it swings). The correct solution, of course, is that the major causative factor is the length of the string: the shorter the string, the faster the oscillation. To solve the problem, the subject was allowed to experiment with the pendulum in any way he pleased. He could, for instance, make the pendulum heavy or light and see what happened. The examiner played a limited and non-directive role. He recorded the subject's experiments and verbal statements, and he intervened in the course of events to question the subject on a few points

2. The model of the 16 binary operations is actually a special case of a larger and more comprehensive system called the *combinatorial system*. This special case applies to situations involving two values (e.g., p and p̄) of each of two factors (e.g., p and q). With a greater number of factors, more complex models are necessary and can be generated from the combinatorial system.

that were not clear. In addition, the examiner also asked the subject to prove his assertions when he did not voluntarily do so. To summarize, the subject assumed the role of a scientist seeking an answer by empirical means to a classical problem in physics, and the examiner recorded his behavior.

To show the true measure of the adolescent's accomplishment, we will first present a brief account of how children in the preoperational and concrete operational periods deal with the problem. Preoperational children below 7 years of age approach the task in a very haphazard way. First, the "experiments" which they devise reveal no overall plan or pattern. These younger children seem to make random tests which in fact yield little information of value. For example, one child began by pushing a long pendulum with a light weight; then he swung a short pendulum with a heavy weight; and then he removed the weight altogether. Such a procedure can tell one nothing about the role of weight or length for reasons that should be clear (and if they are not, they will be later). Second, the child does not even report the results accurately. He hypothesizes, for instance, that his pushes influence the speed of oscillation, and reports that this is what occurs when, in fact, it does not. Apparently the child's expectations influence his observations; and this attitude is hardly a mark of scientific objectivity. Third, the child's conclusions are faulty and unrelated to the evidence. This may occur because the child reports the results inaccurately; for example, he may mistakenly perceive that frequency of oscillation increases as the pendulum is pushed more vigorously. On other occasions the conclusions are inaccurate because the child reasons about the results in a faulty way. For example, if he (correctly) perceives that a short heavy pendulum swings more rapidly than a long, light one, he may incorrectly conclude that weight, and not length, is the causative factor.

The concrete operational child shows considerable improvement in his intellectual ability. He investigates a number of potential determinants of oscillation and observes the results in an accurate way. And he may even discover the correct answer. But there are many features of his procedure which are unsystematic and illogical and which require further development. Consider this protocol:

BEA (10;2) *varies the length of the string* [according to the units two, four, three, etc., taken in random order] *but reaches the correct conclusion that there is an inverse correspondence:* "It goes slower when it's longer." *For the weight, he compares 100 grams with a length of two or five, with 50 grams with a length of one and again concludes that there is an inverse correspondence between weight and frequency.*[3]

3. From *The Growth of Logical Thinking from Childhood to Adolescence,* pp. 70–71.

The child performed well in two respects. First, his answer was at least partially correct, although he mistakenly inferred that weight played a role too. Second, he observed all of the results correctly: for example, the short, light pendulum *did* swing more rapidly than the long heavy one. His objectivity as a scientific observer is no longer in doubt; expectation does not influence observation.

But there were two important deficiencies in the child's approach. First, he did not design the experiments properly. To investigate the role of weight he compared a short, light pendulum with a long, heavy one. This is not the proper procedure. What he should have done was compare a short, light pendulum with a short, heavy one, and a long, light pendulum with a long, heavy one. That is, he should have *held length constant* in order to test the effects of weight and vice versa. Second, the conclusions drawn from the empirical results (which were, as we noted, correctly observed) were imperfect. The judgment that there was an inverse relation between weight and frequency of oscillation (the heavier the weight, the slower the oscillation) does not follow from the observed data. This kind of faulty reasoning can be seen even more clearly in another subject, who (correctly) observed that a short, heavy pendulum swings more rapidly than a long, light one. From this result, he concluded that both length and weight were determining factors; that is, increased length caused slower oscillation, and increased weight caused faster oscillation. This, of course, is not necessarily the correct inference. In the absence of further information, one cannot decide among three possibilities: (a) the above interpretation; (b) that increasing the length slows the oscillation, while weight is irrelevant; and (c) that adding weight increases the speed, while length is irrelevant. Unfortunately, the child did not design his experiment so as to provide the information necessary for deciding among the alternatives, and unwisely settled on one of them without sufficient justification.

Consider, on the other hand, the behavior of the adolescent in the period of formal operations. After passing through a transitional stage, which we will not discuss here, he performs well at three aspects of the problem: (a) he plans the tests adequately, or designs the experiment properly; (b) he observes the results accurately; (c) and he draws the proper logical conclusions from the observations. Here is an example:

EME (15;1), *after having selected 100 grams with a long string and a medium length string, then 20 grams with a long and short string, and finally 200 grams with a long and short, concludes:* "It's the length of the string that makes it go faster or slower; the weight doesn't play any role." *She discounts likewise the height of the drop and the force of her push.*[4]

4. *Ibid.*, p. 75.

Let us consider in turn each of the three aspects of the adolescent's behavior.

(a) *Designing the experiment.* From the outset, and before carrying out any tests, the adolescent believes that there are several possible determinants of the frequency of oscillation. The causative factor could be length, weight, or any other of the factors present. Furthermore, he realizes that it is also conceivable that some combination of factors might be responsible: perhaps weight and length combined increase oscillation while neither by itself is a sufficient cause. In other words, the adolescent begins by imagining a series of purely hypothetical results; before acting, he conceives of all the possibilities. The evidence for this assertion is that later he proceeds to test all *possible* causes of oscillation. The systematically exhaustive way in which he performs the test suggests that he must have imagined all of the possibilities at the outset. Also, these imagined possibilities are abstractions of a sort. While he considers length, for instance, as an isolated and independent determinant of oscillation, it is the case that in reality length never stands alone; it is always accompanied by other factors such as weight. A swinging pendulum is never just long or short; it also has a certain weight, is released from a particular height, and so forth.

The adolescent's next step is an attempt to discover which of the many possibilities is operative. He uses a method which involves holding some factors constant while varying others. Consider EME's approach. She first tested a long string with 100 grams, then a shorter string with 100 grams, then a long string with 200 grams, and finally a short string with 200 grams. A schematic overview of her procedure might look like Table 1.

Note that four possibilities are tested, and that they involve holding one factor constant and varying another. In the case of the first two steps,

TABLE 1

ARRANGEMENT OF
OSCILLATION EXPERIMENT

	Length	*Weight*	*Oscillation*
1.	long	light	?
2.	short	light	?
3.	long	heavy	?
4.	short	heavy	?

TABLE 2

ALTERNATIVE ARRANGEMENT
OF OSCILLATION EXPERIMENT

	Length	Weight	Oscillation
1.	long	light ·	?
3.	long	heavy	?
2.	short	light	?
4.	short	heavy	?

the weight is light and the string is either long or short. In the case of steps 3 and 4, weight is heavy and the string may be long or short. Thus in both steps 1 and 2, and in 3 and 4, weight is held at one level (or is constant) while length is varied. If length is a causative factor, then its effects should be manifest in a comparison of 1 vs. 2, and in a comparison of 3 vs. 4.

We can easily rearrange Table 1 to show the strategy of holding length constant while varying weight. Table 2 shows more clearly what is, of course, already contained in Table 1, namely, that the four tests can be used to get information on the role of weight. If one compares 1 and 3, for example, the length is long in both cases, while weight changes.

Actually, for purposes of illustration, we have simplified the matter somewhat. In dealing with length and weight, the adolescent also holds constant the other factors—height of the drop, and force of the push— since varying them would confuse the results. All these variables are held constant so that the effects of the two factors above, length and weight, may be assessed. Also, after testing the effects of length and weight, EME went on to do the same for the height of the drop and force of the push.

The adolescent's procedure seems very reasonable, of course, and one might even consider a detailed description of it to be trivial; surely, everyone would go about the problem in this way. But as we have seen before, for example, in the case of conservation, what is obvious and trivial to the adult is not necessarily apparent to the child. Similarly, in the case of designing experiments, if you will recall, the child in the concrete operational period does not always follow the "obvious" procedure. Remember the child whose *only* comparison involved a short, light pendulum vs. a long, heavy one (steps 2 and 3 of Table 3), and who felt that this test resulted in sufficient information for firm conclusions.

(b) *Observing the results.* It comes as no surprise that the adolescent, like the concrete operational child but not like the preoperational period child, observes the empirical results without bias.

TABLE 3

OBSERVED RESULTS,
OSCILLATION EXPERIMENT

	Length	*Weight*	*Oscillation*
1.	long	light	slow
2.	short	light	fast
3.	long	heavy	slow
4.	short	heavy	fast

(c) *Drawing logical conclusions.* When the adolescent performs the four step experiment shown in Tables 1 and 2, he obtains the results shown in Table 3. It should be clear from Table 3 that whenever the pendulum is short, it swings quickly; and whenever it is long, it swings slowly. None of the other factors has any effect on oscillation.

Table 4 shows the results which were not observed. The reason for presenting this table will be clear later.

To introduce Piaget's use of logic, we will simplify the tables by means of a few abbreviations. If we let p stand for short and p̄ for long, q stand for light and q̄ for heavy, r for fast and r̄ for slow, and T (true) for observed result and F (false) for non-observed result, then we have Table 5. Therefore, p and q are the factors and r is the result. T and F merely indicate whether the result was observed or not. For example, line 1 says that it was observed (T) and that a long (p̄), light (q) pendulum swung slowly (r̄). Line 7 says that it was not observed (F) that a long (p̄), heavy (q̄) pendulum swung rapidly (r).

TABLE 4

RESULTS NOT OBSERVED,
OSCILLATION EXPERIMENT

	Length	*Weight*	*Oscillation*
1.	long	light	fast
2.	short	light	slow
3.	long	heavy	fast
4.	short	heavy	slow

TABLE 5

SYMBOLIZATION OF
OSCILLATION EXPERIMENT

	Length	*Weight*	*Oscillation*	*Result*
1.	$\bar{p}$	q	$\bar{r}$	T
2.	p	q	r	T
3.	$\bar{p}$	$\bar{q}$	$\bar{r}$	T
4.	p	$\bar{q}$	r	T
5.	$\bar{p}$	q	r	F
6.	p	q	$\bar{r}$	F
7.	$\bar{p}$	$\bar{q}$	r	F
8.	p	$\bar{q}$	$\bar{r}$	F

What does the adolescent conclude from this pattern of observed and non-observed results? In regard to weight, Table 5 shows that it is observed that when heavy or light, the pendulum swings rapidly or slowly. Consequently, the weight makes no difference whatsoever on the speed of oscillation. Piaget writes this conclusion as q * r (read: weight is irrelevant to oscillation) and calls it *tautology* or *complete affirmation*. (Clearly, it could be shown in the same way that force and height are also irrelevant.)

In regard to length, Table 5 shows that it is observed that a short pendulum always swings rapidly and a long one slowly (and it is *never* observed that a short pendulum swings slowly and a long one rapidly). Therefore, the length of the pendulum fully determines the rate of oscillation, and height is irrelevant. Another way of saying this is that short length is a necessary and sufficient cause of fast oscillation.

In propositional logic, the pattern of results for length and oscillation is usually called "reciprocal implication," and is written p $\supsetneq$ r. Thus, the adolescent has found that p $\supsetneq$ r (length determines oscillation), whereas q * r (weight is irrelevant).

To summarize, the adolescent begins in the realm of the hypothetical and imagines all of the possible determinants of the results. To test his hypotheses, he devises experiments which are well-ordered and designed to isolate the critical factors by systematically holding all factors but one constant. He observes the results correctly, and from them proceeds to draw conclusions. Since the experiments have been designed properly, the adolescent's conclusions are certain and necessary.

The Bending of Rods

In order to investigate another aspect of adolescent thought, Piaget presented subjects with a problem involving the bending of rods. We shall first review the logical conclusions drawn from the results of the experiment, and later see how this form of reasoning differs from that observed in the case of the pendulum problem.

Piaget presented the subjects with a series of rods which were attached to the edge of a basin of water. The rods were in a horizontal position (parallel to the water). The rods differed in (a) composition (steel, brass, etc.), (b) length, (c) thickness, and (d) cross-section form (round, square, rectangular). In addition, (e) different weights could be attached to the end of the rod above the water. The subject's task was first to determine which of the rods bend enough to touch the water, and then to explain the results. As in the case of the pendulum problem, the subject was allowed to vary the factors in any way he wished. He might place on the apparatus a long, thin, round, steel rod with a heavy weight; a short, thin, square, brass rod with a light weight; or any other kind that he preferred. Again, the examiner's role was non-directive: mainly he noted the subject's tests, remarks, and initiated a few questions to clarify uncertain points.

Here is a protocol of one adolescent's behavior:

DEI (16;10): "Tell me first [after experimental trials] what factors are at work here."—*"Weight, material, the length of the rod, perhaps the form."*—*"Can you prove your hypotheses?"*—*[She compares the 200 gram and 300 gram weights on the same steel rod.]* "You see, the role of weight is demonstrated. For the material, I don't know."—*"Take these steel rods and these copper ones."*—"I think I have to take two rods with the same form. Then to demonstrate the role of the metal I compare these two *[steel and brass, square, 50 cm. long and 16 mm.² cross section with 300 grams on each]* or these two here *[steel and brass, round, 50 and 22 cm. by 16 mm.²]*: for length I shorten that one *[50 cm. brought down to 22.]* To demonstrate the role of the form, I can compare these two" *[round brass and square brass, 50 cm. and 16 mm.² for each.]* "Can the same thing be proved with these two?" *[brass, round and square, 50 cm. long and 16 and 7 mm.² cross section.]* "No because that one *[7 mm.²]* is much narrower."—*"And the width?"*—"I can compare these two" *[round, brass, 50 cm. long with 16 and 7 mm.² cross-section].*[5]

It should be clear from the protocol that the adolescent's procedure is highly systematized. DEI considered that any one of several factors may

5. *Ibid.*, p. 60.

TABLE 6

ARRANGEMENT OF RODS EXPERIMENT

	Length	Weight	Bending
1.	long	heavy	?
2.	long	light	?
3.	short	heavy	?
4.	short	light	?

be involved in determining the flexibility of the rods. For example, an increase in weight or an increase in length may make the rod bend. To test these hypotheses, the adolescent employed the method of varying one factor at a time while holding the others constant. To test the role of weight, for instance, DEI put first a 200 gram weight and then a 300 gram weight on the *same* rod. Because it was identical in the two cases, the rod obviously held constant the factors of material, length, etc., while only weight varied.

We will now examine the adolescent's procedure in detail. For purposes of economy, let us suppose that only two factors, that is, length and weight, were present in the problem. In that case, a full account of the adolescent's procedure is given by Table 6. This shows that when steps 1 vs. 2 and 3 vs. 4 are compared, length is held constant and weight varied. And when 1 vs. 3 and 2 vs. 4 are compared, weight is held constant and length varied. This procedure should be familiar to the reader, since it is the same as that employed in the pendulum problem.

DEI correctly observed the results given in Table 7, which also lists the data *not* observed.

TABLE 7

RODS EXPERIMENT

	Length	Weight	Bending
			Results Observed
1.	long	heavy	great
2.	long	light	great
3.	short	heavy	great
4.	short	light	little

Results Not Observed

5.	long	heavy	little
6.	long	light	little
7.	short	heavy	little
8.	short	light	great

For example, line 2 says that the subject *did* observe a long, light rod bend a great deal, and line 5 says that the subject did not observe a long, heavy rod bend just a little. At first, the results may seem somewhat confusing. Rows 1 and 2 show that long rods bend a lot, but line 3 shows that short rods also bend a great deal. Similarly, lines 1 and 3 show that heavy rods bend a great deal, but line 2 shows that light rods do so also. Perhaps the results may be clarified if we consider the outcomes for each factor separately. Table 8 shows the results for length (ignoring weight).
It should be clear from the table that a long rod always bends a lot, whereas a short rod may bend a great deal or just a little.

Table 9 shows the same pattern of results in the case of weight. Again, the obvious interpretation is that heavy rods are always observed to bend a great deal (and never just a little), whereas light rods may either bend a little or a lot.

Before going on, let us symbolize the results once again: Table 10 first presents the case of both length and weight, and then shows the cases of length and weight separately. p stands for long length, p̄ for short length; q for heavy weight, q̄ for light weight; r for great bending and r̄ for little bending; and T for an observed result, and F for result not observed.

TABLE 8

LENGTH AND BENDING

	Length	Bending

Results Observed

1.	long	great
2.	short	great
3.	short	little

Results Not Observed

4.	long	little

TABLE 9
WEIGHT AND BENDING

	Weight	Bending
	Results Observed	
1.	heavy	great
2.	light	great
3.	light	little
	Results Not Observed	
4.	heavy	little

TABLE 10
SYMBOLIZATION OF RODS EXPERIMENT

	Length	Weight	Bending	Result
	Both Length and Weight			
1.	p	q	r	T
2.	p	$\bar{q}$	r	T
3.	$\bar{p}$	q	r	T
4.	$\bar{p}$	$\bar{q}$	$\bar{r}$	T
5.	p	q	$\bar{r}$	F
6.	p	$\bar{q}$	$\bar{r}$	F
7.	$\bar{p}$	q	$\bar{r}$	F
8.	$\bar{p}$	$\bar{q}$	r	F
	Length Alone			
1.	p		r	T
2.	$\bar{p}$		r	T
3.	$\bar{p}$		$\bar{r}$	T
4.	p		$\bar{r}$	F
	Weight Alone			
1.		q	r	T
2.		$\bar{q}$	r	T
3.		$\bar{q}$	$\bar{r}$	T
4.		q	$\bar{r}$	F

For example, line 4 under "weight alone" says that the subject did *not* observe (F) a heavy (q) rod bending only a little (r̄).

The adolescent draws the following conclusions from the pattern of observed and non-observed results. First, length is a cause of the rod's bending. Whenever there is a long rod, it always bends. But do not short rods also bend (at least sometimes) and does this not contradict the hypothesis? The adolescent reasons that the hypothesis of causality is not disconfirmed. A special kind of cause—sufficient cause—is involved. In the present case, a long rod is always *sufficient* to cause bending. But the fact that the rod sometimes bends also when the length is short means that length is not the only causative factor. In other words, length is not *neces-sary* for bending; other factors may cause bending too. Second, the adolescent concludes that weight also is a sufficient cause of bending. Whenever the rod is heavy it bends. But as was the case with short length, sometimes light weights bend and sometimes they do not. Again, the result depends on what other factors are present. To summarize, the adolescent makes the judgment that both length and weight are *sufficient* to cause bending, although neither one alone is *necessary*. In propositional logic, these results may be called "implication," and are written $p \supset r$, $q \supset r$ (read: length implies bending, weight implies bending)

Perhaps we may achieve a better understanding of implication if we contrast it with reciprocal implication (previously observed in the pendulum problem). Table 11 shows both the pattern of implication and the (hypothetical) pattern of reciprocal implication in the case of length in the rods problem.

TABLE 11

THREE LOGICAL RELATIONS

	Length	*Bending*	*Results Showing Implication*	*Hypothetical Results Showing: Reciprocal Implication*	*Tautology*
1.	p	r	T	T	T
2.	p̄	r	T	F	T
3.	p̄	r̄	T	T	T
4.	p	r̄	F	F	T

The implication column states, as we have already seen, that long rods always bend a lot, and short rods may bend a great deal or only a little. The (hypothetical) reciprocal implication column says that long rods

always bend a great deal, and that short rods *always* bend a little. Therefore, in this hypothetical case, nothing besides length causes bending.
It should be clear from the table that reciprocal implication and implication differ only in the pattern of T's and F's (observed results and non-
observed results). Finally, to review further, consider the last column,
showing tautology or complete affirmation. This hypothetical case states
that all possible combinations of length and bending can be observed. A
long rod bends both a little and a lot, and so does a short rod. Clearly,
then, length is irrelevant to bending. Thus, we have reviewed $p \supseteq_{\subset} r$ (reciprocal implication), $p \supset r$ (implication) and $p * r$ (tautology).

The Other Binary Operations

In describing the adolescent's behavior on the various scientific
reasoning problems, we have thus far covered three logical relations:
$p \supseteq_{\subset} r$, $p \supset r$, and $p * r$. In Piaget's system, there are 13 more, and the
whole set is called the *system of 16 binary operations*. Rather than discuss
each of the 16 operations in detail, we will instead merely list them all, in
terms of patterns of observed and non-observed results, and briefly discuss
only a few operations. Suppose again we have the variables of long length
(p) and short length ($\bar{p}$); great bending (r) and a little bending ($\bar{r}$).
There are four combinations of p, $\bar{p}$, r, and $\bar{r}$. These are shown in the
extreme left of Table 12. They correspond to possible outcomes of the
experiment. It could conceivably occur that a long rod (p) bends a lot
(r) or a little ($\bar{r}$) and that a short rod ($\bar{p}$) bends a lot (r) or a little ($\bar{r}$):
these are the four possible outcomes of an empirical test. Each of the
possible outcomes may be observed (T) or not observed (F). It is possible
for all of them to be observed or for only some to be observed, while others
are not observed. In other words, there are a large number of ways in which
the experiment might turn out in terms of observed and non-observed
results. Table 12 lists all the ways in which the four outcomes may be
observed or not observed. (It is, of course, understood that instead of p and
r, we could have a and b or any other symbols, and that instead of length
and bending, we could have weight and oscillation or any other factors:
Table 12 is completely general.) For example, column 2 says that if we
did the experiment we could observe that long length produces great bending (p and r) and could fail to observe that long length produces little
bending (p and $\bar{r}$), and that short length produces a great deal of bending
($\bar{p}$ and r) or little bending ($\bar{p}$ and $\bar{r}$).

We have already seen parts of the table before. For example, in connection with the pendulum problem we have seen that the pattern of

TABLE 12

THE 16 BINARY OPERATIONS

	The four possible outcomes of an experiment			
	1.	2.	3.	4.
Length	p	p	$\bar{p}$	$\bar{p}$
Bending	r	$\bar{r}$	r	$\bar{r}$

Name of operation	All ways in which four possible outcomes can be observed or not observed *			
1. Negation	F	F	F	F
2. Conjunction	T	F	F	F
3. Inverse of implication	F	T	F	F
4. Inverse of converse implication	F	F	T	F
5. Conjunctive negation	F	F	F	T
6. Independence of p to r	T	T	F	F
7. Independence of r to p	T	F	T	F
8. Reciprocal implication	T	F	F	T
9. Reciprocal exclusion	F	T	T	F
10. Inverse of independence of r to p	F	T	F	T
11. Inverse of independence of p to r	F	F	T	T
12. Disjunction	T	T	T	F
13. Converse implication	T	T	F	T
14. Implication	T	F	T	T
15. Incompatibility	F	T	T	T
16. Tautology	T	T	T	T

* Only number 14, implication, is actually observed in the case of rods. The rest are hypothetical.

observed and non-observed outcomes shown in column 16 is tautology, or p * r. Column 14 is implication, p $\supset$ r, the obtained relation in the rod experiment, and column 8 is reciprocal implication, p $\underset{C}{\supset}$ r, also found in the pendulum experiment. The other columns involve analogous logical operations. For example, suppose we did an experiment and obtained the hypothetical results shown in column 2. Then, line or row 1 says that it is observed (T) that long (p) rods bend a lot (r), while it is not observed (F) that long (p) rods bend a little ($\bar{r}$), and that short ($\bar{p}$) rods bend a little ($\bar{r}$) or a lot (r). In other words, all we know from the experiment is that long rods bend a great deal. This pattern of results is called "conjunction" and is written as p $\wedge$ r. It means merely that long rods *and* great bending go together: the two occur in conjunction. While this operation seems a bit unnatural in the present context of rods and bending, there are many other situations in which conjunction makes as much sense as implication hopefully does here.

Such, then, are the 16 binary operations. We have seen how the adolescent uses three of them, and have briefly reviewed what the rest are like. Now let us consider another feature of the adolescent's thought, the INRC group.

THE INRC GROUP

Thus far we have seen how the adolescent draws conclusions from the pattern of observed and non-observed results of an experiment. These conclusions may be stated in terms of logical operations, like p $*$ q or p $\supset$ q. In other words, to this point we have been concerned with how the adolescent derives from the results of an experiment the proper logical relations among the factors involved. Each of the 16 binary operations is a logical relation of this type. These logical relations are usually called "functions," and that is the terminology we will use here.

Following the analysis of functions, Piaget goes on to describe how the adolescent manipulates the conclusions which he has derived from an experiment. For this purpose, he introduces another logical model, the INRC group. We will see how the INRC group is an attempt to specify the rules which the adolescent uses in manipulating or transforming functions. There are four such rules: identity (I), negation (N), reciprocity (R), and correlativity (C). We will consider two of them.

Reciprocity

To illustrate R, let us return to the problem of the bending rods. If you will recall, after designing the experiment properly (using the method of holding constant all factors but one), and observing the results accurately, the adolescent came to the conclusion that length was a sufficient cause of bending (p $\supset$ r), and that weight was also a sufficient cause of bending (q $\supset$ r). Another way of phrasing each of these statements is to say that (1) a long rod which is light will bend, and (2) a heavy rod which is short will bend. In terms of our symbols, (1) may be written as (p $\wedge$ $\bar{q}$) $\supset$ r, and (2) may be described as ($\bar{p}$ $\wedge$ q) $\supset$ r. To restate these functions once again, (p $\wedge$ $\bar{q}$) $\supset$ r says that a rod which is long (p) and ($\wedge$) light ($\bar{q}$) implies ($\supset$) bending (r); ($\bar{p}$ $\wedge$ q) $\supset$ r states that a rod which is short ($\bar{p}$) and ($\wedge$) heavy (q) implies ($\supset$) bending (r). In the course of his experiments, then, the adolescent has come to the conclusions which may be described in terms of both of the propositional functions given above. (He has also come to similar conclusions about the other factors in the experiment—material, cross-section, etc.—but we shall ignore these for the moment.)

Having derived the conclusions, the adolescent discovers that in the case of each rod, one factor *compensates* for the other. (Recall our discussions of compensation in the case of conservation.) In the first rod the weight is light, but the length compensates for this and causes the rod to bend. In the second rod the length is short, but the increased weight makes up for this and produces bending. Another way of looking at the matter is as follows. Suppose we observe that a rod of a given weight and length bends a certain amount. Imagine further that we want to keep the amount of bending exactly as it is and make the length shorter. The way to do this is to increase the weight; that is, compensate for a decrease in length by an equivalent increase in weight. Or conversely, if we want to decrease the weight while maintaining the same degree of bending, we would have to increase the length.

Thus far, the adolescent has come to conclusions about the factors causing bending in each rod, and has also noticed, again in the case of each rod separately, that one factor compensates for the other to produce a given degree of bending. In one rod, length makes up for weight $((p \wedge \bar{q}) \supset r)$ and in the second, weight makes up for length $((\bar{p} \wedge q) \supset r)$.

Next, the adolescent sees a certain relation between the compensations affecting each rod; reciprocity is involved. That is, by linking his separate conclusions about each rod, he realizes that the compensation within one rod is the reciprocal of the compensation within the other. While in one rod length makes up for the weight, the reciprocal (weight making up for length) holds in the other rod.

Piaget again states the adolescent's reasoning in logical terms. If you will recall, the functions intended to describe the adolescent's initial conclusions were $(p \wedge \bar{q}) \supset r$ and $(\bar{p} \wedge q) \supset r$. Now, to describe the adolescent's understanding of the relation *between* these conclusions we may write $(p \wedge \bar{q}) = R (\bar{p} \wedge q)$, or a long, light rod is reciprocal (R) of a short and heavy one. Thus, we see how two separate functions, $(p \wedge \bar{q})$ and $(\bar{p} \wedge q)$ are related to one another by means of one operation of the INRC group, namely R, or reciprocity. This is intended to describe how the adolescent perceives relations between his conclusions.

Negation

To illustrate the rule N, consider the following study. Piaget presented the subjects with another problem from physics. Subjects were shown an apparatus in which a spring device launched balls, one at a time, across a horizontal track. The balls were of various weights and volumes. The task was to predict where on the track the balls would stop. In addition, subjects were asked to explain the results. Piaget was particularly interested in whether subjects would come to discover the principle of inertia. This states, in essence, that if no factors impede the motion of the ball, then it will forever maintain a uniform rectilinear motion; that is, keep going at the same speed. Of course, under normal conditions, several factors are always present to impede movement. Friction slows the ball as a function of its weight; air resistance impedes the ball as a function of its volume; and the irregularities of the track, among other factors, hinder motion too. The result of all these interfering factors is that one can never observe the operation of inertia in a pure state. In other words, since the real world always and unavoidably contains impediments like friction or air resistance, it is impossible to view enduring, uniform rectilinear motion. The conservation of motion by inertia is a theoretical possibility, not an empirical fact. For Piaget, the interesting problem is how the subject discovers an ideal principle which is not observable.

The adolescent goes about solving the problem in a systematic way. As we have already seen, he designs a series of experiments properly and uses the method of holding constant all factors but one. Since we have covered this matter before, we will not review it again. The adolescent's observations allow him to construct several valid statements concerning the behavior of balls on the horizontal plane. DEV (14;6), for example, concludes that a ball "stopped because the air resists . . . the bigger they are, the stronger the air resistance." [6] He and other adolescents are successful in identifying additional factors, too; for example, that friction stops the ball. We can conclude, then, that using the experimental procedures already discussed, adolescents are able to derive legitimate causal statements about the forces impeding a ball's motion.

Once again, Piaget describes the adolescent's conclusions in terms of propositional logic. Letting p = the ball's stopping, q = the presence of friction, and r = the presence of air resistance, Piaget writes $p \supset q$ (read: stopping implies friction) and $p \supset r$ (stopping implies air resistance). The functions may be combined into $p \supset (q \lor r)$, where "$\lor$" stands for "or." Furthermore, the function can be expanded to $p \supset (q \lor r \lor s \lor t \lor \ldots)$, where s, t, and . . . indicate an indefinite number of other factors. Thus far, then, the adolescent's thought merely illustrates several of the 16 binary propositions, again a matter we have already reviewed.

Next appears the step which is of particular interest. After coming to a conclusion which may be described by the function $p \supset (q \lor r \lor s \lor t \lor \ldots)$, "the subject asks himself what should be the result of the negation of all these factors, this negation implying a corresponding negation of statement p, that is slowing down. This is equivalent to the assertion of the continuation of motion:

$$\bar{q} \cdot \bar{r} \cdot \bar{s} \cdot \bar{t} \cdot \cdot \supset \bar{p}\text{."} [7]$$

6. *Ibid.*, p. 129.
7. *Ibid.*, p. 130. Piaget uses "." as we have used "∧". Both mean "and."

That is to say that the adolescent begins with conclusions concerning the stopping of motion. The conclusions may be described in terms of the function p ⊃ (q ∨ r ∨ s ∨ t . . .) or stopping implies friction, etc. Then the adolescent transforms the original function by the operation of negation, N, which is one of the INRC group. The result of this transformation is a new function, namely q̄ ∧ r̄ ∧ s̄ ∧ t̄ . . . ⊃ p̄. The new function states the principle of inertia, and reads, the absence of friction (q̄), and (∧) the absence of air resistance (r̄), and (∧) the absence of all other impeding factors (s̄ t̄ . . .) implies (⊃) the absence of stopping (p̄). Since the precise logical rules for applying negation are rather complex, they will not be covered here. The important point is that the adolescent has used certain rules to transform the initial conclusion into yet another. This transformation allows him to discover the principle of inertia which he cannot observe in the world of fact. Without manipulating the initial conclusion, and thus going beyond the evidence provided by reality (the factors causing stopping), the adolescent could not achieve the statement of the ideal (the principle of inertia). It is the adolescent's mental operations, his reasoning, rather than his observations which allow him to discover the ideal possibility. The operation N is simply Piaget's attempt to describe *how* the adolescent manipulates the initial conclusions to go beyond them.

Further Aspects of the INRC Group

Thus far we have discussed two rules of the INRC group: negation and reciprocity. As we have seen in the discussion of conservation in Chapter Four, negation and reciprocity are both forms of *reversibility*, that is, ways of reversing the operations of thought. Of course, the reversibility of the period of formal operations differs from that of the period of concrete operations. In the latter case, operations on concrete objects may be reversed; in the former case, operations on hypothetical propositions (functions) may be reversed.

Piaget goes on to discuss two further aspects of the INRC group, I and C, which we will only mention here. I is an identity operator: when applied to a function, I leaves it unchanged. C is more complex. Applied to a function, C changes conjunction (∧) to disjunction (∨), and vice versa, but leaves everything else unchanged.

THE LOGICAL MODELS

We could go on to describe further aspects of the logical structures or models. Piaget's discussion is quite extensive and complex. It is also very technical. Piaget has a tendency to elaborate on the logical features of his models. He stresses, for instance, that the 16 binary operations have *lattice* properties, and that the INRC operations form a *group* of four transformations. We will not review these logico-mathematical features of the models, since a proper exposition requires far more mathematical development than lies within the scope of this book. (For example, to define a lattice we must introduce the notions of *partially ordered set, relation,* and so on.) Instead, we will offer a few general comments on Piaget's models.

First, like the Groupings which were discussed in connection with concrete operational thought, the 16 binary operations and the INRC group are *not* intended to imply that the adolescent understands logic in any explicit way. Most adolescents do not know propositional logic or group operations. Piaget does not use logic to describe the adolescent's explicit knowledge, but to depict the structure of his thought.

Second, the logical models are qualitative, not quantitative. The adolescent comes to conclusions like "length is involved in oscillation" or "thinness causes bending in rods." His conclusions are statements which do not involve numbers; therefore, the model of the statements must also be non-numerical. Neither the 16 binary operations nor the INRC group involve numbers. For example, a statement of implication might be, "the addition of weight causes bending." Implication would not be expressed by a statement like, "the addition of 5 pounds causes 4 inches of bending."

Third, the logical models are intended to describe the structure of adolescent activities. It is not the case that the models exactly duplicate the adolescent's performance in full detail. The models are not simply protocols which list everything that the adolescent does; instead, they are abstractions which are intended to capture the essence of his thought. For example, in one study, adolescents were required to discover the factors causing the stopping of a roulette wheel type of device. Subjects performed certain tests and made a number of verbal statements. While the details of the study are not of interest to us at the moment, we will review part of one protocol in order to illustrate the function of Piaget's logic.

The following operations can be distinguished in his protocol:

1. Disjunction ($p \lor q$) . . . It's either the distance or the content (or both).

2. Its inverse, conjunctive negation ($\bar{p} \cdot \bar{q}$): changing the position of the boxes verifies the hypothesis that neither weight nor color is the determining factor.

3. Conjunction ($p \cdot q$): both content and distance are effective.

4. Its inverse, incompatibility . . . the effect of the magnet is incompatible with moving the boxes from the center for the needle may stop without the boxes being moved and vice versa, or neither occurs.[8]

8. *Ibid.,* p. 103.

Piaget's account continues for twelve more steps. Note that for almost everything that the adolescent says or does, there corresponds a logical representation. Piaget is able to translate almost the entire protocol into logical form. Such logical representations have the advantage of describing the basics of the adolescent's activities in a *general way*. The logical statements go beyond the details of the particular problem and describe fundamental intellectual skills which the adolescent uses in many situations.

Fourth, like the Groupings, both the system of 16 binary operations and the INRC group are integrated systems. According to Piaget, none of the 16 binary operations nor the INRC group exists in isolation from the others. An operation like implication, for example, does not stand alone; it is part of a larger system which makes implication and other operations possible.

Fifth, like the Groupings, the formal operations describe the adolescent's *competence*. Both the 16 binary operations and the INRC group describe the capacities of the adolescent, and not necessarily what he does on any one occasion at any one time. It may be, for example, that factors of fatigue or boredom prevent an adolescent from displaying the full extent of his capacities. The models do not describe the actual performance, which may be deficient, but define the adolescent's capability.

Sixth, the models may be said to explain and predict behavior. There is explanation in the sense that the models describe basic processes underlying the adolescent's approach to problems. We can say that the adolescent solved a particular problem *because* his thought can utilize the logical operations of implication or negation, and so forth. Such a structural description is one kind of explanation; another kind is prediction in the sense that the models are general. That is, having knowledge of the basic structure of his intellectual activity, we can predict what his performance will be like in general terms in other, similar tasks. Since the models describe the essence of his thought, we can predict how he will operate on problems that are formally similar to ones with which Piaget presented him.

These, then, are the goals of Piaget's theory; to develop formal systems which are clear, adequately descriptive, and general. It is now possible to consider how successfully Piaget's models fulfill his stated intentions. A judgment of this type is unfortunately not a simple matter. For one thing, the models may be successful in some respects but not in others. Also, considerable knowledge of logic is necessary for a fair evaluation of the system. And finally, no model is ever definitive. It is always possible to revise a given model, to state it in another language, to modify its features, and so forth. In fact, Piaget is presently engaged in an elaboration of the models. Consequently, we will limit our comments to one point.

It is not entirely clear that a binary logical model is fully appropriate. (A binary model is one in which only statements involving two values may be made; for example, the rod is long or short, or heavy or light.) Do recall that Piaget feels that one of the advantages of binary propositional logic is that it can deal with non-numerical statements. While this feature of the model is no doubt often advantageous, there are times when it is not. Sometimes, the adolescents' methods and conclusions are not binary in the way Piaget describes. For example, in the rods problem, PEY (12;9) concluded, "The larger and thicker it is, the more it resists." [9] Note that PEY did not deal just with large and small rods, as propositional logic demands, but with the entire continuum of size. The same is true of thickness and resistance with the result that the conclusion applies to rods of *all* possible gradations of largeness and thickness. Thus, PEY's statement is not restricted merely to two values (long and short) of each factor. Or consider EME's behavior in the pendulum problem. To assess the role of weight, she tested first a 100 gram weight, then a 20 gram, and finally a 200 gram. Thus, the weight did not assume just the two values of heavy and light as is necessary for binary propositional logic, but rather involved a scale with three distinct values. It would seem necessary, then, to alter the model in order to bring it closer in line with data of this sort.[10]

GENERAL CHARACTERISTICS OF ADOLESCENT THOUGHT

We have reviewed in some detail the adolescent's methods of problem-solving, and have illustrated aspects of the 16 binary operations and the INRC group. Piaget does not mean to say that the typical adolescent of the formal stage always employs operations of the kind described. Various factors may prevent use of these operations. Under conditions of fatigue or boredom, for instance, the adolescent may not fully display the thought of which he is capable. Piaget's model of the formal operations (and the concrete operations too) describes the adolescent's optimum level of functioning, and not necessarily his typical performance.

There are several general ways in which Piaget describes adolescent thought. One, the adolescent makes reality secondary to possibility. In order to understand this point, let us consider first the behavior of the younger, concrete-operational child. Given the oscillation problem, he makes various experiments and observes the results quite carefully. He may correctly judge that short pendulums swing more rapidly than long ones; or in the rods problem, he may decide quite accurately that rod A bends

9. *Ibid.*, p. 56.
10. The reader interested in pursuing a critique of the logical aspects of the models is urged to consult an incisive paper by C. Parsons, a logician. C. Parsons, "Inhelder and Piaget's *The Growth of Logical Thinking*," *British Journal of Psychology*, 51, 1960, pp. 75–84.

more than rod B, which in turn bends more than rod C, and so forth. Thus, to solve the problem the child can efficiently perform the concrete operations, as in ordering the degree of bending of rods. But there are several major deficiencies in his procedure. He begins his experiments with little foresight and does not have a detailed plan for carrying them out. The concrete child does not consider all of the possibilities before he begins. Instead, he is limited to dealing with empirical results, with things that are available to immediate perception. He fails to make consistent use of the method of holding constant all factors but one. The part played by possibility is very small indeed; it is restricted to the simple extension of actions already in progress. After the child has ordered a set of rods in terms of the extent of their bending, for instance, he could, if given several new rods, place them in appropriate positions in the series. The concrete-operational child does not consider possibilities on a theoretical plane. Instead, he works efficiently with the concrete and real, and has the potentiality to do to new things what he has already done to old ones.

For the adolescent, on the other hand, possibility dominates reality. Confronted with a scientific problem, he begins not by observing the empirical results, but by thinking of the possibilities inherent in the situation. He imagines that many things *might* occur, that many interpretations of the data *might* be feasible, and that what has actually occurred is but one of a number of possible alternatives. Only after performing a hypothetical analysis of this sort does he proceed to obtain empirical data which serve to confirm or refute his hypothesis. Furthermore, he bases experiments on deductions from the hypothetical; he is not bound solely by the observed. In the pendulum problem, he might suppose that length is a causative factor, and then deduce what must occur if such a hypothesis were true. The experiment is then designed to test the deduction. Thus, the adolescent's thought, but not that of the concrete-operational child, is hypothetico-deductive.

The second distinctive feature of formal operations is their "combinatorial" property. For purposes of contrast, recall again the behavior of the concrete-operational child. When confronted with several factors which might influence an experimental result, the child of this stage usually tests each of them alone, but fails to consider all of their combinations. On the other hand, when given the task of discovering which mixture of five chemicals produces the color yellow, the adolescent combines them in an exhaustive way. He mixes one with two, and one with three, and one with four, and so forth, until all combinations have been achieved. This is another way, then, in which possibility dominates the adolescent's encounters with reality. If, like the concrete-operational child, the adolescent had not beforehand conceived of all the possibilities, he would have designed a more limited set of experimental situations.

It can be said, then, that adolescent thought has achieved an advanced state of equilibrium. This means, among other things, that the adolescent's cognitive structures have now developed to the point where they can effectively adapt to a great variety of problems. These structures are sufficiently stable to assimilate readily a variety of novel situations. Thus, the adolescent need not drastically accommodate his structures to new problems. This does not mean, of course, that the adolescent's growth ceases at age 16. He has much to learn in many areas, and Piaget does not deny this. Piaget does maintain however, that, by the end of adolescence, the individual's ways of thinking, that is, his cognitive structures, are almost fully formed. While these structures may be applied to new problems with the result that significant knowledge is achieved, the structures themselves undergo little modification after adolescence. They have reached a high degree of equilibrium.

The adolescent's thought involves a number of additional features. First, the adolescent's thought is flexible. He has available a large number of cognitive operations with which to attack problems. Given some preliminary statements, he can manipulate them by means of the INRC group to derive definitive conclusions. This ability is completely lacking in the concrete-operational child. Thus, the adolescent is versatile in his thought and can deal with a problem in many ways and from a variety of perspectives. Second, the adolescent is unlikely to be confused by unusual results because he has beforehand conceived of all the possibilities. In the pendulum problem, for instance, it would not at all surprise the adolescent if it occurred that the only determinant of oscillation were the combination of weight and length with neither factor by itself being effective; this result was one of the possibilities considered. For the younger child, however, the same result might be seen as inconsistent and not understandable, since it contradicts the simple relationships of which he can conceive. Third, the adolescent's thought is now simultaneously reversible in two distinct ways.[11] That is, he has available both the operations N and R, each of which involves a kind of reversibility. In less technical terms, this means that his thought can proceed in one direction, and then use several different methods for retracing its steps in order to return to the starting point.

The effect of the adolescent's intellectual achievements is not limited to the area of scientific problem-solving. Piaget finds repercussions of formal thought on several areas of adolescent life, although his remarks probably hold more particularly for European cultures than for American. In the intellectual sphere, the adolescent has a tendency to become involved in abstract and theoretical matters. He constructs elaborate polit-

---

11. The concrete-operational child has available the two forms of reversibility too, but they are not integrated into one system. Negation applies only to classes and reciprocity only to relations. See *Growth of Logical Thinking*, ch. 17.

ical theories or invents complex philosophical doctrines. He may develop plans for the complete reorganization of society or indulge in metaphysical speculation. Having just discovered capabilities for abstract thought, he then proceeds to exercise them without restraint. Indeed, in the process of exploring his new abilities the adolescent sometimes loses touch with reality, and feels that he can accomplish everything by thought alone. In the emotional sphere the adolescent now becomes capable of directing his emotions at abstract ideals and not just toward people. Whereas earlier he could love his mother or hate a peer, now he can love freedom or hate exploitation. The adolescent has developed a new mode of life: the possible and the ideal captivate both mind and feeling.

We may now ask how the stage of formal operations is attained. Why does the child pass beyond the period of concrete operations to reach a later state of equilibrium? Piaget is not very explicit on this point, and only gives an outline of equilibration theory as applied to adolescence. He maintains first that it is conceivable that neurological development occurring around the time of puberty provides the basis for the appearance of formal operations. But neurological change is not sufficient: there are cultures whose members lack formal operations but not, presumably, the requisite neurological development. Second, Piaget maintains that the social environment also plays a role. Education in school or other instruction may hasten or retard the development of formal structures. It is also true that the level of intellectual accomplishment of a given culture may affect the cognitive development of its members. But the social environment explanation is not sufficient. One cannot teach a 5-year-old formal operations: the individual must be ready for them by having developed the proper preliminary cognitive structures. In other words, the child must prepare for the development of formal operations by first developing the skills of the concrete period. A third consideration is that the individual's experience with things plays a role. If the adolescent has never had a chance to experiment with anything, he will not develop formal structures. Experience, however, is not a sufficient hypothesis to explain the attainment of formal operations. The 4-year-old and the 14-year-old, given the same experience, will not benefit from it in the same way. Fourth, and finally, the child's own activity is crucial in this development. This is the equilibration factor which we have discussed in Chapter Four. When the child in the concrete-operational period attempts to apply his intellectual methods to complex situations (for example, the scientific problems already covered), he sometimes meets with contradiction and failure. When this happens, he attempts to resolve the contradictions, and to do so must reorganize the concrete operations. Change begins with the felt inadequacy of the current state of affairs and proceeds by a process of internal reorganization.

To summarize, cognitive advance occurs as a function of appropriate neurological development, a proper social environment, experience with things, and internal cognitive reorganization. This, of course, is a point of view concerning growth and not a detailed theory.

SUMMARY AND CONCLUSIONS

In the stage of formal thought, the adolescent develops the ability to imagine the possibilities inherent in a situation. Before acting on a problem which confronts him, the adolescent analyzes it and attempts to develop hypotheses concerning what *might* occur. These hypotheses are numerous and complex because the adolescent takes into account all possible combinations of eventualities in an exhaustive way. As he proceeds to test his ideas, he designs experiments which are quite efficient in terms of supporting some hypotheses and disproving others. He accurately observes the results of the experiments, and from them he draws the proper conclusions. Moreover, given some conclusion, he can reason about it and thereby derive new interpretations. The adolescent's thought is now so flexible and powerful that it has reached a high degree of equilibrium. Piaget describes this entire process in terms of two logical structures or models, the 16 binary operations and the INRC group. He believes that such models are clear and capture the essence of the adolescent's mental activities.

It is apparent from the above description that Piaget has made a definite contribution to our understanding of adolescent thought. First, his empirical data seem relatively straightforward. The adolescent's methods of solution are shown fairly directly in the protocols. Little inference is required to decide what the adolescents were doing or thinking. Second, Piaget's findings suggest that there are basic differences between the adolescent and younger child as far as scientific reasoning is concerned. It seems clear that as age increases there is an improvement in systematic experimentation, in the design of crucial tests, in attempts to isolate variables, in the appreciation of the complexity of problems, and in the ability to draw reasonable conclusions from empirical data. Third, Piaget has made a beginning in the task of developing formal models to describe and explain the adolescent's behavior. While we have doubts as to the adequacy of the proposed logical system, it is nevertheless true that Piaget is one of the very few theorists of child development who have even attempted to construct models of this sort.

6

genetic epistemology and the implications of piaget's findings for education

Up to this point, we have reviewed Piaget's overall theory of intellectual development which covers the period from birth to the inception of mature thought during adolescence. We have seen examples of various behavioral responses which provide the empirical basis for the theory. In addition, we have briefly discussed the methodologies which Piaget and his collaborators have employed. In short, our concern until now has been Piaget's psychology, which indeed represents a substantial and valuable contribution. However, in recent years, Piaget has turned from purely psychological studies and has devoted much of his attention to the problems of genetic epistemology.

GENETIC EPISTEMOLOGY

It was not Piaget's intention at the outset of his career to contribute only to the field of experimental child psychology. We saw in Chapter One that Piaget was no usual psychologist whose major purpose was to reach an insight into the child's thought processes. Even though he has devoted some 45 years of his life to this subject, his ultimate objective, when turning to the study of child psychology, was far more ambitious. It was essentially to elucidate problems in the branch of philosophy known as *epistemology*. Epistemology is concerned with the theory of knowledge. It asks questions like the following. Is genuine knowledge indeed attainable? If so, what are the origins of such knowledge? Do we acquire knowledge by reasoning or through direct experience with the external world? What are the relations that exist between the subjective and the objective components of the knowledge situation; that is, between the person and his environment? Is there a difference between what things seem to be and what they really are? All these and many other issues are dealt with by the epistemologist as he tries to probe into the nature of knowledge.

With his scientific background Piaget felt that purely philosophical methods were not adequate for the solution of these kinds of epistemological questions. A new approach, one which involved the psychological study of the child, was needed in this area.

Science and Philosophy

In order to understand Piaget's approach to epistemological questions, we must first consider his views on the nature of science and philosophy and understand the distinctions that he draws between the two disciplines.

Piaget distinguishes between science and philosophy on the basis of two major criteria: subject matter and methodology. Philosophy, he feels, purports to study many aspects of reality simultaneously in order to provide an overall picture of man's place in the world and his purpose in living. This understanding of reality is achieved by various methods, the most important of which is reflection. The philosopher observes diverse aspects of reality, evaluates them, and after careful thought or inner speculation, reaches a philosophical position as to the essence of reality and human nature. This approach is both general and subjective. It is general because philosophical principles attempt to cover a great many manifestations of life; it is subjective because the conclusions are drawn primarily as a result of the philosopher's reflection. The scope of philosophy is, therefore, too broad and its methods too fallible for any sort of consensus to be reached regarding the fundamental questions it raises. Each philosopher, or school of philosophy, has a group of followers or disciples who firmly believe in the validity of their premises, but who have no objective method of evaluating their beliefs, and thus they fail to convince those who support different premises. Philosophical schools are consequently rarely in agreement with each other.

Science differs from philosophy both in the extent of the phenomena studied and, more especially, in methodology. While philosophy attempts to grasp many aspects of reality concurrently, science, on the contrary, limits itself to the study of a limited domain of phenomena. In doing so it does not rely on either introspection or reflection as a means of reaching conclusions, but on objective methods of observation and collection of data. It endeavors to subject its conclusions to empirical test and possible refutation. By limiting its scope to restricted and observable aspects of reality, science hopes to reduce the influence of subjective factors. It is possible, therefore, that agreement can often be reached in science, at least insofar as the limited sector under study is concerned, whereas this is seldom the case in philosophy. The boundary between science and philosophy is not necessarily fixed. Gradually more and more problems, originally considered philosophical in nature, are being investigated by the scientific method. Psychology is itself an example of a discipline which began by being purely philosophical and is now well established in the field of science.

Rationale for Genetic Epistemology

Because of his views concerning the inadequacies of philosophy—and especially its incapacity to reach a definitive understanding on fundamental questions—Piaget felt that it would be desirable to deal with the philosophical issues of knowledge by the use of scientific methods. One might reach agreement by this technique on the problems of a relatively limited area of speculation. He believed that it might be fruitful to investigate epistemological problems from a psychological point of view particularly by applying the scientific methods used in psychology. Many epistemological problems are in fact basically psychological. For example, the questions of the relationship between the knower and his environment or the innateness of certain forms of knowledge both relate to human behavior, and are, therefore, psychological issues. It might, therefore, be possible for them to be resolved by the application of scientific methods. The issues should no longer be left solely for the speculation of philosophers but should be treated in a more objective manner.

Piaget also felt that a developmental study would be especially useful. Knowledge undergoes a long period of evolution in the individual as well as in society. The study of this development at both levels might yield insight into the most mature (or at least latest) forms of collective and individual knowledge. For these reasons, both the *genetic* (or developmental) study of the child, and the *historical* study of knowledge, are relevant for problems of epistemology.

Piaget approached these problems within a biological framework as well as a psychological one. When concerned with the problem of the individual's acquisition of knowledge, Piaget tended to think in terms of embryology: with development, mental structures take on qualitatively different forms, but at the same time they retain some continuity since each one evolves from previous structures. Piaget was interested also in relating the increase of knowledge in the individual to the increase of knowledge in a society. This is analogous to comparing the development of a species (phylogeny) with that of an individual (ontogeny).

In brief, Piaget did not think of himself purely as a child psychologist, but rather as a "genetic epistemologist"—one who uses information concerning cognitive development of the child and historical development of culture as a foundation for theories aimed at understanding the nature of both individual and social knowledge. Moreover, Piaget approached this endeavor within a biological, evolutionary framework which postulates some element of continuity in development. In this sense his work attempts to bridge the gap between biology and philosophy.

Psychogenetic Method

Piaget uses two methods in the study of epistemological problems. To understand the growth of individual knowledge he uses the *psychogenetic* method, and to deal with collective knowledge, he employs the *historico-critical* method.

The psychogenetic method deals with the individual development of certain scientific notions such as space, geometry, number, or time from their initial appearance to the stage when these notions achieve their most mature forms. This approach may be compared to a type of mental embryology of the child. The results derived from the use of this method have given rise to the main body of data and theories described in the present book. These findings, as they deal with the growth of knowledge in a particular area, can then be used in the clarification of certain epistemological problems. One example concerns the notion of causality. The nature of cause and effect in physical phenomena has been a source of discussion among philosophers for quite some time. One interpretation of the origins of the notion of causality has been provided by the Scottish philosopher, David Hume, who believes that a person's explanation of physical phenomena is purely a result of past experience. If two events usually occur contiguously, that is, with little spatial or temporal separation between them, the person will create an association or link. Over time this link becomes strengthened with repetition. The association leads to a "habit"; that is, it produces an expectation as to what event will follow another. Without being aware of how the first event affects the second, the person attributes a causal connection between the two occurrences as a result of past experience and habits. He sees the first event as the cause and the second as the effect. Such an emphasis on contiguity means that any two events can stand in a cause-effect relation, provided there is some sort of spatial or temporal proximity between the two events. Causal inference, then, is felt to be merely a question of habit; that is, the observation of regular associations between events.

Maine de Biran contributes another philosophical interpretation of causality, and maintains that causality is an extension of the experience of our own voluntary bodily movements. We are constantly experiencing our own movements as affecting certain events in the world. For instance, if we hold an object in our hands and we move our arms upward, this results in the lifting of the object; if a ball is lying in front of us and we move our feet forward, this results in the kicking of a ball. These experiences remind us that we are agents of causality. The feeling of causality is more than the recognition of certain habits of the past whereby two external events become linked together. It is our own voluntary movements and their ensuing results that move us to predicate cause-effect relationships in the world. In other words, voluntary movements and their effects serve as a model for our ascribing causality to events. So for Maine de Biran it is our volition and not, as for Hume, the observation of regularities that gives rise to the original sentiment of causality

Piaget's observations of children from infancy onward have served to clarify the issue to a certain degree. Some of the infant's actions seem to speak in favor of Hume's interpretation. The baby of 6 or 7 months does indeed seem to associate anything to anything else, simply on the grounds of spatial or temporal contiguity. For example, Jacqueline at one time pulled a string in her bassinet, and Piaget simultaneously moved a book back and forth before her eyes. When Piaget stopped, Jacqueline again pulled the string, clearly expecting that this action would cause the book's movement. Thus, an association between string and book had been formed on the basis of mere temporal contiguity.

These observations seem to confirm Hume's theory of causality as a result of connections formed through habit. However, Piaget's observations have also shown that, contrary to Hume's theory, it is not just anything which can become connected with anything else. The infant forms a causal association only between his own actions and events. In the example mentioned above, a causal relation was formed between Jacqueline's own action of pulling the string and the movement of the book. Such connections are not random, according to Piaget, but are related to the child's voluntary bodily movements. So we can see that Maine de Biran's interpretation also is equally valid. During the initial stages the child's feelings of causality are a consequence of his own actions. Maine de Biran's interpretation is not altogether adequate as he believes that the person is aware of his own volition in provoking the bodily movements. This concept does not appear to be true of the young infant who does not know that it is *he* who makes his arm move. It is only after a period of development that the child eventually becomes aware that his actions are indeed a source of causality.

In the problem of the origins of causality, only one of the innumerable notions studied by Piaget, psychological data can make some contribution toward an increased understanding of problems of an epistemological nature. No agreement had been reached in the past on this point, because philosophers had speculated on the problem from the point of view of adult notions of causality and had failed to take into account the early stages in its evolution. This unfortunately also seems to occur fairly frequently in many areas of science. In particular, many psychologists have attempted to understand certain manifestations of human behavior such as language, memory, or perception by concentrating only on their mature versions. They restrict their studies to adult performance alone. If one believes in the continuity of development, then the addition of another dimension, the temporal one, should provide valuable information on the end product. A new perspective is introduced to the whole problem by means of an analysis of psychological facts from a developmental point of view. This approach can be applied in a similar fashion to other epistemological problems and help to provide valuable insights. Thus, we can see that the genetic method of psychology has an important contribution to make to both psychology and other fields.

Historico-Critical Method

The second method which Piaget employs, the historico-critical method, consists of an analysis of collective thought over a period of time. In these studies he no longer deals with the growth of knowledge in the individual, but with the historical evolution of a set of notions on a given subject matter. After having analyzed the historical development of a particular notion, Piaget then attempts to look for some sort of parallel between the individual acquisition of knowledge and the development of collective knowledge. In other words, he uses a psychological model to study the evolution of collective thought. Although he does not always find a perfect fit between the two, he does nevertheless find a number of similarities in the mechanisms of development. The example of mathematical thought might help to clarify the use of the two methods.

A mathematician, P. Boutroux, has analyzed the evolution of mathematical thought from the Greek period to the present day and finds that this can be divided into three distinct periods. Piaget agrees with this division and tries to show that there is an analogy between the development of mathematics and the intellectual development of the child.

The first period in mathematical thought begins with the Greeks when the major portion of mathematics was essentially arithmetic and what we now call Euclidian geometry. The mathematicians of that time tended to concentrate on the geometric forms, or the spatial configurations, rather than on the operations underlying these forms. They were interested in the results of certain mathematical operations, and not in the operations themselves. To illustrate this orientation, let us consider one example: the problem of bisecting and trisecting an angle.[1] Euclid discovered an easy ruler-and-compass method of bisecting any angle. He had thereby achieved a limited understanding of this geometric form. But the trisection problem, which on first sight appears to be similar to that of bisection, defied solution for two thousand years, because he had not grasped the basic operations which are necessary to fully understand these problems. What interested the Greeks here was the question of *attributes* of angles. Can all angles be bisected? Can all angles be trisected? Indeed, all of Greek geometry was concerned with describing the attributes of geometrical objects in general but not the basic operations underlying them. As a consequence of this concentration on the result of mathematical operations rather than on the operations themselves, the mathematical notions of the Greeks, although extremely diversified and containing the germs of many later developments in mathematics, tended to be quite sterile. They were not able to progress beyond a certain point. Accent was laid on external reality, or the thing known in the knower-known relationship.

This period of mathematical thought, Piaget feels, could be compared with the stage of preoperational thought in the child. During this period the child can perform certain actions and discover some of the attributes of objects and figures. He recognizes some geometrical shapes and forms. He can establish the spatial relationships of objects and can find his way in familiar surroundings, which implies that he can perform certain actions or transformations on his environment. He is, nevertheless, largely unaware of the processes which determine his mental or motor activity. Like the Greek mathematicians, although he is able to apprehend certain limited aspects of reality, he is not concerned with the means by which he interacts with his environment.

The second period in the history of mathematical thought occurred during the 17th century. Algebra and analytic geometry were discovered. At this time mathematicians shifted their attention from the result of mathematical operations (the thing known) to the operations themselves (how this knowledge is attained). In its early stages, analytic geometry was used to provide alternative proofs to the problems which the Greeks

1. Recall that in Euclidean geometry only ruler-and-compass methods are used: the measurement of lines and angles is never permitted.

had first studied. The significance of this lay in the fact that the new proofs were "better." Euclidean proofs, although logical and elegant, were often discovered haphazardly. Analytic geometry, however, by reducing all the problems of Euclid to algebraic problems, allowed them to be tackled in an orderly fashion.

The importance of this advance is well illustrated by our earlier example of bisecting and trisecting angles. The fact that the bisection problem could be solved by algebraic procedures was not of great interest —since Euclid had already solved it anyway. But these same algebraic operations enabled mathematicians to reduce the (unsolved) trisection problem to an algebraic form: trisecting an angle is equivalent to solving a certain equation. Eventually the 19th century algebraist, Galois, proved that, in general, this equation *cannot* be solved; therefore the trisection problem is essentially insoluble. The Greeks, by concentrating their efforts on the specific question (the attributes of angles) rather than on the operations involved in answering the question, could never have arrived at this conclusion. Clearly this concentration on operations led mathematicians to a deeper understanding of their field.

The second period in the history of mathematics corresponds to the moment in individual development when the child becomes capable of concrete operations. At this point not only can he classify things, order them, or perform a series of mental operations on them, he is also becoming aware of the transformations which he performs on objects. At first this awareness is far from complete. For instance, in the experiment of conservation of liquid mentioned in Chapter Four, he will say that the liquid in the second beaker is the same because one can pour it back to the original beaker and there will still be the same amount of water (operation of reversibility), or else that it is the same because nothing has been added or taken away (operation of identity). Contained in these justifications is the implicit discovery of the role of operations. The child no longer centers on the states (or attributes) of reality, but now also takes into consideration the transformations or operations.

The third period in the history of mathematics began in the late 19th century, although one could argue that the new insight was implicit in much earlier work. The Greeks, while interested in mathematical "objects" (number, angles, triangles, circles, etc.) were highly selective in their choice of these objects. The reasons for this do not concern us here, but it should be noted that all these objects were intuitively appealing. Abstruse notions, such as the number π, disturbed the Greeks.[2] They

2. The Greeks ascribed "perfection" to lines and circles, so naturally they expected to find a simple and intuitively appealing ratio between the length of the circumference of a circle and its diameter. The number π, which is approximately 3.1416, is neither simple nor intuitively appealing. Greek mathematicians were outraged by this monstrosity.

were unhappy that their ideas of perfection in geometry and arithmetic seemed to be challenged by the existence of such a number. To modern eyes the Greeks failed to realize that the objects of mathematical study ought to be quite arbitrary (sets with structures). For example, modern mathematicians on encountering the number π, ask: why not enlarge the number system to include π? The result is the construction of the "real" numbers. Why not generalize the number system further, to study abstract groups, fields, etc.? Why not study different types of geometries, rather than solely Euclidean geometry? Why not generalize further to study abstract topological spaces? And so forth.

In the child this may be likened to the period of formal operations. Here the child, or rather the adolescent, becomes more aware of his power of operating on things which is now abstract as well as concrete. Reality becomes secondary to possibility. He is not interested solely in the actual results of a given experiment, but in its possibilities and in the generalizations it might lead to.

However, there is something more to be said of the third period in the development of mathematics. While the modern mathematician feels free to decide what objects he will study (the real numbers, groups, fields, abstract geometries, etc.) he is constrained by the basic laws of logic. Thus, the structure of mathematics still appears to have some property akin to that of objective reality which Boutroux terms the "intrinsic objectivity" of mathematical reality. In other words, the mathematician is not completely in control of his subject. Similarly, the adolescent acquires knowledge of certain constraints in his environment over which he has no control, as, for instance, gravity. Despite his increased capacity for hypothetico-deductive reasoning, there are still features of his environment which elude his control.

We can see, then, how the collective development of mathematical thought parallels that of the individual. At first the child is not aware of his mental operations, although he can successfully perform a number of actions on the things around him. Slowly, with the increase in his intellectual capacity, this awareness of the inner workings of his mind comes about and with it a greater facility in understanding and controlling intricate concrete situations. Later in life, at a time when he is able to operate mentally on abstract events, he comes to realize that, despite his capacity to understand a great deal more of external reality, there are still certain features which he cannot fully control. Just as the child's intellectual development seems to start with a period of intense egocentrism, characterized by phenomenalistic thought which concentrates on the superficial, or peripheral aspects of reality, so the history of mathematical thought seems at first to reflect these same characteristics. In both individual and collective thought, the initial period betrays a lack of awareness of the more profound and subtle features of reality and of the complexities of thought and mental activity. Then gradually, a process of decentration occurs which leads to a deeper awareness of both inner and outer reality and to a state of greater objectivity and understanding.

Piaget has used the same approach for a number of scientific notions and has found that ontogenesis, or individual development, frequently patterns or recapitulates sociogenesis, or collective development. He therefore feels that the study of the development of scientific thought in the child might prove a useful complement to the study of collective thought. By combining the two methods, a better understanding of the nature of knowledge might eventually be reached.

Knower-Known

Another problem of an epistemological nature which has had repercussions on psychology can be defined as the subject-object relationship. Here an attempt is made to understand the respective roles of the knower and the thing known in the act of knowledge. This problem is reflected in philosophy by the controversy between the rationalists and the empiricists. To state it briefly and somewhat crudely, the rationalists believe in the inherent capacity of human intellect to apprehend the world. This implies that human intellect is in some ways preadapted to the world. In a sense, the structure of the world has been incorporated into the structure of the mind, and this enables human beings to adopt a certain approach toward reality without first learning it. A representative of this type of philosophical view would be Kant who postulates the existence of *"a priori* categories of understanding," such as those of cause and effect. These categories direct the person in such a way that he will automatically think of things in terms of causality, and will not need to learn this orientation. The rationalist, therefore, accentuates the role of the knower at the expense of the object known in the knowledge situation. The knower comes to the knowledge situation with his *a priori* structures which determine what will be known. External reality therefore plays a minor part in knowledge since the knower imposes on it certain structures of his own. To some extent, the Gestalt psychologists may be located in this tradition.

Empiricists, on the other hand, stress the role of experience in the knower-known relationship. We gain knowledge and learn modes of reasoning by experiencing the world through our senses; we do not create or impose our own structures of thought on external reality. Objects exist by themselves and the knower merely produces a copy of them, rather as a mirror reflects the properties of objects by means of images. The role of the knower is therefore minimized since he merely discovers, by his use of the senses, what is outside himself. In psychology, empiricism has been popular. Both the structuralists (like Wundt) and the early behaviorists stressed that knowledge and thought were the results of empirical experience. According to Watson, for example, a person is a *tabula rasa*, a blank slate, on which impressions of the environment are stamped. The individual's contribution to the knower-known situation is viewed as extremely passive, and the importance of the environment is emphasized. External reality, therefore, plays a predominant part in the acquisition of knowledge.

Piaget attempts to provide a synthesis of the two opposing points of view by proposing what he calls an interaction theory. This theory stresses the interrelationship between the knower and the known in the act of discovering reality with each element making a more or less equal contribution. Piaget consequently acknowledges the importance of the environment which undoubtedly determines the development of thought to a certain extent. Obviously the type of experience he acquires and the situation to which he is exposed will channel the child's mental performance. But they will not determine development entirely because the child in no instance comes to a situation with a *tabula rasa*. He comes with a mental structure, or accumulation of past experience in the form of schemes, and these will influence his apprehension of reality. This means that for the child reality is not an objective phenomenon which has its own independent existence. Reality is determined by the type of structure with which it is apprehended. The reality of a 4-year-old child is not the same as that of a 7-year-old, nor the same as that of a 14-year-old. Yet the different "realities" are equally legitimate, since the things that a 4-year-old sees and believes are as real to him as the things a 14-year-old sees and believes. For a child in the preoperational period, his world does, in fact, present the various characteristics which we have repeatedly stressed throughout the book, and which constitute the expressions of thought of this stage of development. For him liquid does indeed change in form as well as in quantity or size, just as for him a row of candies does become longer and contain more when the spatial layout is changed. So Piaget feels that the role of the knower and the development of his mental or cognitive structures is very important in the dual relationship between knower and known. As the one changes, so does the other. With development the child acquires a less superficial view of reality. Knowledge proceeds from the periphery to the center of reality, but at each level there is a constant interaction between the knower and the external world.

These are some of the ways in which Piaget has applied psychological data to problems of an epistemological nature. By using his twofold method to probe into questions concerning the nature of knowledge, Piaget has drawn attention to the fruitfulness of interdisciplinary cooperation. Part of the reason why research in the humanities or social sciences has failed to progress as rapidly as might be hoped for has been due to the relative isolation of the different disciplines. This isolation prevents the ideas or discoveries of one discipline from permeating to related problems falling within the scope of another. Recognizing the potential of such interdisciplinary cooperation, Piaget set up in Geneva in 1956 an International Center for Epistemological Research. This center, composed of a group of specialists representing the various fields of scientific and philosophical endeavor, has studied a number of problems since its inception and the various discussions of research and theories have proved beneficial to all members.

The preceding brief description of some of Piaget's work in epistemology, although it is sketchy and does not do him full justice, will perhaps provide the reader with a glimpse of the extent of Piaget's interests. He has come a long way from the young scientist whose first article was on an albino sparrow observed in the park. He has contributed to biology, logic, mathematics, philosophy, sociology and psychology. In some areas he was a pioneer who opened up new vistas for exploration. In others, his contribution was to provide a different approach to the problem, a new way of looking at old things, a reorganization into an original pattern of what might previously have appeared banal or commonplace. One may not always agree with all his views. In fact, he is frequently modifying some aspects of his theories to adjust them to new evidence. One cannot, however, help but admire and respect a man who has had so great an impact on such a wide variety of fields, and who continues, at an age of more than 70 years, to bring to research a curiosity, a lucidity, and a breadth of experience that is difficult to match.

IMPLICATIONS FOR EDUCATION

In the present section, we will consider some general implications of Piaget's views for education. While Piaget himself has hardly dealt with the problems of education or with other practical applications of his work, it is clear nevertheless that his theories are particularly relevant for educational practice. Piaget's investigations into the development of a number of logical, physical, and mathematical notions, as well as other aspects of the child's thought, implicitly contain a number of ideas which, if suitably exploited and developed, could prove valuable to educators and educational planners. The potential of his findings for education has so far scarcely been acknowledged, and it is only fairly recently, during the past ten years or so, that psychologists and educators have begun to appreciate the importance of Piaget's theories. Attempts are currently being made in various countries, especially in Great Britain, to modify existing school programs in line with the discoveries of the Geneva group, and these attempts could profitably be extended to other parts of the world. We will therefore attempt to extract from his theories a number of general principles which may be of value to the educator. It should be emphasized at the outset, however, that our intention is not to propose particular curricula or materials on the basis of Piaget's work. We will not describe, for example, a teaching sequence on number or on logical implication; rather, our concern is with general guiding principles which emerge from Piaget's psychological research. The implementation of these principles requires the special skills of the educator, not the psychologist.

Differences Between Adults and Children

Piaget's theory as a whole suggests a proposition, which, although quite general, should have important consequences for education. The proposition is that the young child is quite different from the adult in several ways: in methods of approaching reality, in the ensuing views of the world, and in the uses of language. His investigations concerning such matters as the concepts of number, or verbal communication, have enabled Piaget to contribute to a change, indeed one might almost say to a metamorphosis, in our ways of looking at children. As a result of his work we have become increasingly aware that the child is not just a miniature, although less wise adult, but a being with a distinctive mental structure which is qualitatively different from the adult's. He views the world from a unique perspective. For example, the child below the age of 7 years truly believes that water, when poured from one container to another, gains or loses in quantity, depending on the shape of the second container. For him there is no inconsistency in stating that a given amount of water gains or loses in quantity merely by being poured from one container to another. Or in the case of number, the young child, although able to count to 20 or more, has no conception of certain fundamental mathematical ideas. He may think, for example, that a set of five elements contains more than a set of eight elements, if the physical arrangement of the sets takes on certain forms.

These and many other unexpected discoveries concerning the child's notions of reality lead us to the surprising recognition that the child's world is in many respects qualitatively different from that of the adult. One reason for the child's distinctive view of reality is a distinctive mental structure. The young child (below about 7 or 8 years of age) centers his attention on limited amounts of information; he attends to states rather than transformations; he is egocentric, and fails to take into account other points of view; and he is incapable of forms of thought, like reversibility, which allows symbolic manipulation of the data of experience. Even the older child (between 7 and 11 years), although capable of fairly subtle mental operations, is strongly tied to concrete situations. He reasons best only about immediately present objects, and fails to take into account the possibilities inherent in a situation.

One result of the child's cognitive structure is a view of reality which seems chaotic and unnatural to the adult. Another consequence is that the young child's use of language is different from the adult's. That is, the words that the child uses do not have the same meaning for him as for the adult. This point has sometimes been overlooked in the past. It was usually assumed that if a child used a particular word, this word naturally would convey the same meaning as when an adult used the same word. Adults believed that once a child has learned the linguistic label for an object, he has available the underlying concept. But Piaget has shown that this is often not the case. The child does learn his words from the adult, but assimilates them into his own mental structure, which is quite different from the adult's. The words "same amount to drink," for example, are interpreted in one way by the 4-year-old, and in another way by the adult. Only after a period of cognitive development does the child use these words and understand them in the same way as the more mature person.

The implication of this very general proposition—that the young child's thought and language are qualitatively different from the adult's—is also very general. It must follow that the educator must make a special effort to understand the unique properties of the child's experience and ways of thinking. The educator cannot assume that what is valid for him is necessarily valid for the child. For example, while the educator himself may learn a great deal by reading a book or listening to a lecture, similar experiences may be far less useful for the young child. While the educator may profit from an orderly arranged sequence of material, perhaps the child does not. While the educator may feel that a given idea is simple and indeed self-evident, perhaps the child finds it difficult. In short, it is not safe to generalize from the adult's experience to the child's. The educator's assumptions, based as they often are on his own learning experience, may not apply to children. What the educator needs to do is to try to improve his own capacity to watch and listen, and to place himself in the distinctive perspective of the child. Since the meaning expressed by the child's language is often idiosyncratic, the adult must try to understand the child's world by observing his actions closely. There are no easy rules or procedures for the educator to use in order to understand the child. What is needed chiefly is considerable sensitivity—a willingness to learn from the child, to look closely at his actions, and to avoid the assumption that what is true or customary for the adult is also true for the child. The educator needs to interact with the child in a flexible way in order to gain insight into the latter's current level of functioning. With this attitude—a willingness to observe the child, to learn from him—the educator can begin to understand the child, and tailor the educational experience to the child's needs.

Activity

Perhaps the most important single proposition that the educator can derive from Piaget's work, and thus use in the classroom, is that children, especially young ones, learn best from concrete activities. We have seen throughout this book that Piaget places major emphasis on the role of activity in intellectual development, especially in the early years of life. In Piaget's view, one of the major sources of learning, if not the most essential one, is the intrinsic activity of the child. The child must act on things to understand them. Almost from birth, he touches objects, manipulates them, turns them around, looks at them, and in these ways he develops an increasing understanding of their properties. It is through manipulation that he develops schemes relating to objects. When new objects are presented, the child may at first try to apply to them already established schemes. If not successful, he attempts, again through manipulation, to develop new schemes; that is, new ways of acting on and thereby comprehending the world. This understanding may not be on a verbal level. In fact, verbal understanding is not usually accomplished at the outset; it takes a long time. The child must begin by acting on objects, that is, by manipulating them. Over a period of time, these overt, sensori-motor schemes can become internalized in the form of thought. Still later the child may be able to express on a verbal level the notions he has developed on the basis of interaction with the world.

For these reasons a good school should encourage the child's activity, and his manipulation and exploration of objects. When the teacher tries to bypass this process by imparting knowledge in a verbal manner, the result is often superficial learning. But by promoting activity in the classroom, the teacher can exploit the child's potential for learning, and permit him to evolve an understanding of the world around him. This principle (that learning occurs through the child's activity) suggests that the teacher's major task is to provide for the child a wide variety of potentially interesting materials on which he may act. The teacher should not teach, but should encourage the child to learn by manipulating things.

Acceptance of the principle of active learning requires a considerable reorientation of beliefs concerning education. Teachers (and the public at large) usually consider that the aim of education is to impart knowledge of certain types. According to Piaget's theory, this conception is in error for several reasons. First, teachers can in fact impart or teach very little. It is true that they can get the child to *say* certain things, but these verbalizations often indicate little in the way of real understanding. Second, it is seldom legitimate to conceive of knowledge as a *thing* which can be transmitted. Certainly the child needs to learn some facts, and these may be considered *things*. But often the child does not learn facts if the teacher transmits them; the child must discover them himself. Also, facts are but a small portion of real knowledge. True understanding involves action, on both the motoric and intellectual levels. Consider for example the understanding of class properties. A traditional view might propose that the child learns some facts about classification; for instance, that a square is a geometric form. Piaget's view, on the other hand, argues that understanding of classification consists of a sequence of activities. First the child physically sorts or otherwise manipulates objects. He feels various forms and in this way, among others, perceives the differences among them. He may put different forms in different places. Later, he can sort the objects solely on a mental level. He does not need to separate things physically, but he can do it mentally. Later still, he can perform inclusion operations on the (imagined) classes of objects. He can consider that a hypothetical class includes and is "larger than" its constituent sub-class. Thus, knowledge of classification does not merely involve facts, but actions as well: physical sorting, mental sorting, mental inclusion operations. Furthermore, most of these actions are non-verbal.

The teacher's job then is not so much to transmit facts or concepts to the child, but to get him to act on both physical and mental levels. These actions—far more than imposed facts or concepts—constitute real knowledge. In this connection it may be useful to conceive of the child's understanding in terms of three levels.

The first of these levels is motoric understanding. Knowledge at this level implies that the child can act directly on objects and manipulate them correctly. He can adjust his movements to fit the properties of the objects, and thus indicate that he has understood them at the level of motor responses. For instance he can move objects, or lift them up, or turn them around. Another level of understanding is that of internal activity on an intuitive basis. The child performs actions on the objects in a very abbreviated and internal manner. Because the activity can be performed so much faster on a mental level than on an overt level, the child is able to do more in a given period of time. He is also no longer limited by spatial and temporal restrictions. Finally, there is the level of verbal understanding. The child is able to deal with concepts on an abstract verbal level, and he can often express his mental operations in words.

Several important comments can be made concerning these levels of understanding. First, the higher levels—intuitive and verbal—depend upon the lowest; that is, the motor. Manipulation of things is a prerequisite for higher, verbal understanding. The young child cannot jump to the higher levels before establishing a basis in concrete manipulation. Therefore, concrete experience should precede learning from verbal explanations or written materials. Second, these different levels need not necessarily be restricted to given ages. It is unlikely, for example, that the preoperational child is completely intuitive in his approach, or that the adolescent is completely verbal. Rather it seems probable that at a given period of development one mode of understanding will predominate over, but not exclude the rest. For both these reasons, that is, the priority of concrete manipulation and the presence of all modes of understanding at all age levels (at least beyond infancy), children must have a chance to be active in the classroom, to touch and feel things, to find out what they do, to explore, and so forth. This is what real knowledge is about.

Cognitive Structure, New Experience, and Self-Regulation

Piaget's theory stresses the interaction of current cognitive structure and new experiences for the arousal of interest and the subsequent development of understanding. One way of putting the matter is to say that interest and learning are facilitated if the experience presented to the child bears some relevance to what he already knows but at the same time is sufficiently novel to present incongruities and conflicts. If you will, recall the moderate novelty principle as an example which was discussed in the case of infancy (but applying to older children as well). Piaget's proposition is that the child's interest is aroused when an experience is moderately novel; the experience is not so radically novel as to be unassimilable into current cognitive structure; and it is not so familiar as to surfeit the child. This principle is relativistic: the experience does not contain in itself any intrinsic properties of interest. Rather, interest derives from the interaction between the state of the child's mind and the thing to be known.

Equilibration theory emphasizes that self-regulatory processes are the basis for genuine learning. The child is more apt to modify his cognitive structure in a constructive way when he controls his own learning than when methods of social transmission (in this case, teaching) are employed. Do recall Smedslund's experiments on the acquisition of conservation. If one tries to teach this concept to a child who does not yet have available the mental structure necessary for its assimilation, then the resulting learning is superficial. On the other hand, when children are allowed to progress at their own pace through the normal sequence of development, they regulate their own learning so as to construct the cognitive structures necessary for the genuine understanding of conservation.

These principles, if taken seriously, should lead to extensive changes in classroom practice. They imply, first, that teachers should be aware of the child's current level of functioning. Unless such an assessment is made, the teacher will find it difficult to judge what is apt to arouse the interest of his students. Second, the principles imply that the classroom must be oriented more toward the individual than the group. Since there are profound individual differences in almost all areas of cognitive development, it is unlikely that any one task or lesson will arouse the interest of or promote learning in all members of the class. For some children the task may be too easily assimilated into current mental structures, whereas for other students the problem may require a greater degree of accommodation than the student is at present capable of mastering. The result is boredom for the first group and confusion for the second. Third, children must be given considerable control over their own learning. Some may need more time than others to deal with the same material; similarly, children may approach the same problem in different ways.

To promote interest and learning, then, the teacher should tailor the curriculum to the individual. This means that the group should effectively be disbanded as the only classroom unit, that children should often work on individual projects and that they should be allowed considerable freedom in their own learning. Several objections are usually raised to this sort of proposal. First, if this were done, how could the teacher assure that all the children learn some common, required material? The answer is that he could not, unless the children's interests overlapped. But why is it essential for all children always to learn the same things? Second, under an individual learning arrangement, would not the children just waste their time or engage in mere play? This attitude, shared by many teachers, reveals a derogatory opinion concerning children's intellectual life, and a lack of faith in them. The attitude is clearly wrong too. Piaget has shown that the child is quite active in acquiring knowledge, and that he learns about important aspects of reality quite apart from instruction in the schools. In the first two years of life, for example, the infant acquires a primitive understanding of causality, of the nature of objects, of relations, of language, and of many other things, largely without the benefit of formal instruction or adult "teaching." One need only watch an infant for a short period of time to know that he is curious, interested in the world around him, and eager to learn. It is quite evident, too, that these are characteristics of older children as well. If left to himself the normal child does not remain immobile; he is eager to learn. Consequently, it is quite safe to permit the child to structure his own learning. The danger arises precisely when the schools attempt to perform the task for him. To understand this point consider the absurd situation that would result if traditional schools were entrusted with teaching the infant what he spontaneously learns during the first few years. The schools would develop organized curricula in secondary circular reactions; they would develop lesson plans for object permanence; they would construct audio-visual aids on causality; they would reinforce "correct" speech; and they would set "goals" for the child to reach each week. One can speculate as to the outcome of such a program for early training! What the student needs then is not formal teaching, but an opportunity to learn. He needs to be given a rich environment, containing many things potentially of interest. He needs a teacher who is sensitive to his needs, who can judge what materials will challenge him at a given point in time, who can help when he needs help, and who has faith in his capacity to learn.

Limitations and Opportunities

There are certain limitations on what the child can learn. His thought develops through a series of stages, each showing both strengths and weaknesses. Any one stage is characterized by the ability to perform certain actions typical of the particular stage, and, on the other hand, by the propensity to commit certain typical errors. Intellectual development is a progressive process. New mental structures evolve from the old ones by means of the dual processes of assimilation and accommodation. Faced with novel experiences, the child seeks to assimilate them into his existing mental framework. To do this, he may have to adjust and modify the framework, or accommodate to the requirements of novel experience. New knowledge is never acquired in a discontinuous fashion, but is always absorbed into preexisting structures in such a way that prior experience is used to explain novelty, and novelty is adapted to fit previous experience. Mental development is more than a mere accumulation of isolated and unrelated experiences; it is a hierarchical process with the later acquisitions being built upon, and at the same time expanding upon the earlier ones.

One implication of the stage theory is in a way "pessimistic." Since intellectual development seems to follow an ordered sequence—a sequence which, until proof of the contrary, appears to be universal—the young child is incapable of learning certain kinds of concepts. It would serve no purpose, for instance, to try to teach a child of the preoperational period the principle of inertia, or any other abstract notion which requires the existence of reasoning at a formal operational level. A current trend pre-

vails in the United States which believes that it is possible to teach anything to a child of any level of development, providing the appropriate
method is used. Piaget's findings tend to stress the contrary. Certain things
cannot be taught at any level, regardless of the method adopted. It is. of
course possible to accelerate some types of learning to a certain extent by
use of suitable environmental stimuli. For instance, if a child of the preoperational period is fairly close to achieving the structure of concrete
operations, suitable physical experience may expedite the process, with
the result that the structure may be acquired somewhat earlier than if no
such experience had been presented. But presentation of the same experience to an infant would not have the same effect. The infant lacks much
of the experience and mental development necessary to achieve concrete
operations and would consequently not have available an appropriate
mental structure into which he could fruitfully assimilate the planned
experience. In all likelihood, the infant would assimilate the experience
to fit his own level of understanding. He might learn something from it,
but not what the teacher had had in mind. The experience, therefore,
although being suitable to accelerate the achievement of concrete operations for the preoperational child, would have quite a different effect on
the infant. The effects of experience are limited, then, by the intrinsic
ability of the child at a particular stage of development.

Thus, one aspect of Piaget's stage theory is "pessimistic"; that is, it
assumes that there are some things children cannot learn. But there is an
"optimistic" side to his theory too. At each stage of development the
child is capable of certain forms of thought, and he has spontaneously
developed certain notions of reality. For example, Piaget has found that
concepts of topological geometry (distinctions between closed vs. open
figures, etc.) develop in the child before those of Euclidean geometry
(measurement of angles, distances, etc.) and projective geometry (measurement of perspectives, coordinates, etc.). Understanding of topological
notions appears fairly early in life, whereas the child only begins to understand the notion of Euclidean and projective geometry at around 7 years
of age. Thus, while the 5-year-old may be incapable of learning projective
concepts, he has already developed an intuitive understanding of topological notions. Each stage of development is characterized by both
strengths and weaknesses.

There are several implications stemming from Piaget's proposition
concerning the strengths and weaknesses of each stage of development.
First, as we have already stressed, the teacher must try to be aware of
the child's current level of cognitive functioning. To some extent the
teacher can rely on Piaget's discoveries for this information. But Piaget's
work is not sufficient, since it covers only a limited number of the subjects which are usually studied in schools. Therefore, the teacher himself

must make an assessment of his students' capabilities. Even if revelant research were available, the teacher must still perform such an assessment since it is extremely likely that there are wide individual differences with respect to the understanding of any concept at almost any age level. The teacher's job is not easy. He should not place great reliance on standardized tests of achievement. Piaget's clinical method has shown that the child's initial verbal response (the type of response that is given to a standard test) is often superficial and does not provide a reliable index of the real quality of his understanding. Tests often tap only the surface, and they also often test the wrong things. Again the teacher must observe the children carefully and attempt to discover both their intuitive competence and weakness in any area.

Second, once the teacher has some awareness of the child's current level of functioning, he can make available to the child experiences which facilitate development. For example, in the case of geometry, the teacher might first present his students with opportunities to learn about topological concepts (these opportunities would not, of course, involve teaching, but perhaps acquiring materials which emphasize topological distinctions and at which the child, under the teacher's general guidance, can work on independently). If such an arrangement were followed, the young student would feel comfortable with topological notions. His available mental structures would assure understanding of some topological concepts and others could be elaborated without great difficulty. Thus, his first school experiences with geometry should build upon and exploit what he already knows in an intuitive way.

Social Interaction

In Piaget's view, physical experience and concrete manipulation are not the only ways in which the child learns. Another type of experience leading to understanding of the environment is social experience, or interaction with other persons, be they peers or adults. The effects of this type of experience, although almost negligible during the first few months of life, become increasingly important as the child grows older. We have pointed out earlier that one of the prime deterrents to an objective understanding of reality is the child's egocentric thought. He cannot view things objectively at first because he can only see them as related to himself. The very young child assimilates external events directly into his own action schemes. Things are only relevant to the extent that they concern his own private preoccupations. He cannot view objects or events from any other perspective besides his own. This egocentrism naturally prevents the child from gaining an objective view of objects or of persons. Gradually, as the child becomes capable of decentering his attention, as he begins to focus on various aspects of reality simultaneously, as he comes to understand another person's point of view, then he gains a more objective knowledge of reality.

One method which promotes the relinquishing of egocentrism is social interaction. When one child talks to another he comes to realize that his is not the only way of viewing things. He sees that other people do not necessarily share his opinions. Interaction inevitably leads to conflict and argument. The child's views are questioned. He must defend his ideas, and he must justify his opinions. In doing this he is forced to clarify his thoughts. If he wants to convince others of the validity of his own views, his ideas must be expressed clearly and logically. Other people are not as tolerant of his inconsistencies as he is himself. So we see that, apart from the more commonly stressed affective side of social interaction, or the need to get along with other people, there is an important cognitive component. Social experience not only helps people to adjust to others at an emotional level, it also serves to clarify a person's thinking and helps him to become in some ways more coherent and logical.

In both types of experience, physical and social, the teacher can help the child to develop his potential for activity. By providing a variety of objects which the child can manipulate, the teacher provides a setting for the empirical discovery of physical properties of things or the opportunity for understanding at the motoric or intuitive level. By providing the opportunity for social interaction, the teacher promotes an exchange of opinions which ultimately leads to understanding or learning at the verbal level.

It should be made clear that social experience is not independent from physical experience. Verbal exchange of opinions is not feasible on certain subjects until the prior physical experience which gave rise to the opinion has occurred. In fact during the early stages of development, it seems that physical experience, or motor activity, plays a relatively more important role than language in the discovery of reality. Once the child has acted on an object or a situation, language can then serve as a major tool to internalize the experience into a compact category of experience. But the child's activity or experience is of paramount importance especially during the early stages of development.

The implication of Piaget's view is that social interaction should play a significant part in the classroom. Children should talk with one another. They should converse, share experience, and argue. It is hard to see why schools force the child to be quiet, when the results seem to be only an authoritarian situation and extreme boredom. Let us restrict the vow of silence to selected orders of monks and nuns.

Traditional Methods of Instruction

Piaget's theory implies that there are grave deficiencies in "traditional" methods of instruction, especially in the early years of school. By "traditional" methods, we mean cases in which the teacher uses a lesson plan to direct the students through a given sequence of material; attempts to transmit the material to the students by means of lectures and other verbal explanations; forces all students to cover essentially the same lessons; and employs a textbook as the basic medium for instruction. Under such an arrangement, the students take fixed positions in a classroom; talk to one another only at the risk of punishment; are required to listen to the teacher; must study the material which the teacher feels is necessary to study; and must try to learn from books. It is, of course, the case that teachers differ in the degree to which they employ traditional methods. No two classrooms are identical, and it would be difficult to find one which is traditional in all respects and at all times. Nevertheless, traditional methods are still highly influential in education today, as even casual observations of the schools reveal.

Traditional procedures of instruction are based on several assumptions concerning the nature of children and their learning. One assumption is that students of a given age level should learn essentially the same material. There is some truth to this assumption. Children of a given age level in a particular cultural context are usually of a similar level of cognitive development and, therefore, generally cannot learn certain concepts but are capable of dealing with others. But traditional schools often implement this principle in a ludicrous manner. By forcing all students to cover the identical material each day, the traditional method ignores the fact that there are individual differences in the pace of learning. Also such a procedure fails to take account of the factors producing interest and genuine learning: these occur when a new experience is characterized by a moderate degree of novelty in relation to the individual's current cognitive structure. In a classroom if different children who possess different cognitive structures are presented with an identical experience, then some will either find the experience boring or so new as to be unassimilable.

A second assumption is that children learn through verbal explanation on the part of the teacher, or through written exposition in books. Of course, this is sometimes true. But as we have seen, children require concrete activity for genuine learning. Verbal explanation or written exposition can be effective only after a basis in concrete activity has been established.

A third assumption of traditional education is perhaps implicit in the first two. It is that if students were given a greater degree of control over their own learning, that is, if they were allowed to select what is to be learned and the ways in which it is to be learned, then they would waste their time and learn little. There is some truth to this assumption; if the students did not have some adult guidance they might indeed waste some time. But this does not imply that students should have almost no control over their own learning. As Piaget has shown, a major part of learning depends on self-regulatory processes. Also, outside of school, children manage to acquire an understanding of certain aspects of reality. Therefore, students can be trusted to take a major share of the responsibility for directing the learning process. Adults can certainly help, but an attempt to take complete control of the child's learning is self-defeating.

A fourth assumption is that uncontrolled talking in class is disruptive to the educational process. Certainly, a great deal of noise may prevent students from learning (although our observation is that they are bothered by noise much less than teachers). But Piaget points out that conversation, and the resulting clash of opinions, is often beneficial for mental growth. To exclude intelligent and spontaneous conversation in schools is therefore unnnecessary.

Summary and Conclusions

We have reviewed some of the major implications of Piaget's views for educational practice. While Piaget has not been mainly concerned with schools, one can derive from his theory a number of general principles which may guide educational procedures. The first of these is that the child's language and thought are different from the adult's. The teacher must be cognizant of this and must therefore attempt to observe children very closely in an attempt to discover their unique perspectives. Second, children need to manipulate things in order to learn. Formal verbal instruction is generally ineffective, especially for young children. The child must physically act on his environment. Such activity constitutes a major portion of genuine knowledge; the mere passive reception of facts or concepts is only a minor part of real understanding. Third, children are most interested and learn best when experience is moderately novel. When a new event is both familiar enough so that it may be assimilated without distortion into current cognitive structure, and novel enough so that it produces some degree of conflict, then interest and learning are promoted. Since at a given age level, children's cognitive structures differ, all children will not find the same new event interesting, nor will they learn from it. This implies that successful group instruction is almost impossible. Children should work individually, with freedom, at tasks of their own choosing. Piaget finds too that an important aspect of learning is self-regulation. Before he enters school, and without adult instruction, the child learns in many ways.

Fourth, the child's thought progresses through a series of stages, each of which contains distinctive strengths and weaknesses. Teachers should respect both of these. Children should not be forced to learn material for which they are not ready; and they should be allowed to apply their intuitive understanding to subjects covered in school. In order to accomplish this, the teacher must once again display high sensitivity: he must perceive each individual child's inadequacies and strengths. He must circumvent the former and exploit the latter. Fifth, children should talk in school, should argue and debate. Social interaction, particularly when it is centered about relevant physical experience, promotes intellectual growth.

It should be clear that these views are at variance with many of the assumptions of traditional education. According to Piaget's evidence and theory, students of a given age level do not and cannot learn essentially the same material; they learn only in a minor way through verbal explanation or written exposition (concrete experience must come first); they can and do exert control over their own learning; and they should talk to one another. It should also be clear that these ideas are not particularly new. The "progressive" education movement has proposed similar principles for many years. Piaget's contribution is not in developing new educational ideas, but in providing a vast body of data and theory which provide a sound basis for a "progressive" approach to the schools. A long time ago, John Dewey,[3] in rejecting traditional approaches to education, called for and attempted to provide a "philosophy of experience"; that is, a thorough explication of the ways in which children make use of experience in genuine learning. Piaget has gone a long way toward meeting this need.

We would also like to point out that these educational ideas are not only "idealistic," but practical as well. Many primary schools in England (and a few in the United States) have been approaching education in line with the principles described above, and have drawn directly on Piaget's work for their inspiration. These schools represent a very promising experiment in educational innovation and have already achieved a good measure of success.

We will close this section on education, and this book, with a quote from Piaget. It states Piaget's educational goals and at the same time describes his own accomplishment.

The principal goal of education is to create men who are capable of doing new things, not simply of repeating what other generations have

3. John Dewey, *Experience and Education,* (New York: Collier Books, 1963).

done—men who are creative, inventive, and discoverers. The second goal of education is to form minds which can be critical, can verify, and not accept everything they are offered. The great danger today is of slogans, collective opinions, ready-made trends of thoughts. We have to be able to resist individually, to criticize, to distinguish between what is proven and what is not. So we need pupils who are active, who learn early to find out by themselves, partly by their own spontaneous activity and partly through material we set up for them; who learn early to tell what is verifiable and what is simply the first idea to come to them.[4]

4. Piaget Rediscovered, p. 5.

index

Abbreviated behavior, 47, 54, 119
Accommodation, 18–19, 23, 35–36, 45–46, 52, 56, 60–62, 77
Action as source of thought, 6–7
Activity
    and education, 221–223
    in sensorimotor period, 31, 35, 70
Adolescent thought
    and equilibration theory, 205
    general characteristics of, 202–206
    summary and conclusions, 206
    See also Formal operations
Adaptation, 17–19, 23
Animism, 98–99
Anticipation, 36–38, 54–55
    passive, 43
    visual, 49
Artificialism, 99
Assimilation, 18–19, 23, 62, 80, 110
    functional, 30–33, 35, 38, 40–41, 45, 52, 59, 89–90
    generalizing, 30–33, 39, 52
    recognitory, 30–33, 36, 47
Autistic thought, 115–116
Automatic behavioral reaction. *See* Reflex

Behaviorism, 70, 153
Bergson, H., 2

Binet, A., 3
Biography of Piaget, 1–13; summary, 24–25
Biologie et connaissance, 12
Biology
    and genetic epistemology, 209–210
    Piaget's interest in, 1–4, 12, 15
    role in Piaget's theory, 5, 14, 16–19
Bleuler, E., 3
Boutroux, P., 212, 215

Categories of reality, 41
Causal relations, 92, 110–111, 210–212
Centration, 68, 126, 137, 145, 148, 151, 157, 159, 161, 166, 168
Child's Conception of Geometry, The, 9
Child's Conception of Number, The, 8
Child's Conception of Physical Causality, The, 6, 16
Child's Conception of Space, The, 9
Child's Conception of the World, The, 6, 16
Circular reaction
    deferred, 50–51
    primary, 34–36
    secondary, 43–46, 53–54
    tertiary, 58–60
Claparède, E., 5

Classes, Relations, et Nombres, 8
Classification, 21–22, 119–133
    inclusion relations, 119, 121, 124–127,
        131, 133
    in infancy, 46–48, 119
    part-whole relations, 109, 112–113
    properties of, 120–121
        extension, 121–124
        intension, 121–124
    stage 1, 121–123
    stage 2, 123–126
    stage 3, 127
    summary, 133–134
Clinical method, 4–5, 16, 94–98, 116;
        revised, 4, 7, 117–121, 123, 181–
        182
Cognition, figurative and operative aspects
        of, 152–153
Collective monologue. *See* Language
Compensation and conservation, 151, 165.
        See also Reciprocity
Competence, 179. *See also* Formal opera-
        tions
Concept. *See* Meaning
Concrete operational thought, 127, 133,
        151
    general characteristics of, 161–168
    in relation to formal operations, 183–
        184, 199
Conservation
    of continuous quantity, 162–163
    definition of, 164
    development of, 164–165
    of discontinuous quantity, 165
    of length, 158
    of substance, 163, 165
    of volume, 163–165
    of weight, 163, 165
    See also Number
Conservative behavior, 46, 52–53, 58
Construction of Reality in the Child, The,
        7
Content of thought, 16, 94–99
Coordination of schemes, 42, 51–53
Cornut, S., 2
Cultural influences on thought, 166, 169
Curiosity, 38–39, 58–60, 70

Darwin, C., 27
Décalage
    horizontal, 162, 165
    vertical, 113, 127
Decentration, 68, 115, 127, 151, 158, 161,
        167–168
Development, 168–179
    in infancy, 69
    and learning, 175–176
    summary, 177–179

*Développement de la Notion du Temps
        chez l'Enfant, Le,* 9
*Développement des Quantités Physiques
        chez l'Enfant, Le,* 8
Dewey, J., 231
Directed behavior, 46, 61
Discovery of new means, 60–61
Discrimination. *See* Assimilation, recog-
        nitory

Early Growth of Logic in the Child, The,
        11
Education, 218–232
    and activity, 221–223
    and assessment, 227
    and equilibrium, 223–224
    and interest, 223
    and qualitative differences in thought,
        219–221
    and social experience, 227–228
    and stages of thought, 225–227
    and understanding, 222–223
    traditional methods of, 229–230
Egocentric speech. *See* Language
Egocentrism, 101, 103–104, 108, 115
Einstein, A., 8
Emotions, 15
Environment, role of, 69–70
Epistemology
    definition of, 208
    Piaget's interest in, 2–3, 5, 12, 15, 179
    See also Genetic epistemology
Equilibration theory, 172, 174–175
    critique of, 178–179
    and education, 223–224
    summary, 177–179
    See also Adolescent thought
Equilibrium, 23, 172, 174, 181
    in adolescence, 204
    and assimilation-accommodation, 172
    properties of, 172–173
*Essai sur les Transformations des Opera-
        tions Logiques,* 10
Études Sociologiques, 11
Euclid, 213–214

Formal operations, 181–202
    combinatorial property, 203
    and competence, 201
    critique of, 201–202
    general characteristics of, 199–202
    qualitative nature of, 200
    See also INRC group, 16 binary opera-
        tions
Freud, S., 3–4, 33, 74, 108, 115–116, 128,
        172
Functional invariants, 17–19, 23, 30

Galois, E., 214
Genèse de l'Idée du Hasard chez l'Enfant, La, 10
Genetic epistemology, 10, 207–218
  historico-critical method, 212–216
  knower-known relation, 216–217
  and mathematics, 212–215
  parallel between collective and individual thought, 213–216
  psychogenetic method, 210–212
  rationale for, 209–210
Gesell, A., 71, 169, 178
Gestalt psychology, 8, 216
Grouping I, 129–133
  associativity, 130, 132–133
  binary operator, 129–131
  characteristics of, 132–133
  composition, 130, 132
  identity, 130
  inverse, 131
  negation, 131
  resorption, 131
  special identity, 131–132
  tautology, 131
Growth of Logical Thinking from Childhood to Adolescence, The, 10

Heredity
  general, 38
  of physical structures, 16–17, 20, 29, 33, 168–169
Hull, C. L., 33
Hume, D., 210–211

Identity and conservation, 152, 165
Image Mentale chez l'Enfant, L', 12
Imagery
  anticipatory, 158–160
  auditory, 77
  and concrete operations, 160
  evolution of, 159
  history of research on, 153–154
  kinetic, 155–159
  mental, 152–161
  reproductory, 158–160
  role of boundaries in, 157–158
  static, 158–159
  summary, 160–161
  transformational, 157–159
  visual, 74, 77–78
  See also Mental symbols
Imitation, 39–41, 48–49, 55–56, 64–65, 153
  deferred, 65, 73–75
  and mental symbols, 75–77, 79
  mutual, 40
  of new models, 61–62
  vocal, 40

Index, 78
Individual differences, 14–15, 68–69
Inference, 62
Inhelder, B., 8–10, 12, 181
INRC group, 196–199
  correlativity, 196
  identity, 196
  negation, 196–199
  reciprocity, 196–197, 199
Intelligence, definition of, 3, 13–15
Intelligence tests, 3
Intention, 45–46; definition of, 53
Interaction theory, 217
Internalization of behavior, 47, 64–65, 119
Interrupted prehension, 49–51
Introduction à l'Épistémologie Génétique, 10
Invariants. *See* Functional invariants

Judgment and Reasoning in the Child, 5
Jung, C., 3
Juxtaposition, 92, 109–113, 120

Kant, I., 216

Language, 86–94
  collective monologue, 88, 90
  early use of, 81–83
  egocentric, 87, 89–94
  functions of, 86–87, 91
  monologue, 87, 89–90
  repetition, 87, 89–90
  socialized, 87–89, 91
  and thought, 85, 171–172
Language and Thought in the Child, The, 5
Learning, 168–179
  and conservation, 176
  summary, 177–179
Logic
  Piaget's interest in, 9
  use of, 4–5
Logico-mathematical experience, 169–171
Logico-mathematical models, 142, 180; Piaget's rationale for, 127–129

Maine de Biran, 211
Maturation, 70, 168–169
Meaning
  in early childhood, 78–81
  in infancy, 46–48, 55, 61, 70
Mécanismes Perceptifs, Les, 8
Mémoire et Intelligence, 12
Mental symbols, 63–64, 66, 73–75, 80–81, 154
  formation of, 75–78
  and imitation, 75–77, 79
  role of language in, 74–75

Mental symbols (*cont.*)
  See also Imagery, Symbolic function
Methodology
  informal-experimental, 27–29
  naturalistic, 27–29, 82, 89, 95–96
  in study of imagery, 154–155
  See also Clinical method
Mobility
  and equilibrium, 173
  in infancy, 53
Moderate novelty principle, 39, 46, 58–59,
    70, 223
Moral behavior, 100–103
  definition of, 100
  egocentric stage, 101
  genuine cooperation, 102
  incipient cooperation, 101–102
Moral judgment, 102–109
  absolutistic stage, 102–105
  realistic stage, 106–108
  subjective stage, 106, 108
Moral Judgment of the Child, The, 6
Motivation, 38–39, 70; theories of, 33

Negation and conservation, 151–152, 165,
    167–168
*Notions de Mouvement et de Vitesse chez
    l'Enfant, Les*, 9
Novelty. *See* Moderate novelty principle
Number, concept of, 142–152
  and classification, 150
  conservation of, 142, 144, 146, 148, 151
  construction of equivalence, 145–148
  and counting, 147
  definition of, 142
  in infancy, 54
  and ordinal relations, 150
  stage 1, 145–147
  stage 2, 147–148
  stage 3, 148–152
  summary, 152
  vicariant ordering of, 149–150
  See also One-to-one correspondence

Object concept, 41–43, 49–51, 56–57, 62–
    63, 65–66
One-to-one correspondence, 139–144, 146,
    148–150
Operations, definition of, 150. *See also*
    Concrete operations, Formal oper-
    ations
Ordinal relations. *See* Relations
Organization, 17–19, 23
Origins of Intelligence, The, 7

Participation, 99
Perception, 8, 77, 153

Philosophy. *See* Epistemology
Physical experience, 169
Piaget's early work, summary, 113–116
Plane of action. *See* Understanding
Plane of thought. *See* Understanding
Play, Dreams, and Imitation, 9
Preconcept, 120
Preoperational thought
  general characteristics of, 161–168
  relation to formal operations, 183
Psychoanalytic theory, 115–116; Piaget's
    early contact with, 3, 6
Psychologie de l'Enfant, La, 12
Psychology of Intelligence, The, 9

Reasoning, 109–113; in preoperational pe-
    riod, 83–84
Reciprocity and conservation, 151, 165,
    168
Reflex, 17, 20, 29–31, 33, 37
Regulations, 148
Relations
  in infancy, 48, 53–54, 135
  ordinal, 109, 112–113, 134–142
    properties of, 135–136
    stage 1, 136–137
    stage 2, 137–141
    stage 3, 141–142
Representation, 65. *See also* Mental sym-
    bols, Symbolic function
Reversibility, 131, 151–152, 167–168, 199;
    empirical, 151–152, 167

Sagesse et Illusions de la Philosophie, 11
Scheme, definition of, 20–22
Sensorimotor period
  stage 1, 29–34
  stage 2, 34–43
  stage 3, 43–51
  stage 4, 51–57
  stage 5, 58–63
  stage 6, 63–66
  summary, 66–71
Signified, 47–48, 54–55, 78–80
Signifier, 47–48, 54–55, 77–78
Simon, T., 3
16 binary operations, 182–196
  complete affirmation, 188, 194
  conjunction, 195
  implication, 193–195
  reciprocal implication, 188, 193–195
  tautology, 188, 194–195
Smedslund, J., 176, 223
Social learning theory, 94, 104–105, 108,
    116
Social transmission, 171; and education,
    227–228

Speech. *See* Language
Stages, 23, 71
    age norms of, 29, 68, 161
    continuity of, 69, 162
    invariant sequence of, 29, 69, 162
Structure
    description of, 22; *see also* Logico-mathe-
        matical models
    physical, *see* Heredity
    psychological, 17, 19, 20–24, 33, 36
Symbolic function, 64, 72–83; summary,
    84–85. *See also* Mental symbols
Symbolic play, 79–81; and emotions, 80–
    81
Syncretism, 109–113, 116, 120
Szeminska, A., 8–9

Tests, standard, 3–4, 95–96
Theoretical framework, 13–24; summary,
    24–25

Tolman, E. C., 128
Traité de Logique, 9
Transductive reasoning, 83–84
Trial-and-error learning, 33–34, 46, 60–61,
    65

Understanding
    and education, 222–223
    on plane of action, 41, 113
    on plane of thought, 41, 113
    verbal, 93
Unilateral respect, 104–105, 107–108

Verbal communication. *See* Language

Watson, J. B., 217
Wish fulfillment, 89–90
Wundt, W., 153–154, 217
Wurzburg psychologists, 153